CUSTOM
CAR PAINTING
ON A
BUDGET

Rick Bacon and Dennis W. Parks

S-A DESIGN

CarTech®

CarTech®

CarTech®, Inc.
6118 Main Street
North Branch, MN 55056
Phone: 651-277-1200 or 800-551-4754
Fax: 651-277-1203
www.cartechbooks.com

Edit by Wes Eisenschenk
Layout by Connie DeFlorin

ISBN 978-1-61325-693-0
Item No. SA511

Library of Congress Cataloging-in-Publication Data Available

Written, edited, and designed in the U.S.A.
Printed in China
10 9 8 7 6 5 4 3 2 1

All photos are courtesy of Rick Bacon or Dennis W. Parks unless otherwise noted.

DISTRIBUTION BY:

Europe
PGUK
63 Hatton Garden
London EC1N 8LE, England
Phone: 020 7061 1980 • Fax: 020 7242 3725
www.pguk.co.uk

Australia
Renniks Publications Ltd.
3/37-39 Green Street
Banksmeadow, NSW 2109, Australia
Phone: 2 9695 7055 • Fax: 2 9695 7355
www.renniks.com

Canada
Login Canada
300 Saulteaux Crescent
Winnipeg, MB, R3J 3T2 Canada
Phone: 800 665 1148 • Fax: 800 665 0103
www.lb.ca

CONTENTS

Dedication

Rick Bacon

I dedicate this book to my biggest cheerleader, my mom, who recently lost her battle with cancer. Her encouragement and unconditional love and support have been driving forces in my life and sustained me through some dark times. She was always looking forward to seeing my latest creation, and her honest and sometimes-brutal input will be sorely missed.

I also dedicate this book to my dad, who instilled a work ethic that drives me every day to do as much as I can with every hour. It is dedicated to my two children, who look to me for guidance, wisdom, and protection.

Last, but certainly not least, this book is dedicated to my employees and customers. Without you all, I'd be awfully bored, broke, and miserable. Many people have enabled me to do what I love and make a living doing it. Thank you!

Dennis W. Parks

This book is dedicated to my best friend, Roger Ward, who taught me more about painting than anyone. He gladly answered my questions and made me laugh whenever I was feeling down. Roger could have moved to California and made millions painting cars. Luckily for those of us in the Midwest, he stayed true to his roots and lived in Kansas, painting some of this area's most well-known hot rods and customs.

Acknowledgments

Rick Bacon

I'd like to thank Kevin Tetz for getting Wes Eisenschenk and me together to lay the foundation for this book. Thank you, Dennis Parks, for the help writing and assembling this project when my personal life got too crazy.

Dennis W. Parks

Thank you to Wes Eisenschenk for giving me the opportunity to write this book, to Rick Bacon for providing most of the photos, and for my significantly better-half, Sandy, for putting up with my writing habit.

Rick Bacon

In 1984 as a high school junior, Rick Bacon picked up a paint gun and began finishing cabinets and furniture for fellow students in his wood shop class. He never put down the paint gun. Opening his first auto body repair shop in 1995 provided the opportunities to explore custom work and expand his skills with custom paint. This work was seen by TV producers in Tennessee, and Rick spent several years showing his skills on MuscleCar TV and *Overhaulin'*. In 2014, he moved to Sonora, California, where he opened his current shop, Rick Bacon Customs.

Dennis W. Parks

Aside from a few Ford hot rods (a 1929 Ford Model A Tudor sedan and a 1927 Ford Track T roadster), all my vehicles have been Chevy trucks. Beginning with a 1957 GMC, I have owned a 1976 Custom Deluxe, a lowered 1982 Custom Deluxe, a 1990 S-10, a 1951 Advanced Design pickup, a 1991 Silverado, a 2002 Silverado, a 1955 Task Force pickup, a 1968 C10 Stepside, a lowered 2008 Silverado extended cab, a 2014 Silverado four-wheel drive, and, most recently, a 1970 C10 Stepside. While I have lost track of the miles I have driven, most all of them have been behind the wheel of a GM truck.

I have also spent quite a bit of time writing about and photographing hot rods and vintage trucks. My magazine articles have been published in *Street Rodder, Hot Rod, Midwest Rod and Machine, Truckin', Rodder's Digest, Musclecar Classics, Street Rod Pickups, Street Rod Action, Supercar* (Australia), *Classic Trucks, Street Rod Pickups, Custom Rodder, Rod & Custom, Super Chevy, Custom Classic Trucks, American Rodder, Hot Rod Trucks, High Performance Pontiacs, Rodding USA,* and *Hot Rod New Zealand.*

In addition to being a full time senior technical writer for a pharmaceutical benefits manager, I have authored several automotive how-to books: *How to Build a Hot Rod Model A Ford; How to Build a Hot Rod; How to Paint Your Car; How to Restore and Customize Auto Upholstery & Interiors; How to Plate, Polish, and Chrome; How to Build a Cheap Hot Rod; The Complete Guide to Auto Body Repair; Hot Rod Body and Chassis Builder's Guide; Automotive Wiring: A Practical Guide to Wiring Your Hot Rod or Custom Car; How to Restore and Customize Automotive Interiors; The Complete Guide to Auto Body Repair; Automotive Rust Repair and Prevention;* and *Chevrolet Trucks 1955–1959: How To Build & Modify.*

Introduction

Custom Car Painting on a Budget. Wow, that sounds like an ominous title. Most automotive enthusiasts will tell you that those terms are mutually exclusive. The words "custom car" and "budget" sure do not go together. "Car painting" and "budget" do not go together very often, either. Everyone seems to think of "cheap" when they hear the word "budget."

The reality is that everything is done on a budget. Everything. We merely forget that the budget is sometimes larger than other times. Projects sometimes are completed within budget, while other times they are not.

Regardless of the size of the budget or the scope of the project, the success of completing the task within budget lies squarely on getting the project completed correctly while minimizing errors. Errors require rework, which translates to additional time and material. Keeping these things in check goes a long way toward finishing the project under budget.

Two other principle factors are: 1) proper planning and 2) having a reasonable budget. Changing plans midstream will ultimately lead to an increase in time and material. There is also no denying that paint products are not cheap.

This book provides insight on planning a realistic budget, what materials are needed, and how to do the work required to paint your custom car.

PAINT JOB COSTS, MATERIALS, AND EQUIPMENT

Painting an automobile involves more than an investment of money. It requires labor, materials, equipment, and a work space. Some of those things are less expensive than others. Perhaps the most potentially expensive component of a high-quality automotive paint job is labor. Many people believe that performing a paint job consists of squeezing the trigger on a spray gun and avoiding runs in the paint. While that technically may be the only true painting component of a paint job, that task involves the least amount of time to perform.

There is lots of tedious, labor-intensive work that goes into a custom paint job. This is the very work that will make or break a paint job. When these tasks are done correctly, you will achieve a paint job of which you can be proud. Yet, if you skimp, you will be less than satisfied with the results. With such a significant percentage of the cost of a paint job being labor, this is where your efforts can save you substantially by doing the work yourself. After all, your time is significantly cheaper than paying for anyone else's.

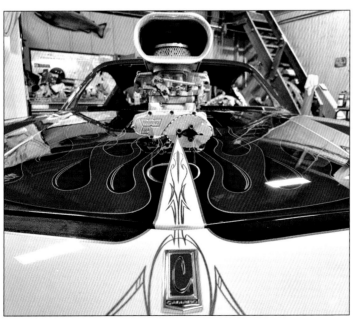

Before metaphorically jumping down the scoop, there's a lot to consider before custom painting your car. Do you have the equipment? How much will it cost? Do you have the skills required? Determine the answer to these questions before you begin.

Skill

Before you set out to perform a custom paint job on your car, ask yourself a few questions. Give each question some thought and provide yourself with an honest answer. When you jump in without first assessing your skills, you may end up with a partially finished project or one with less-than-acceptable results.

Do you have the necessary skills? Doing minor bodywork, masking, spraying primer, spraying paint, and reassembly of automotive components is not for everyone. If you have not done at least some of these tasks, you might not be ready to perform a complete custom paint job. But, if you own a spray gun that is designed for use with automotive paint and you can manage common hand tools, you can probably learn the required skills.

However, consider doing some smaller projects first as an opportunity to hone your skills a bit. Even if you do not have any automotive parts to work on, you can always buy a scrap fender, door, or hood from a salvage yard on which to practice. It is certainly better to do an excellent job refinishing one scrap part than totally screwing up your only drivable automobile. Even if that perfectly finished scrap part seems like a waste of time, it may be what you need to rekindle courage and enthusiasm when a larger project is not going as well.

Do you have the required time? Whether you are paying a premium shop rate or doing the work yourself, doing a complete custom paint job is a time-consuming process. Regardless of the vehicle's vintage, to obtain the best possible finish, a seemingly endless list of tasks must be performed on every surface that you plan to refinish.

If you start a project, will it have a firm must-be-finished date, or does it come with a flexible time frame? Everything takes longer than expected. You must remember that going into the project. When you are tied to a fixed completion date, you may want to pass if this is your first time painting an automobile. However, you are never going to learn a new skill if you do not try. So, if you have the time available to learn a new skill and there are no time constraints, go for it.

Quality

What are your expectations? How good does the finished product need to be? If you are simply making a used car look a little better for your first-time-driver child, the bar is not going to be very high. While you don't want your kid to be embarrassed to drive the vehicle, realize that it will probably be involved in a few fender benders. That does not mean that kids are bad drivers, but statistically, they do not have the experience to avoid some collisions. Your insurance broker will confirm

this. For this situation, simply repair any existing body damage, scuff the existing paint, prime, seal, and paint with a single-stage paint system. Single-stage paint in a solid color is the easiest to touch up, should that ever be necessary.

Perhaps it is your daily driver that needs a little freshening up. This is going to be a car that you want to look nice. In addition to repairing any existing body damage, you will most likely need to do some block sanding prior to applying sealer. Depending on your intended use for the vehicle, you may want to use a single-stage paint system, or you may choose to use base coat/clear coat. Each have their pros and cons, but those will be discussed later. Either system can provide a superb refinish for your automobile. The substantial difference is the investment in both time and money.

Maybe it is that dream-car project you have been waiting forever to build. This will be much like the previous situation but requires significantly more labor. For all intents and purposes, the paint, primer, and other materials cost the same, so you might as well get the most out of them, right? Besides, your time is free. The amount of love and dedication you put into the project is where you will see the biggest differences. Most of that dedication will be in the form of block sanding during the bodywork phase, along with wet sanding, buffing, and polishing after painting.

Experience

The best way to learn to do something is to do the work. Read everything you can about how to do the desired task, do the work as

instructed, evaluate your work, and figure out what you did wrong on anything that did not yield the best results.

A complete car or truck is probably not the best choice for a first-time paint job, but you or your neighbor probably have a wheelbarrow. These usually have some surface rust or worse, which will give you some experience in working with surface rust. A wheelbarrow is usually simple to disassemble and reassemble and provides an opportunity to prime and paint both the inside and outside of the sheet metal. This is a good project on which to learn, as it will have some contours to smooth out with some block sanding.

It also does not require more than a quart of paint. Most auto paint distributors usually have a few quarts of paint that was ordered and mixed but never picked up by the customer. This paint is usually sold at a reduced price. Even if you have to buy paint at regular price, a wheelbarrow will not require a lot. Even if you cannot find a wheelbarrow, many things can be used to learn how to paint. Bicycles, lawn mowers, and trash barrels can all be made to look better with a new coat of paint.

Materials

When selecting automotive paint products, do not attempt to play chemist. That work has already been done by the chemists that work for the paint manufacturing companies. What you should do is determine which type of paint you want to use and ensure that you use compatible products.

Any automotive paint system has various primers and substrates that are designed to adhere to and cover various surfaces, such as steel, fiberglass, and aluminum. Each of these products will have certain top coats with which they are compatible. Top coats (color) have certain products onto which they can be applied, as well as certain products that can be applied over them, such as a clear coat.

Premium Products

Just as there are premium automobiles and lesser automobiles, there are different grades of automotive paint products. Most paint manufacturers have a good, better, and best line of products. They all have their valuable properties and weaknesses and are priced accordingly.

Some of those properties include the ease of application, good coverage, long-lasting shine, and durability in all types of climates. As with clothing, a vehicle that is driven every day in all types of weather requires different protection than a vehicle stored in a climate-controlled showroom under bright lights. Premium products also have a wider variety of special effects, such as pearl, candy, or translucent.

For premium products, you typically need to contact a distributor in your area that deals primarily with auto body repair shops and custom auto shops. These are the primary sources of business for these distributors, so they may not always be available to answer your specific questions.

However, you can ask when they're typically less busy, and they will probably be more than happy to earn your business. In most cases, these distributors will not be open on the weekend. That is always something that the nonprofessional must keep in mind if you are planning to work on a paint job over the weekend. As long as you can remember to ensure you have all of the products you need when you need them, it is not a problem.

Shop-Grade Products

Not all automotive part stores carry automotive paint products, but those that do typically carry what is known as shop-grade products. These shop-grade product lines are perfectly acceptable if you are looking for standard colors of paint and the basic primers and clear products. The downfall is that this product line may not include candy, pearl, metallic, or other exotic paint products.

They will be somewhat less expensive than the premium lines and are available whenever the parts store is open. That might be reason enough to use these products. When your local auto-parts store is part of a chain, there is a distinct possibility the chain will mix color top coats only at one location due to the cost of mixing machines and the amount of inventory required. This might mean you are forced to pick up your actual paint at a different location, or they may be willing to transfer between stores for you. The store transfer may be limited to certain days or a specific time of day, so allow for that when you are planning your work.

Different Colors, Different Costs

While it does not necessarily make sense, different colors of paint have different prices. Reds, maroons, and purples are typically more expensive than yellows, blues, and silver due to the contents that provide the color. You should still paint your car the color that you really want, but if your budget is tight, one color might be just as desirable as another.

Additional Materials, Additional Cost

When planning your paint scheme and/or paint type, realize that more materials are going to increase the cost. Any time you are painting a vehicle, be sure to have enough paint, primer, and everything else

Besides primer, sealer, and masking tape, even a simple paint job requires at least three more products to get color on your vehicle. A single-stage paint, such as acrylic urethane, requires the paint itself along with hardener and reducer.

you are going to be using. Unless you can determine exactly how much of each color you are going to need for a multicolor paint job, multiple colors will cost more than a single color due to the additional colors.

In most cases, paint suppliers mix paint in quarts or gallons. So, if a vehicle requires 1 gallon of one color to paint and you have some left over for touch-up, a gallon is sufficient. However, if you desire to make it a two-tone paint scheme, you need at least a quart for your secondary color. This example requires you to purchase a gallon of your primary color and a quart of the secondary color. With experience, you might be able to better determine that two quarts of the primary color and one quart of the secondary color is sufficient, but you might not want to take that chance.

Additionally, you must choose between a single-stage paint or base coat/clear coat. Both require the same amount of bodywork and substrates (primer and sealer). However, using clear will not only cost you more in material, but it will cost more in time (spraying, color sanding, buffing, and polishing).

An important note is that you can make single-stage paint shine just as much as you can the base coat/clear coat. If shine is what you are after, you can accomplish that with single-stage paint and additional labor in the form of color sanding, buffing, and polishing to save some money, but you will not have the ultraviolet (UV) protection that base coat/clear coat provides. This is fine when your vehicle sits inside a garage when it is not being driven.

Multicolor paint schemes or special effects (pearl, candy colors, or metallic) are going to cost more for materials as well as labor. But again, your labor is cheap, so if you can afford the materials, there is nothing to keep you from pulling off an exotic paint scheme that is just as high quality as your local custom paint emporium.

Equipment

To perform any operation or complete any task, there is always some tool or piece of equipment required. When the task is more complex, more tools are usually involved. However, that does not mean that all of them are an absolute necessity. Some make the task easier, while others save you time. Most of these fall into the classification of being nice to have but not necessary. Others are good to have if you make your living painting automobiles or even if you do it on a somewhat regular basis but are probably too expensive to justify for your first automotive paint job.

Required

Unless you are going to use rattle cans to paint your car (no, we are not going to go there), you must have a spray gun, an air compressor, and an air hose. You can buy, borrow, or rent them, but these are must-have items for painting a car. Also, you need some sandpaper, a sanding block, masking tape, mixing cups, stir sticks, and paint filters. If you can gather all of these items and know how to use them, you can get your car painted. We will go into more detail on these a little later.

Optional

It is nice to have two separate paint guns or at least two different-sized tips for one gun. The reasoning for this is that primer and other substrates are substantially thicker than top coats. To attempt to use the same paint gun with the same paint tip for both is a struggle.

When there is no bodywork to do, one small sanding block can be used to scuff the entire surface prior to applying paint. However, when bodywork is necessary, you will appreciate having a longboard sander for large, flat surfaces. If you are going to be doing lots of bodywork, a pneumatic or electric orbital sander is nice to have to remove surface rust. This also doubles as a buffer later in the project after the paint has been applied and you are buffing it out.

Auto body workers have been using dual-action (DA) sanders forever when doing bodywork. If you know how to use it, a DA sander can save time and effort. However, when used by someone who is inexperienced, it is easy to create more work for yourself.

Long-Term Use

A paint tree is handy to use for painting small parts. Just hang them on the tree. The one I have is a round pole mounted to a mobile base. It has arms that can be rotated around the pole and at different heights. Each of these arms have a hook on the end from which you can hang parts. It works well but was not cheap. A common and economical alternative is to suspend a piece of electrical conduit or pipe from the ceiling of your work area in a horizontal orientation. Tie pieces and parts to it using welding wire.

If you are doing lots of masking, a masking station that dispenses masking paper and applies masking tape to one edge as it dispenses can save you some time. Masking paper can be cut with scissors or a razor blade, so a fancy dispenser should not be your first purchase. Money is better spent on a second spray gun if you do not already have one.

Perhaps at the top of the list of things that makes the paint job easier but is a large investment is an automobile rotisserie. These are designed to rotate an automobile body or chassis around a horizontal axis to provide full access to the inner, outer, top, and bottom sides.

Work Space

Wherever you paint your car or truck, you need a suitable work space. In addition to potentially learning new skills and working with expensive materials, painting an automobile requires a sizable work area. While most passenger cars will easily fit into a parking space that is a mere 171 square feet (9 feet x 19 feet), that same vehicle, when disassembled, takes up much more space than that.

Room to Work

You need space to disassemble parts, store parts, and prime and paint parts. You need at least an arm's length of distance away from the parts you are painting simply to maneuver yourself and your spray gun. Other than the car body itself, any other parts that are to be painted separately should be hung, if possible, to allow you to paint both sides at one time. If necessary, you can lay parts across sawhorses, but this requires longer drying times before you can turn the parts over to paint the opposite side.

Another option for a painting area is a portable, inflatable paint booth. Much like an inflatable

While a lift is great for disassembly and reassembly, it is not an absolute must for doing automotive paint work. This area is not an ideal paint location, as the lighting is not suitable and there is too much clutter. Everything in the corner would be full of overspray if a vehicle was painted in this space.

This painting area is much better suited for painting, as the walls reflect all available light. Other than the vehicle and/or parts being painted and the roll-around cart that the body is on, the only other things in the painting area are the air hose, spray gun, and the painter.

bounce house for children, these can be purchased through Amazon or other online stores. Available with built-in fans and filters, they are a growing, attractive option for occasional painters.

Lighting

You need light and plenty of it. No painter has ever complained about having too much light to paint. Having adequate light makes obtaining a perfect body prior to applying paint much easier. If the body panels are not correct before you apply sealer, they are not going to be correct after you apply paint. It simply does not work that way. Good light also helps to avoid runs, drips, and errors, all of which require rework. LED or fluorescent lighting is the best for painting, so if you are going to purchase new lighting for your garage for this painting project, that is the best bang for your buck.

Good ventilation is a necessity. While a commercial spray booth is the best option, many vehicles have been painted in a home garage with the door opened slightly and a box fan under the door to pull the fumes out.

Your work space must have an adequate electric supply to power the air compressor. You may be able to get by with a 110-watt air compressor, but a better alternative is a larger two-stage air compressor that typically requires 220 watts.

If you do not have access to a garage in which to paint, it is worth your while to inquire with local body shops about the possibility of renting their paint booth during some off hours. If you are not familiar with any of the local shops, check with the people at the counter where you buy your paint products, as they are going to know the latest on which shops are busy and which ones might be willing to collaborate with you. While a busy shop would probably not do this, a smaller shop may consider it. You definitely need to respect their allotted time frame and most likely need to have all of the bodywork done beforehand to use their booth for spraying final color (and clear, if applicable).

Another possibility is to check with a local community college or technical school that offers classes in automotive painting. You may have to register for a class or two to be able to use its spray booth, but that would not be all bad. You might even meet some new friends who could help you with some of the grunt work.

Regardless of where the spray booth is located or how you get to use it, if you need to transport your painting project to it, try to get it as close to being ready to paint as you can. That means all bodywork done and parts that are to be removed are removed and left at home. Unless you are using an enclosed trailer, transport your project car on a dry day. You need to do any masking after you get to the spray booth, and that takes time.

Unless you are spraying in an actual spray booth that is empty, cover everything in the immediate area with some type of drop cloth. If you do not, you will find just how far overspray will float through the air before it lands on something. The quick way to cover everything in the garage that you do not want to yield to overspray is to purchase a roll or two of clear plastic. Anything between 2 to 6 mil thickness will work great. With some help from

A great advantage of having access to a spray booth is that it will have great lighting. This helps ensure that you achieve adequate coverage in all areas high, low, or in tight places. Professional spray booths are also heated, which allows you to paint year-round. A good ventilation system is another benefit.

a friend or two, use a staple gun to secure one edge of the plastic sheeting to the ceiling or rafters. Let the other edge fall to the floor. Use duct tape to secure the plastic sheeting to the floor if desired. Depending on how fancy your garage may be, you may want to cover the floor as well. However, plastic sheeting can be very slippery, so it is a fall hazard.

Unless you have some sort of exhaust fan in the area where you are painting, plan to leave the garage door open at least a few inches while spraying to avoid a buildup of overspray. After giving the paint a few minutes to flash, open the door a bit more to evacuate any residual overspray. Close it to within a few inches when applying the successive coats. Make sure that nothing is going to blow in from the outside and land on your fresh paint while the door is open. Early morning is often a suitable time to paint.

If the area outside your garage is dusty, sprinkle it down prior to painting to keep the dust down. Before spraying, sweep or vacuum the floor in your painting area. You are going to use lots of air pressure, so you will stir up dust if there is any. However, avoid the temptation to water down the floor as this will add humidity into the paint, which may cause more problems than it would solve.

Environmental Regulations

Environmental laws regarding automotive paint are constantly under review and subject to change, so if you have any questions, consult with the local supplier of your paint products. They should know the local laws regarding the use of and disposal of used or excess paint products. Waterborne paint products are largely required for use on the east and west coasts of the United States and are becoming available throughout the Midwest. On the local level, if the product is on the shelf, it has been considered acceptable for that area.

You will most likely have some paint left over during a painting project. Since automotive paint is mixed with reducers and hardeners, you cannot pour it back into the bucket like house paint. One way to dispose of leftover paint is to pour it into an open container and let it cure. Eventually, it will turn into a rubbery blob at the bottom of the container. When it gets to that point, it can be disposed of in the trash. Check with your paint supplier for other suggestions. One thing is for sure: never pour it on the ground.

Safety

For years, car painters did little to protect themselves from the dangers of the chemicals we call paint. Often, a bandana over their nose and mouth was the extent of any personal protective equipment (PPE). Quite sadly, those painters who are still alive will tell you that they should have done more to protect themselves. It should be obvious to most people that inhaling paint overspray, mixing solvents, and sanding dust is not a good thing.

With most contemporary solvent-based paint products, including hardeners that contain isocyanates, inhalation protection is necessary. At a minimum, a spray mask with replaceable filter cartridges should be used. If you are not painting cars for a living, this will usually be sufficient. To extend the life of one of these masks, store it in a resealable bag when not in use. If you are a smoker or have other pre-existing health conditions, that might not be enough. If you plan to paint multiple vehicles, seriously consider investing in a full-face, fresh-air respiratory system. The price may seem expensive, but you only have one set of lungs.

A multitude of products are used in a complete paint job, so the recommendations for the specific products vary. However, the National Institute for Occupational Safety and Health (NIOSH)-approved respiratory protection recommendations are included in each of these products. The local dealer that supplies

At the very minimum, protect yourself with a charcoal mask, goggles, and gloves when doing most painting tasks. You only have one set of lungs and eyes, so they are worth protecting. Wearing disposable gloves helps prevent you from having to clean paint off your hands.

When spraying any automotive paint products that contain isocyanates (almost any paint product with a hardener in it), you must protect your body. Isocyanates can enter your body through your mouth, nose, eyes, or pores in your skin. A paint suit protects your body.

If your paint suit does not include a hood, a separate head sock will provide coverage for your head. This also helps minimize overspray that lands on your face.

your paint products will have these safety products available.

Isocyanates can enter your body through tear ducts or skin contact. Therefore, whenever you are mixing or spraying paint, wear goggles, gloves, and a paint suit or disposable coveralls. Aside from perhaps a full-face, fresh-air respiratory system, all of these safety-related items should be figured into the costs of doing a paint job.

Not only are paint products bad for your internal organs but they are also flammable. You must always be aware of any ignition sources that could spark overspray into a fireball. As with any project going on in a garage, always have an easily accessible fire extinguisher nearby.

Paint Products

Contemporary paint materials consist of resins, additives, catalysts, and solvents. Resins are the bulk of the material, whether it is paint or clear. The resin is what determines how the material sprays, cures, and holds up over time. The resin itself must be mixed with a hardener in exact ratios to yield the desired results. Additives are used to enhance the application properties. Catalysts can be used to alter the reaction time between resin and hardener. Solvents are used to adjust the flow capabilities of the mixture.

Historically, those applying automotive paint chose between enamel or lacquer-based paint. In most cases, two or three coats of enamel covers and provides a decent shine after a good coat of wax has been applied. For a custom paint job, lacquer paint was applied in several coats with extremely fine sandpaper used between coats for a super smooth surface. Then, acrylic enamel and acrylic lacquer came about. They were an improvement to their respective predecessors and offered greater durability.

Continued improvements led to urethane and polyurethane paint products. These include products that are quick drying and allow for less time in a body shop for repairs, and they provide greater durability and resistance to airborne pollution and oxidation.

While not required everywhere, waterborne paint is becoming common throughout the United States. Its use is mandated on both coasts of the United States, as well as in most of Europe and Canada. The largest difference in this waterborne paint is that water (instead of harsh solvents) is used to make it a sprayable liquid. Application is still similar, with air movement over the surface rather than evaporation being the essential component in drying.

Paint/Clear

Paint is what gives your car the color that makes it so appealing. Paint and the optional clear coat are considered top coats, as they are applied atop the sealer.

When it comes to automotive paint, it is all mixed upon purchase. Even if the paint you request is a stock color from a late-model vehicle, the paint is mixed by adding specific amounts of toners to a base to provide the exact color you request. The code and the color (along with other information) will be listed on the label.

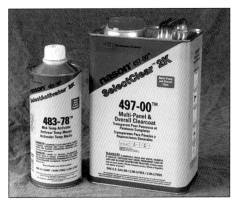

Using clear atop the color adds a layer of UV protection as well as gloss. However, there are a wide variety of clear products, all designed for specific uses. Some are designed specifically to air dry, while others require force dry. Some require reducer, while others do not. Do your research prior to applying clear so you do not mess up a perfectly good paint job.

Primers

Primers are substrates, as they are applied beneath the sealer. These primers include elements to enhance adhesion and promote corrosion protection. They also serve as fillers

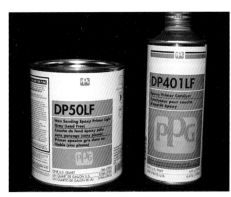

One of the most popular epoxy primers on the market is PPG's DPLF. It is available in five colors and can be applied directly to bare metal to provide strong corrosion protection and adhesion. It requires being mixed with a catalyst prior to application. It can also be used as a sealer, which eliminates the need for another product.

Primer-surfacer is typically mixed with a reducer to make it sprayable. Older primer-surfacers did not require being mixed with hardener, but most do now.

in various forms to provide a smooth surface.

Sealer is technically a primer, as it is composed of primer-type products, but sealer serves as a convenient milestone between substrates and top coats.

Fillers

Fillers are typically plastic in nature and can be in the form of a solid (as in body filler) or liquid (as in

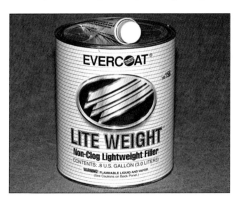

A wide variety of body fillers are available with various characteristics. Some are designed for large areas of bodywork, while others are designed for small divots. Some are easier to sand than others. Body filler can usually be found at your local auto-parts store and from paint suppliers.

sprayable body filler). In either case, the bulk of the material is mixed with a hardening agent, applied to the surface, and then sanded to the final contour.

Fillers are used to fill shallow low spots in the body panels. sheet-metal panels that are more than 1/8-inch deep should be metal-worked prior to being filled. Composite panels that are low should be repaired first with similar composite components prior to being filled.

Thinners, Reducers, and Activators

Various primer, paint, or filler products require activators (also known as hardener) to set off the chemical reaction that transforms the product from a soft or pliable solid or liquid into the finished product. Primers or paints require thinner or reducer to make them sprayable. The same product that makes the

While it is a best practice to use one of the specific thinners/reducers suggested from the same manufacturer when mixing primer, paint, or clear, it is always a good practice to have some cleanup thinner around. This is used to clean your spray gun and other cleanup chores. You can always find this type of product at your local auto-parts store for a reasonable price.

product sprayable can also be used to clean.

Since most paint products involve a chemical reaction, they are developed under controlled conditions. This research and development allows for some of the components to be interchangeable depending on the actual condition in which it is being used. Reducers and thinners are often rated for certain temperature ranges. When spraying paint products in relatively cool temperatures, use a faster-evaporating solvent. In relatively warmer temperatures, use a slower-evaporating solvent. However, you do not need to remember what products to use, as the label on the container typically indicates the appropriate temperature range for the product.

Masking

Masking a vehicle prior to spraying primer and paint requires multiple rolls of masking tape. Do not skimp on masking tape, as there is a definite difference between the masking tape that is used to paint your home and the tape used for painting your vehicle. To ensure you are using the correct type of masking tape, purchase it where you purchase your paint products. Automotive paint products include solvents that are much stronger than anything used in house paint and will soak through conventional masking tape.

In addition to automotive paint-grade masking tape that is typically available in widths from 1/2 inch to as wide as 3 inches, there is fine-line tape. This is available in widths from 1/16 inch to 1/4 inch. Since this tape is much narrower, it is considerably more flexible. This makes it ideal for laying out flames, scallops, and other graphics.

Automotive paint-grade masking tape is available in a variety of widths, commonly ranging from 1/2-inch wide to 2 inches wide. The 3/4-inch-wide size serves most needs, but during a complete paint job, you most likely need narrower and wider sizes as well.

For covering larger areas, use masking paper that is secured by masking tape. While newspaper has undoubtedly been used to mask large areas, it is certainly not designed to use for masking automotive paint. The solvents soak through the newsprint, render it useless, and cause a real mess in the process. Additionally, it creates newspaper lint or dust that you would need to pick out of your fresh paint.

Automotive-grade masking paper is similar to butcher paper or kraft paper, which is typically either white or brown. It is comparable in weight to paper that goes in a standard office copier machine. Regardless of the color, it is used the same in that it covers a large area when compared to masking tape. Masking paper has no adhesive, so it must be secured with masking tape around the edges.

Frisket paper can be used to cover large areas, just like masking paper. However, the difference is that frisket paper is self-adhesive with a peel-off backing. This is extremely conve-

nient when masking large areas that include intricate paint schemes. You can lay out your graphic design, such as flames or scallops, with fine-line tape. Peel the backing off the frisket paper, apply it to the area to be masked, and press it firmly in place to ensure that there are no trapped air bubbles. Using a razor blade, cut the frisket paper along the fine-line tape and peel the frisket paper off the surface that is to be painted. Using frisket paper allows the user to mask precise shapes and paint them with no overspray.

Sandpaper

There is no denying that the bulk of time spent on a high-quality paint job is spent prepping the sheet metal. The actual painting takes little time. Prepping the surface is what really matters, and most of that is spent sanding. Obviously, any necessary bodywork (collision damage or rust repair) must be done first, but even with new sheet metal, sanding must be done.

Sandpaper is rated based on how many grits appear within a square inch of the sandpaper surface. A rating of 18 grit is very coarse, as the grits are exceptionally large. A rating of 2,000 grit is extremely fine, as the grits are exceedingly small. Even 3,000- and 4,000-grit sandpaper is available.

Coarse 40- to 80-grit sandpaper is commonly used to remove existing paint, 80- to 240- grit sandpaper is generally used to smooth body filler, and 280- to 600-grit sandpaper is commonly used to smooth the entire body prior to applying sealer and paint. For a daily driver, this is most likely sufficient. For any type of vehicle where bodywork and paint quality will be judged, finer-grit

Sandpaper is available in a wide variety of grits and different shapes and sizes to fit a variety of DA sanders, sanding blocks, and boards. Be sure that you know how the sandpaper attaches and is secured to your sanding device.

sandpaper is used to perfect the painted surface prior to and after the application of clear.

A common mistake made when sanding is to not use a sanding board or sanding block to provide a uniform surface and even pressure on the sandpaper. The human hand consists of hard knuckles and soft muscle tissue, which results in a surface of varying hardness. This inconsistency causes waves in the surface.

Tools

Just as with any other task, there are certain tools and equipment to use. Some are essential, while others simply make the task easier. Some are inexpensive, some are handmade to solve a specific issue, and others are pretty much just for the professionals (due to cost).

Basic Tools

Most of the basic tools associated with painting are bodywork tools: sanders, grinders, body hammers, slide hammers, filler spreaders, and sanding blocks. Sanders and grinders are often the same tool with different attachments. They have a hand-held motor (electric or pneumatic) to which grinding wheels, sanding discs, or wire brushes can be attached. These are commonly used for removing paint and rust. They can be used with sanding discs to smooth body filler, but this can do more damage than good if used improperly.

Body hammers and slide hammers are used to shape metal. Body hammers can be used with or without a dolly to form metal back to its original shape or into a shape from flat stock. Hammers have heads of different shapes, sizes, and textures to effect various changes to the metal. Slide hammers attach to studs or pins attached to the sheet metal, and a weighted cylinder is pulled away from the sheet metal to pull the sheet metal back into position. This work with body hammers, dollies, and slide hammers should be done until the sheet metal is as close as possible to the desired shape.

Filler spreaders of assorted sizes are used to spread body filler over a recessed area to bring it back to the desired shape. Sanding blocks are

With the various lengths of sanding boards available, it is more economical to purchase the sandpaper for them in a roll. You can tear off a piece that fits your sanding board, whether it be long, short, or somewhere in between. Not all auto-parts stores provide this option, so you may need to find an auto-body supply store or order it online.

Hammers and dollies come in various shapes and sizes, and so do automotive body panels. Some hammers and dollies are used to form or repair gentle, large-radius curves, while others are for working in tight areas. When using hammers, it's important to know when to use brute strength and when to use finesse. With automotive bodywork, the latter is more common.

used with sandpaper for final shaping and smoothing of the body filler and/or the sheet metal.

Pneumatic Tools

A spray gun and a dual-action (DA) sander are the most-common pneumatic tools used when painting an automobile. For a one-time painting project, the spray gun is a necessity, while a DA is a luxury.

An air compressor is an electric-powered motor that compresses air into a cylinder to power pneumatic equipment. This process creates moisture that collects in the bottom of the reservoir. This compressor's reservoir should be large enough to provide enough air for the task at hand without being required to stop to allow the compressor to catch up. To help your compressor do this, drain any fluid out of the reservoir daily when using it. The air compressor should deliver clean, dry air. While using an external air drier in your air lines should always be done, you should still drain water out of the reservoir daily.

A regulator on the air compressor allows you to control how much air comes out of the compressor. To properly adjust the air pressure coming through the spray gun, adjust the air pressure controls while holding the gun's trigger fully open. Using this process, set the spray gun's air pressure to the recommended setting for the material you are spraying. A filter is required to prevent water, oil, and rust that gather in the compressor's reservoir from contaminating your spray gun and ruining your paint job.

A compressor must have adequate power and a large enough reservoir to provide the necessary volume required to spray paint (or any task for which it is to be used). Compare the air requirement for the intended spray gun to the capabilities of the compressor. If the air available is more than the air required, you should be able to complete the task at hand.

When applying paint, you want to have enough air available to apply a complete coat without stopping. This may call for an air compressor with a larger reservoir tank (not just more horsepower). For example, many air compressors designed for use with a roofing nail gun are small for portability but run all day to keep up with demand. This type of air compressor is not suitable for automotive painting.

Spray Guns

If you are looking to purchase a spray gun, this is your first question: Will you use waterborne or solvent-based paint products? For waterborne products, use a spray gun that utilizes non-corrosive, stainless-steel internal components to prevent rust from forming on the inside of the spray gun. While these components should also work for solvent-based paint products, you cannot use the same spray gun for both, as the water and solvent tend to gel. Regardless of how meticulous you may be with cleaning your spraying equipment, once it is used, you will never get it to brand-new condition again.

This is the second question to ask yourself before purchasing a spray gun: Do you want a conventional gun or a high-volume, low-pressure (HVLP) gun? While a conventional spray gun that uses lots of pressure undoubtedly costs less money to purchase, the HVLP saves money in the not-so-long run. Since this HVLP gun

An HVLP spray gun is shown that applies material at a significantly lower pressure than a siphon-feed spray gun. This type of spray gun is more efficient because it causes less overspray (paint bouncing off the surface) and, therefore, uses less paint.

Most HVLP spray guns come with different-sized spray tips to compensate for the various material thicknesses. Most primer substrate materials are much thicker than the paint and clear top-coat products. Having the correct-size tip for the material you are spraying provides a better finish.

uses less pressure, less paint goes up in overspray. The less paint you use, the lower the overall cost will be.

One specific thing to remember when potentially buying a spray gun and an air compressor is that the air compressor needs to generate about 60 psi. A conventional spray gun will use all of this to apply the paint at that same 60 psi, causing overspray and stirring up any dust in your painting area. An HVLP gun will require 60 psi but will slow down the air pressure considerably (to around 10 psi) as the paint or primer comes out of the spray gun.

If you are going to spray primer and paint, having multiple spray tips for one spray gun or, ideally, having multiple spray guns is a distinct advantage. Primer and other substrates are substantially thicker than paint and clear top coats. Using one tip to spray both products will clog when spraying primer and not atomize correctly when spraying thinner top coats. For the hobbyist, there are some high-quality package deals that include both a primer gun and a top-coat gun, along with various accessories for a reasonable price.

Detail or Jamb Gun

When doing automotive painting, you will quickly realize that a detail (doorjamb gun) is good to have. Whether painting small areas (such as doorjambs) or spraying intricate parts, a detail gun makes your job easier. The biggest difference between a full-size spray gun and a detail gun is the size of the paint reservoir. This significantly smaller size makes a detail gun easier to maneuver around small parts and allows the painter to adequately cover small parts that may not be accessible with a full-size spray gun.

The top-mounted trigger on a conventional detail gun is operated by the full length of a user's index finger. This comfortable position allows painters to operate these lightweight units in confined spaces with maximum control.

Regardless of the type of spray gun or the material it sprays, it is essential to clean it thoroughly after each use, as dry paint or primer can clog up the small passageways in a spray gun. For most automotive paint products, the related information sheet includes the pot life (the amount of time before the paint is unusable) of the product.

The spray gun must be emptied and the material thoroughly cleaned before the material has a chance to harden. If not, the paint product dries up in the small passages of the spray gun and renders it useless. When the spray gun gets clogged and cannot be cleaned, it will not lay down a good coat of paint. In addition to the cost of a new spray gun, a faulty spray gun quickly begins to cost money in both time and materials. If paint was applied but not correctly, that paint may require additional sanding time to make it right, or you could possibly sand it off and reshoot it. When you must reshoot, it requires additional paint and related materials.

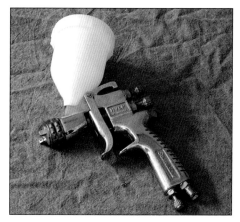

An HVLP detail gun looks and operates just like a full-sized spray gun, albeit with a much smaller reservoir. A detail gun works great when spraying a small amount of paint, such as when doing touch-up work.

Each primer or paint product (solvent or waterborne) requires specific cleanup materials. For solvent-based products, it is usually the same reducer that is used to spray the product. With waterborne, it is often a mixture of water and alcohol.

Fully enclosed cleaning cabinets in commercial body shops force cleaning solvent through the spray gun while the trigger is held in an open position. With the workflow and the amount of paint (not to mention different paint colors), professional shops must ensure their spray guns are clean and function properly.

When you are finished spraying, pour any remaining contents into an old paint mixing cup. This allows the product to dry so it can be disposed. Fill the spray gun cup about 1/3 full of the cleaning solvent and swish it around, turning the gun in various directions. This removes most of the paint product. Then, pour fresh cleaning solvent into the spray cup and spray until nothing but clean solvent is coming from the

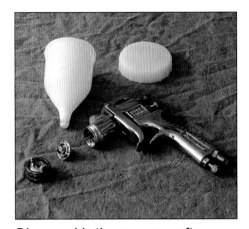

Disassemble the spray gun after emptying any paint product from the paint cup. Put the air cap, air nozzle, needle, and the air-control knob into a mixing cup full of cleaning solvent to soak while you clean the rest of the spray gun.

This palm-type orbital sander can be used for a variety of sanding tasks, depending on the grit of the sandpaper used with it. Sand-paper discs for this type of sander usually have a self-stick backing that allows you to quickly change the disc as necessary.

spray-gun tip. This cleans all of the passageways.

Lastly, disassemble the spray gun and wipe down the internal parts with cleaning solvent. Use a bristle brush (one that has been designed for cleaning a spray gun) dipped in cleaning solvent to clean paint from the larger passages in the housing and the air cap. Never use any sort of sharp object to clean any part of the spray gun, as any scratch to the fine spray-gun parts can disrupt the fan spray.

Reassemble and blow nothing but air through the spray gun to remove any cleaning solvent that can clog the air passages. Wipe down the exterior of the spray gun with clean solvent to remove any paint drips or splotches. After drying the spray gun's exterior, hang it in a vertical position for storage.

DA Sander

Having a DA sander and the experience to know how to use it will save you lots of time when sanding

This coarse wheel is used with a pneumatic die grinder to remove paint from intricate areas. A variety of accessories can be used with a die grinder to cut, grind, sand, or buff a surface. Many of these accessories can also be used on an angle-head grinder. With a die grinder, surface contact is usually made with the thin edge of the wheel.

With this angle-head grinder, surface contact is usually made with the larger face surface of the disc. In this case, a Roloc disc is typically used to remove lesser amounts of surface rust or provide a good surface for applying body filler or primer.

an automobile body. It is good practice to first use a DA to remove paint from an area to get down to bare metal. This gives you an idea as to how fast it works. If your first time using a DA is to smooth some body filler, you may end up replacing that same body filler after you erroneously remove it with a DA.

Pay attention to what type of DA sander you are using or purchasing. Some have a longer orbit and are designed for roughing in bodywork. Others have a smaller orbit and are designed for finish work. The size of the orbit cannot be changed on a given DA, so choose one that matches the work you will be doing.

For general purpose, a hand-held 8-inch rotary sander can be used to strip paint and filler. Just keep speeds low (400 to 600 rpm) and keep the pad as flat to the surface as possible so that you do not build up excessive heat. This tool can be equipped with a polishing bonnet later in the project to buff and polish the paint, which makes it a versatile tool.

Masking Paper/Tape Machine

Since you are doing lots of masking, having a roller that dispenses masking paper with masking tape

applied along one edge is a convenience. However, it is not a necessity. It may take a bit longer to apply, but if you learn how to properly mask a vehicle by yourself, you will ultimately do a better job of masking. We will talk a lot about masking in Chapter 4.

Paint Trees/Panel Stands

Whether you spend the money to purchase a paint tree and/or panel stands from your body shop

supplier or build something on your own, you need a method of holding individual parts, such as a hood, fenders, and doors. Depending on the complexity of your paint project, you will need to paint significantly smaller parts, such as gas-filler doors, ashtrays, wheels, and exterior mirrors. These are usually painted while being hung from something. Being creative with what you have will potentially save you some funds.

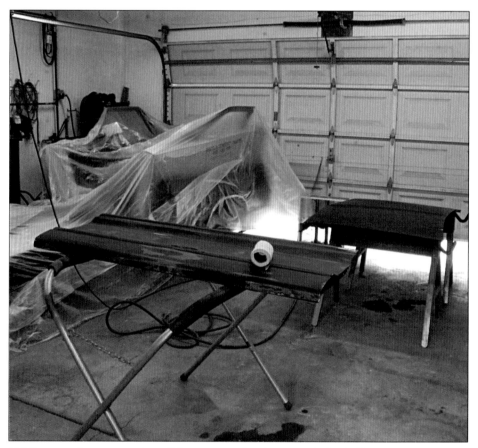

Folding sawhorses work well for supporting large, relatively flat parts when sanding, prepping, and painting. Having a method of hanging small parts is also a good idea. For parts that are not real heavy, hang a piece of electrical conduit from a few rafters. Then, hang pieces to be painted from it with welding wire. Various paint stands are commercially available but are often too expensive for use on your first paint job.

While you can hold a piece of masking paper in place with one hand and tape it down with the other, it is much easier to pull a piece of masking paper off the roll that has masking tape applied to one edge already.

BODYWORK

From this angle, this mid-1950s Buick looks to be solid. It appears the right rear quarter panel has been stripped of paint but not protected by epoxy primer, which led to the formation of surface rust. The fact that the back glass is still intact is a good sign of it being restorable. Obviously, it needs a trunk lid and hood, but this could be the makings of a very cool cruiser.

Whether your next automotive painting project is for a vehicle that you already own or one that you are contemplating purchasing, you must first assess the entire project. It is very rare that a paint job is all that the vehicle will need.

You must have an idea of what your plans are for this project. Does it need a new body panel, new floors, or does it even have a drivetrain? If you are looking for an inexpensive daily driver, an operable drivetrain is more important than a paint job. If you have a running, driving car that requires some freshening up, you are in the right place.

Presumably, your next project car can start, drive, and stop. Drive it for a few days and make notes of what it needs versus what you want to do

The two most exciting times of an automotive paint project occur before you begin and after you are finished. In the beginning, there are dreams of perfection and you behind the wheel of the best-looking car on the road. When you are finished, the reality of how well you succeeded sets in. By following the steps in this book and doing the work required, the dream and the result can be the same.

with it. As you begin to compile this list, make note of what must be done before a paint job and what should be done after applying paint.

For instance, if the vehicle requires new wiring before being drivable, wiring can be done after painting. This saves you from masking all the wiring to keep your color-coded wiring intact. Other interior upgrades, such as air conditioning or new upholstery, should be made after painting.

Chassis or suspension upgrades or repairs should be completed before painting. The same goes for the engine and/or transmission because you do not want anyone leaning over a freshly painted fender to install a new engine or major component. An exception to any of this might be on a total frame-off rebuild, where many upgrades are being completed simultaneously by different people.

Hidden Issues

Besides the upgrades that you know you want to make, look for hidden issues that require attention. Many of these, if left unresolved, will quickly ruin a good paint job. Yes, I am talking about rust. With almost all makes and models, some areas are prone to developing rust. With any vehicle you are planning to paint, do some research beforehand to gain more knowledge of these rusty pitfalls.

If your vehicle is largely supported by the automotive aftermarket, check out all the relevant catalogs that cater to your vehicle. When there are patch panels available, that will give you a good idea of where to be suspicious of rust issues. Any areas of a vehicle that can trap moisture are places of suspicion. This

can be around the headlights, in the front fenders, above the wheel wells, on the bottom of doors, on rocker panels, on floors, and on the trunk floor.

Other places that are not so obvious are around the windshield and rear glass. These are areas where patch panels are usually not available but rust can still form. There may be two or more pieces of metal that come together in this area, yet it is all covered by trim or rubber molding. The rust forms out of sight, so it is often out of mind until it becomes an expansive area of rust that is difficult to repair. It might not be any easier to repair before painting, but addressing it before painting will eliminate rework that adds to the budget in time and money. To check some of these areas, drive the vehicle through a car wash and watch for leaks around the glass.

Purchase Price versus Expense to Finish

When you are looking to purchase a project, keep in mind not only the purchase price but also the expense to finish. While you can always find projects that have been started, there is always some reason they are not finished. Perhaps the seller really enjoys doing chassis and engine work but does not like painting, wiring, and upholstery. You may be able to get a great deal, especially if the work that has already been completed was done just the way you want it. However, if you are going to redo some of that completed work, it is already costing you more time and money.

Regardless of how good of a deal it may be, if it is not what you want, you may need to pass. If it is what

you want but the purchase price plus cost to finish exceeds your budget, you will have to do some soul searching prior to saying yes or no. Only you can make that decision. It is not a comfortable place to be when you are in way over your head, whether that is monetary or your skill level.

Have a Budget and Stick with It

Painting a car can take a long time. Sure, you can mask a car and paint it in an afternoon if you want, but you most likely will not be happy with the result. If you are happy with it, your expectations are way too low. To perform the work properly, there is disassembly of some items, repair and/or replacement of others, preparation for all, painting, drying, and reassembly. That all takes time. Do you have that time to budget into painting a car? You can make the time if you want to, but that is up to you. Are you willing to make the time?

Then, there is the financial budget. Do you have the disposable income necessary to paint an automobile? Depending on what you are looking for, the money spent for a paint job is going to be close to $1,000 for a bargain-basement price with no upper limit. It is obvious that a smaller vehicle requires less paint product than a larger vehicle. However, some automotive paint sells for $300 to $400 per gallon, and there is a substantial market for paint that sells for $3,000 to $4,000 per gallon. For most vehicles, you need to purchase at least a gallon of paint. Not all will require that, but on average it will.

Shop around before you make a decision on a paint scheme and the type of paint you want to use. It is advisable to stop in at your local automotive paint supplier to discuss the following: 1) what you are working on, 2) your plans with the vehicle when it is finished, and 3) which paint system they suggest will help you meet your goals.

When you have a paint system (acrylic enamel, polyurethane, or waterborne) determined, begin to calculate how many of each component you will need and the prices for that material. At this point, you can decide if you really want a paint job that everyone at the SEMA Show will be talking about or if you just want a single color with some pinstriping.

Remember, good taste is important and holds its value much longer than a flash in the pan at some big event. Despite your wildest imagination, there will always be something bigger, badder, and brighter than anything you may have thought of. Still, it is your budget and your car, so do whatever you want. Just make it the best paint job it can be.

An Adequate Work Space

Ideally, you would have enough working space to completely disassemble your project vehicle to the point deemed necessary, paint everything at one time, and then reassemble it. The amount of space needed depends on two variables: 1) the type of vehicle on which you are working and 2) the level of detail you desire.

For instance, if you are painting a two-door passenger car, it is typical to paint the body shell from the firewall back in one sitting in the designated spray area. Then, paint the front fenders, hood, and anything else that is the body color in a second sitting. This is common on most any

While it would be nice to have the opportunity to do all the paint work in a climate-controlled spray booth with plenty of lighting, it can be done in your home garage. This 1968 Chevy pickup did not require excessive bodywork, so it was simply scuffed, primed, and painted with satin black in a two-car garage. Trim and other easily removable items were removed, and the glass and tires were masked.

While it is a small vehicle, this 1927 Ford Track T was built and painted in this two-car garage. Multiple sawhorses made it possible to paint several body pieces at the same time.

passenger car that was manufactured after World War II.

On automobiles manufactured prior to World War II, the rear fenders were most likely painted off the car and reassembled after paint. If you are doing a simple repaint without any detailing, such as painting the firewall or insides of the fenders, mask everything that does not get painted and spray the entire vehicle at one time.

If you are going to do a total color-change paint job, considerable storage space is required, as this requires taking everything out of the car. All seats, interior panels, the steering column, gauges, stereo, and glass needs to be removed from the vehicle and stored. If you are going to paint the chassis, engine, transmission, or any other components something other than the body color, be able to store those other parts somewhere as well.

All of this can be done, but to be successful and efficient, plan to paint all or as many of the same color parts at one time so that they are ready when you need them for reassembly. You will obtain a better understanding of this as you gain experience doing this type of work.

Push Your Limits or Contract It Out

You need to decide if you want to push your limits and gain experience or contract the work out to someone else. That is purely up to you and is okay whatever you decide. It is not my intent to talk you out of learning how to do something. That is never the case, but the reality is that most if not all reality automotive shows are far from reality. Painting an automobile is not for everyone. However,

whenever someone sees your car and says, "Wow, that paint job looks great. Who did it?" It is cool to be able to answer with, "I did. Thank you."

Perhaps there is a part of the project with which you simply do not feel comfortable. That is okay too. Auto body shops have employees who are painters and those who do bodywork. Each of them possesses a different skillset. While some can and do both jobs, doing both of those tasks might be beyond the skillset of someone that is not already doing it professionally.

There is nothing wrong with hiring a local body shop to hammer out dents, weld in patch panels, or do any other bodywork. If you decide to go this route, be sure to clarify and verify with the body shop what you expect them to do and what you expect to do, along with what it will cost.

Strategy Development

Presuming that you are still reading this and still want to paint your car, the next step is to develop a strategy. Whether you write down the following lists or just keep them in mind, your painting project can be broken down into two distinct lists. One list describes what must be done to the part.

Paint Job Strategy	
Part	Condition
Hood	New, epoxy prime, sand, seal, and paint
Right front fender	Original, strip existing paint, epoxy prime, and paint
Left front fender	Original, requires bodywork prior to paint
Inner front fenders	Original, sand, prime, and paint

The second list describes the color to be painted.

Parts Color Guide	
Part	Finish
Hood	Body color
Front fenders	Body color
Glove box door	Body color
Bumper brackets	Gloss black
Grille	Argent silver
Headlight buckets	Satin black

While these lists may seem silly, planning will help you have parts ready when you want them. Being able to mix enough primer or paint to spray parts at one time is more efficient than spraying a group of parts, cleaning your spray gun, and realizing you forgot two parts that you need for reassemble right away.

Painting a car includes several various tasks that (when executed properly) will culminate into a long-lasting paint job that looks great. No single task can cover up for mistakes made along the way beforehand. Sure, someone with more experience is going to be able to do a more thorough, ultimately better job than you because of their experience.

However, you can do just as well on your first paint job. That may require doing part of it over, perhaps even twice. But, if you know it is not done correctly, you almost always can make it right before moving forward.

Start with a Small Project

If you have convinced yourself that you can meet all the requirements outlined thus far, you are ready to paint your car. Even though the excitement is building, if this work is new to you, you may want to work through a few small parts first. It is much easier and reassuring to

The Track T was not really a small project, but it was the first complete automotive paint job by Dennis W. Parks. It was not perfect, but it was not bad. It was a learning experience.

sand, prime, and paint a glove-box door and a gas-tank-filler lid and be able to say, "These parts turned out good and it was easier than I suspected," than to ruin a few fenders and ask yourself, "How can I possibly fix this?"

Determine the Type of Existing Paint

Unless your plan is to remove all existing paint from your car before repainting it, determine what type of paint is currently on it. If the current paint on your vehicle is from the factory, it is probably urethane based or possibly waterborne, depending on the vintage. Given the vehicle identification number (VIN) and/or paint specification tag, your paint supplier can probably tell you the factory color and the type of paint that was used at the factory. This is

the most-efficient method for matching paint for a partial repair or a full repaint when you want to use the same color.

If you suspect that clear has been applied over the color coats, use 600-grit sandpaper to sand an inconspicuous spot. If the sanding residue is white, clear coats have been applied over the color. If the sanding residue is the color of the paint, no clear coat has been applied.

When you know or suspect the existing paint is older, evaluate it for being enamel or lacquer. Pour a small amount of lacquer thinner on a clean white cloth and rub it on an inconspicuous area. If the spot begins to wrinkle or the paint comes off immediately, the existing paint is enamel based. If the color begins to wipe off after vigorous rubbing, the existing paint is lacquer based. If none of the paint wipes off, the paint is some

form of urethane.

Do not only be concerned with paint type. Also, consider brand compatibility. There is no need for you to pretend to be a chemist. Most brands of automotive paint products are good when used with related products within the same system. However, do not mix reducer from one company with hardener from a different company into primer or paint from another company and expect them to work together properly.

Disassembly

While many people may not even give it a thought, auto painters who care about their work always want everyone to think the paint on any specific vehicle is factory original. Obviously, there are exceptions. Any color other than black on a Ford Model T is not stock. Wild, multicolored paint schemes most likely are not stock, either, but we are getting away from the point that needs to be made. Even the slightest bit of paint overspray where there should not be paint is a flaw. Paint on light assemblies or on any chrome or stainless trim is a giveaway that at least part of the vehicle has been repainted.

Photos or Videos

Before you get carried away with the disassembly (and have parts that you do not know how to put back together), consider taking photos or short videos of the disassembly process for any assemblies with which you are not already familiar. The more detailed the assembly, the more photos are necessary. You do not need a professional-quality camera to do this. Most likely, your smartphone can take some pretty good photos.

Removing the Trim, Chrome, Grille, and Lights

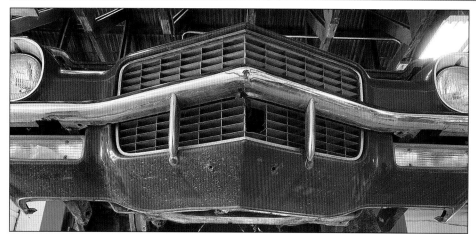

1 On most vehicles, there are lots of trim pieces that should be removed prior to doing body and/or paint work. These trim pieces may be steel or plastic and may be painted, chromed, or anodized. Regardless of the material or finish, they cover edges of sheet metal that should be painted like the rest of the body panel.

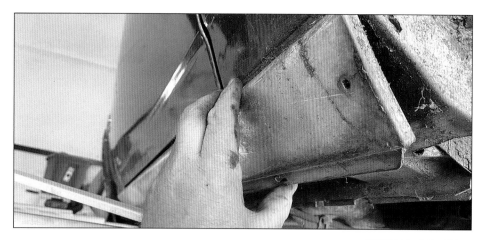

2 Removing trim, such as this piece that fits beneath the door, may reveal rust. This is especially true on the lower areas of the vehicle. Dirt and moisture splash up from the tires and rain or car-wash water gets in from the top. We do not see the rust forming like we might on sheet metal that is not covered with trim.

3 It may be necessary to consult a make- and model-specific service manual for information of how trim or other pieces are secured to the vehicle. Some trim is held in place with screws that are easily accessible from the outside, while other trim is held in place by hidden fasteners.

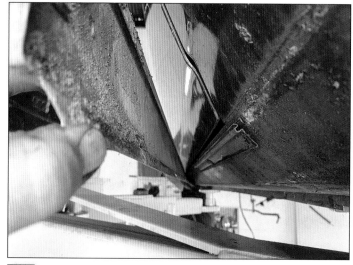

4 In this case, the top edge of the trim slips down and behind another piece of metal that is fastened to the sheet-metal body panel. Working with a variety of vehicles increases your knowledge of how vehicles are assembled.

5 *After removing the trim panel, it is common to find that the attachment panel may be rusty. Depending on the vehicle, a replacement may be available, but there might not be, so it should not be removed unless a replacement is in hand.*

6 *Years ago, vehicle-specific emblems were bolted on from behind. This required welding the mounting holes shut if you decided to remove the emblems permanently. Emblems are now commonly secured in place with adhesive, which makes replacement easy.*

7 *As the front bumper is removed from the front of this Camaro, it is obvious that the bumper covers a fair amount of the front sheet metal that would not be able to be painted if the bumper was not removed. Do yourself a favor by retaining the mounting hardware in a resealable bag and labelling it.*

8 *Some trim panels are secured with sheet-metal screws. After removing the screws to remove the trim from the body, the screws can be reinstalled in the trim panel and held in place with masking tape during storage.*

Removing the Trim, Chrome, Grille, and Lights *continued*

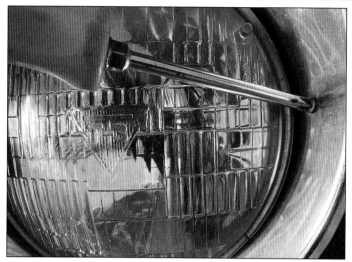

9 *Trim that is designed to be removed on a regular basis, such as for routine maintenance, is usually easier to remove. Headlight bezels are often removed easily by removing two or three sheet-metal screws. These can be taped to the back of the bezel or put into a resealable bag during storage.*

10 *Larger items, such as this grille, should be wrapped up with bubble wrap secured by masking tape to protect it from damage and paint overspray. Cleaning overspray from the grille area is difficult and time-consuming.*

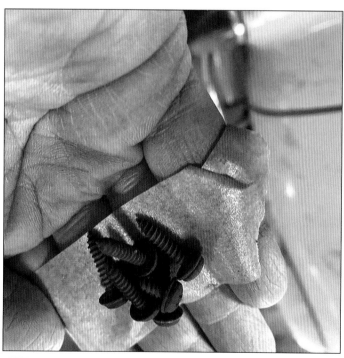

11 *Screws that secure the grille to the front fascia can be wrapped in masking tape. They should be labeled on the outside and/or taped to the back side of the grille during storage. Taking some effort to store and label small items and hardware saves you money by not having to replace them during reassembly.*

12 *With all the trim removed from the front clip, it can be refinished without additional disassembly. However, it can be disassembled a bit more for a thorough paint job. This decision is up to you but depends on a variety of factors, such as time available for labor, the quality you want to achieve, and the end use of the vehicle.*

How do you avoid the telltale signs of a car being repainted? The only method to guarantee that no paint ends up where it should not be is to completely disassemble the parts being painted. Some people do not care if a vehicle has been repainted. However, when a potential buyer begins to wonder if new paint is hiding possible damage, you may quickly realize you should have been more meticulous in masking or disassembly.

However, disassembly can lead to broken parts when you are not familiar with the proper procedure for the removal of a specific part. A parts repair manual for your vehicle (or some internet sources) can be quite handy for finding out how to do a lot of this type of work.

Prior to grabbing a handful of wrenches and tearing into the disassembly of your vehicle, give the process some thought. Where are you going to store everything and how are you going to organize it? Unless you organize everything and label it, you probably will not remember where the part goes, the size of screws that secure it in place, or where that hardware is now. Believe me, it does happen. Coffee cans, boxes, and sealable bags have all been used successfully to store parts, but you must make the effort to make it work.

Otherwise, you will spend a lot of time and a fair amount of money replacing nuts and bolts that you already have somewhere in your garage. Even if pieces will not fit into a bag or box, keeping some notes can help. Knowing the number of fasteners and the size of wrench needed to reassemble a component makes reassembly much easier and faster.

Many of the removable components in a vehicle simply bolt on. However, there is now such a plethora of screw- and bolts-head types that to attempt to describe all the possibilities is way beyond the scope of this book. A factory manual for the vehicle you are working on is a worthwhile investment.

Keep Track of Parts

Earlier in this chapter, we touched on developing a strategy. Now that parts of the vehicle are being disassembled, it is a good time to fully evaluate their suitability for reuse. Before going any further, it must be said that you should not get rid of anything until the project is completed.

It may be tempting to say, "I don't plan to reinstall this piece of trim" or "This piece is too far gone to be reused." While those are often acceptable reasons to dispose of parts, a replacement may not always be as easy to obtain as you might suspect. Even when it is available, it will come with a cost. This is where being well-versed in the availability of collectible or potentially rare parts is a good thing. You can always clean out the garage when the project is over.

Some pieces and parts, such as door handles and other trim pieces, can often be used as is. Place them and the mounting hardware in a resealable bag and stash them out of the way.

Most parts are going to fall into the category of "can be used with some repair." In addition to sheet metal that may need to be straightened or receive some rust repair, it can apply to parts that need to be sanded, primed, and painted. These parts may require some additional sorting so that related parts can be repaired or reconditioned and reinstalled at the same time.

Any cracked or broken glass should be replaced. Replace the weatherstripping around doors and windows because it will probably be deformed if it has been removed.

Replace any light bulbs that are known to no longer work, but do not get rid of anything until a replacement is in hand. Even if you do not replace burned out bulbs right away, you will need to know the shape and size for the replacement.

Know When to Say "When"

All repainting projects have a point at which the disassembly can stop, but that varies depending on the vehicle, the person doing the work, and the intended use for the vehicle after it is painted. For example, most vehicles have a type of door, hood, or trunk hinge. By design, these hinges must be two pieces, but unless you are doing a concourse-quality restoration of a multi-million-dollar hand-built coach, the hinge probably does not need to be disassembled. You will not be able to refinish the hinge to as high a quality as the rest of the vehicle, but in most vehicles, you are not going to see much of it anyway after reassembly. The more your car resembles a daily driver than a show car, the more assemblies you can justify not totally disassembling.

While total disassembly allows you to perfect and detail any assembly, disassembly also requires reassembly. Depending on the complexity of the pieces and parts, they may be too difficult or time-consuming to reassemble. There is also the possibility that a part could be damaged during reassembly. Therefore, use discretion before you decide to disassemble everything merely to apply a new coat of paint.

Collision Repair

Almost all automotive paint jobs require at least some bodywork prior to paint. Bodywork in this context refers to everything from parking-lot door dings to collision and rust repair. It is easy to see the collision- and rust-repair needs, so these items usually get resolved prior to paint. However, all too often, new paint can be seen over old dents. This is purely a rookie mistake that can and should be avoided. If you take your paint prep seriously, this will not be an issue with your paint job.

Simple Door Dings and Dents

Door dings are the easiest to repair, so that is a good place to start if you are first learning bodywork. Of course, small dents that are in the middle of a larger dent should remain undone until the bulk of the larger repair is completed.

Hammer and Dolly

When you can access the back side of a small dent, use a body hammer and a body dolly in combination to hammer out the dent. With some experience, you may be able to remove the dent completely. If you cannot

metal finish it completely, do your best to return the metal to its original contour (within 1/8 inch). When the metal is that close, safely use a bit of body filler to smooth the slight imperfection. Ensure that none of the damaged metal ends up higher than the surrounding metal. It is much better to fill a small low spot with filler than to fill a larger area to blend in with a high point. This is covered in more detail in the next chapter when we discuss block sanding.

For the most part, a body hammer should always be used in conjunction with a body dolly. If you do

Hammer tips are available in assorted sizes and shapes. This part of the hammer is extremely useful when recreating precise body lines that may have been damaged in a collision or when making patch panels.

Without a dolly behind it, striking the top side of this sheet metal with a hammer bends it downward in an irregular shape. With the dolly behind it, the sheet metal conforms to the shape of the dolly when struck by a hammer. It takes multiple strikes, but it will conform to that shape. Depending on the variety of dolly shapes available, it may be necessary to slightly move the dolly before each strike.

When shaping sheet metal to precise shapes, it is essential to hammer the metal against a dolly to form the desired crown or recess. This is sometimes referred to as body-on-dolly hammering. When hammering without a dolly, one simply distorts the sheet metal. However, there is hammer-off-dolly, which does not sandwich the sheet metal between the hammer and dolly. When hammer-off-dolly is used, the hammer strikes one area while the dolly is placed beside that area. The hammer strike lowers the high spot and raises the area where the dolly was used.

Textured hammers such as this are for shrinking the sheet metal and are therefore referred to as shrinking hammers. This textured surface helps shrink the metal that has been stretched during collision or prior bodywork.

not follow this theory, you are typically going to do more damage to the sheet metal. Using a dolly tends to sandwich the sheet metal between it and the hammer to bring the sheet metal back into the desired shape. Automotive sheet metal originates as flat sheets but is stamped into complex shapes by large presses that consist of two pieces. One shapes the outside of the sheet metal while the other shapes the inside. It is the same with a body hammer and a body dolly but on a significantly smaller scale.

For this reason, hammers and dollies come in a variety of shapes and sizes. Hammers typically have a larger surface on one side of the hammer's head, with a relatively smaller pick on the other side, to give two styles of hammer with each tool. The larger side is typically square or round and differs in surface size and contour. Likewise, the pick end may be small or large with a sharp or blunt point.

Dollies also come in a variety of shapes and sizes. The dolly serves as an anvil to hammer the sheet metal against, so having multiple contours makes any single dolly more compatible with the surface you are trying to recreate.

Whenever damage is inflicted onto sheet metal, whether from a hammer, tree, or other vehicle, the sheet metal stretches. For this reason, some body hammers are called shrinking hammers. Their patterned surface shrinks the sheet metal when it is used. This helps "undo" the dent.

Slide Hammer

When you cannot access the back side of a dent, small or large (but not so large that it requires panel replacement), pull the sheet metal back into shape with a slide hammer. Years ago, using a slide hammer meant drilling a series of holes into the dented sheet metal, inserting the threaded end of the slide hammer into one of the holes, and quickly pulling back on the weight that slides along the axis of the hammer. The force of this pulls the sheet metal outward somewhat.

Move the slide hammer to another hole and repeat the process. This process has been used to remove dents from many pieces of sheet metal. However, this was before metal inert gas (MIG) welders were common, so all the holes drilled in the sheet metal were usually filled or covered with body filler, which led to rust, which is not a good thing.

Beside the fact that MIG welders are now very affordable and common, improvements have been made to slide hammers. At the risk of oversimplifying the process, a stud gun can be used to essentially weld a stud to the piece of sheet metal. Instead of creating a hole that must be filled, the stud welded to the sheet metal is used to pull the sheet metal out. The slide hammer has been updated to fit over this protruding stud. Then, with a quick pull of the hammer, the sheet metal is pulled outward. This process is repeated by moving to other studs until the area is close enough to the original contour for body filler to

In the repairman's right hand is the handle, and in his left hand is the hammer. Pins (nails) have already been welded to the bare sheet metal in the deepest portions of the dent. The slide hammer is slid over and tightened onto a pin. In some cases, the operator pulls on the handle to pull the sheet metal outward. In most cases, the weighted hammer is slid outward against the handle to pull the dent outward.

be applied. Prior to applying body filler, each of the studs are cut off the sheet metal and smoothed up with a grinder.

Undoing the Dent

Whether you are using a body hammer and dolly or incorporating a slide hammer to carefully remove a dent, you must learn how to read the dent and then undo it. It makes sense, but it is easier said than done. While this is not a skill that comes overnight, it does come with experience.

As you look at a dent in a piece of sheet metal, you will see that the dent is three-dimensional. There is a point or group of points that are the deepest dents. These are most likely the points of impact, while dents that are less deep are reactionary on the part of the sheet metal. Amateur body workers will start hammering out the deepest dents first. All that does is stretch the metal more and deforms it in the process.

Instead, begin your dent repair by pulling or hammering out the dent around the outer edges of the crater first. This was the last part of the dent to be created, so it should be the first to be repaired. Continue by spiraling toward the deepest part of the dent. Do not attempt to pull out the dent all at one time. Pull or hammer out around the edges a bit. Then, move in toward the deepest part a little and hammer or pull that out some. When you have worked your way to the deepest portion of the dent, start back at the outermost portion that still requires bodywork and repeat the process.

Glue-Pull Repair

Some dents, such as those from hail that does not break the paint, can often be repaired by using a glue-pull repair. This is commonly referred to as paintless dent removal (PDR). This process can be used to pull some dents, even if painting is going to be involved. The glue-pull repair system includes multiple pulling fixtures to pull studs that are temporarily glued to the painted surface.

While the glue-pull repair process is less intrusive than using a slide hammer to pull out a dent, it is not cheap. A professional-grade starter kit is about $200, and a full-on repair system tops out at about $6,000. A full-time professional body shop will recoup this investment quickly, but for an amateur car painter, that price is steep. Less-expensive versions are available on the internet, with some kits retailing for less than $50. How well they perform is anyone's guess.

Depending on the number and severity of the dents in the vehicle that you are preparing to paint, you may consider having a body shop perform the dent repair. You must be clear in your request that you just want them to do the bodywork but none of the paint work. Some shops do this, while others will not. It also depends on how busy the shop is.

Pulling out a Dent Using Glue-Pull Repair

1 A glue-pull repair system includes multiple pulling tabs to be used with several types of pulling fixtures. Rather than welding a stud to the vehicle's sheet metal, the pulling tabs are temporarily attached with hot glue. When the dent has been pulled out completely, the hot glue is removed by spraying it with alcohol and peeling the glue away.

2 This dent is a perfect candidate for paintless dent repair (PDR) since the paint has not been cracked or otherwise damaged. When the dent can be removed without the need for painting, the repair can be made quicker and without the need to match paint.

Pulling out a Dent Using Glue-Pull Repair *continued*

3 It is common to use multiple pulls on the same dent with the same tab. The smaller dent is seen just to the left in the photo. This shows the original depth of the damage with the tabs glued in place prior to any pulls taking place.

4 The blue translucent tabs are rigid and offer little deflection when pulled. These lend themselves quite well to pulling bodylines back into sheet metal without pulling uneven highs and lows into the surface. This tab also has a pre-formed curve that matches the original shape of the bodyline. When pulling like this, ensure the shape of the tab represents the lines you want to restore.

5 Verify that the shape of the tab matches the shape of the area to be pulled. In this case, the line in the fender.

6 All surfaces retain moisture, and that moisture must be removed for the glue to stick properly. Using a heat gun, raise the surface temperature to a minimum of 170°F to burn off the surface moisture. You will see the mist swirl and come off the panel as it warms up and reacts to the heat gun's hot air moving over the surface. Be careful not to overheat the panel, as it can scorch or bubble the paint.

Pulling out a Dent Using Glue-Pull Repair *continued*

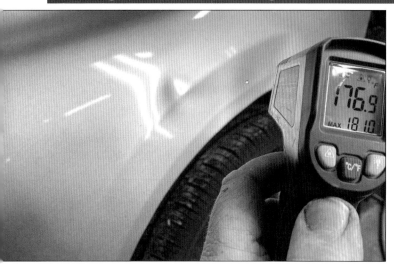

7. There are distinct types of glue, and each one has a different purpose. Much of the pull strength is determined by the heat range. The sheet metal must be heated and allowed to cool to the desired temperature prior to making a pull.

8. After the surface of the sheet metal has cooled to the recommended temperature for the glue you have selected, apply a bead of glue along the length of the tab. Make sure there is enough to completely squish out the edges of the tab and still have about 1/64-inch of thickness between the tab and the metal. When it is too thick, the glue splits apart and does not make a proper pull. When it is too thin, it pulls off the surface with little pressure.

9. There are several ways to attach and pull the tabs. The pull bar shown in the photo is designed to brace against a strong point of the vehicle using a flat, padded base (shown braced against the rim), while the adjustable attachment grips the previously glued tab. The actual pulling pressure is applied and adjusted by pulling on the handle and using leverage to pull the metal into shape.

10. After the bodyline and larger areas are pulled back correctly, begin using the smaller, more precise tabs. The slide hammer is used, much like a traditional welded-pin slide hammer, but the glued tab will not withstand the pressure of a welded tab.

11 Peaked bodylines are the hardest to completely remove whether you use a GPR system or a traditional PDR system. This small tab does a respectable job pulling the metal close to the original shape.

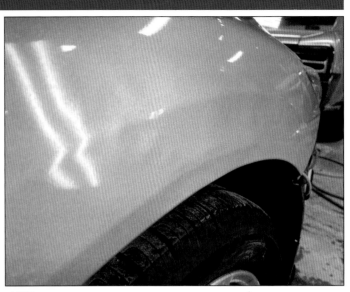

12 At this point, the metal is close enough to the original shape that a thin layer of plastic filler will finish correcting.

13 By getting the metal as close as possible to the original shape, the bodyman can use a finer, easier-finishing filler to reduce the repair and finish time for a higher-quality repair once completed.

14 This filler is Rage Optex. It goes on pink, but as it cures, the color changes to a light green. This tells you when the filler is cured and ready for finishing. Smoother, higher-quality fillers allow the repairer to finish with finer grits of sandpaper prior to priming. This is important when dealing with a high-metallic finish like silver, due to the fact that primer dries and shrinks into the underlying filler. Scratches can appear days or weeks after finishing the job. Here, the fender is final sanded with 320-grit sandpaper in preparation for primer.

Pulling out a Dent Using Glue-Pull Repair *continued*

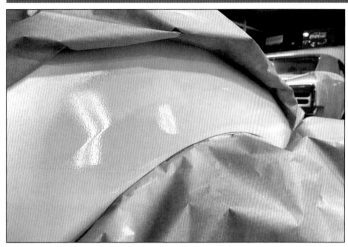

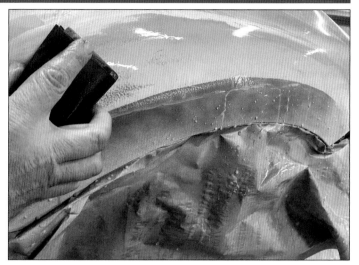

15 *A back-masking technique is used here where the paper is used in a way to create a soft roll along the primed edge. This helps avoid a hard line of primer buildup, which can be a pain to sand flat and will show through the final paint if not corrected. It is much better to avoid it in the first place. The primer being used here is Tamco 3105.*

16 *After applying the guide coat and unmasking, the repair can be blocked out. It is important to know that the bodyline needs to be sanded up to and not over. When the blocking is done, a very narrow line of guide coat along the bodyline should remain.*

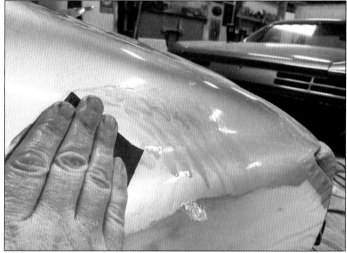

17 *After the dent is all sanded out, pour some water over the panel, and the temporary shine helps show you how it will look once it is painted. When it looks good and you are happy, move onto prepping the rest of the panel.*

18 *Sand the rest of the panel with 1,500-grit sandpaper. This allows the silver base coat to be blended from the primed area over the top of the original silver color. By covering the primered area and blending the color off before the edges of the panel, the color match can be retained between the fender/hood and fender/door. Then the entire panel can be cleared.*

19 *The finished repair is ready to be unmasked and delivered.*

Slide Hammer Repair

There are always going to be dents and dings where you cannot access the back side, which makes hammer-ing them out virtually impossible. When presented with that situation, the dents must be pulled out. This is tradi-tionally done with some type of slide hammer.

Pulling out Dents with a Slide Hammer

1 The white spots are holes presumably from previous slide-hammer work that were incorrectly filled with body filler. Surprisingly, the rear fascia is not rusted out. That is usually what happens with this type of repair.

2 Pins (nails) such as this are used with a stud gun that temporarily welds the pin to the sheet metal. For a small, localized dent, it may require just one pin to pull the dent out. When the low area is spread out, several pins are required.

3 To install the pins, slide the straight end of the pin into the stud gun, press the flat end of the pin against the sheet metal, and then squeeze the trigger for about a second.

4 The stud gun welds the pins to the sheet metal. The pins should be posi-tioned in the deep-est part of the dent or recess. Be sure to space the pins far enough apart so that the slide hammer can fit onto each of the pins.

5 Slide the tip of the slide hammer over a pin and secure the tip onto it. Grasp the handle in one hand with the opposite hand on the hammer. On thinner sheet metal, you may be able to simply pull the handle enough to pull the metal outward. On thicker sheet metal, pull the hammer against the flange of the handle with a quick motion to pull with more force.

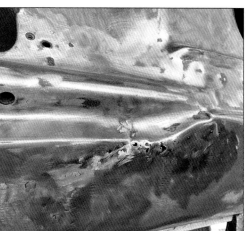

6 When the entire area is pulled out sufficiently to be fin-ished with no more than a skim coat of filler, the pins can be cut off. When there are remaining holes, such as from a previous repair (in this case), those holes can be welded shut.

Body Filler

When the sheet metal is pulled out as close to original as you can get it, check to ensure there are no high spots above what the final surface should be. Before applying body filler, ensure that the surface is free of any other body filler or paint that can diminish the integrity of any additional applications of substrate. To be on the safe side, use 36-grit sandpaper on an orbital sander to remove any paint, primer, or body filler from the area that requires filler.

Now that you are down to bare metal, wipe down the area with wax and grease remover and a clean towel. Note that some wax and grease removers leave a slight film. This can be removed with a final wipe-down with pure denatured alcohol and a clean towel. The same denatured alcohol can be used for detaching the glue-pull repair tabs. Dry the area with another clean towel. Repeat if necessary. You will be amazed at how much dirt, grease, and grime will be on the towels. To provide good adhesion and serve as a deterrent to rust, apply two coats of epoxy primer. This step is significantly more important in high-humidity areas or if the bare metal will be left exposed for an extended period. After waiting the designated time for the epoxy primer to dry, sand it with 80 grit. Then, mix plastic body filler and spread it onto the low area using a filler spreader with slight pressure. This pressure helps eliminate any air bubbles that end up as voids.

The amount of hardener to be added to the filler can vary depending on the ambient temperature. However, keep in mind that too much hardener added during cold weather to speed up cure time may cause it to shrink and crack when the weather warms. Likewise, too little hardener during hotter weather to slow down the curing time can result in soft, poorly adhered filler that will split and peel. Evercoat offers retarders for filler to use in hotter weather so that the proper amount of hardener can be used regardless of the ambient temperature. Honey is also available that can be used to thin out the filler for finer coats. It is a pure resin and can be added to any brand/type of filler.

After the filler has begun to tack up enough that it can maintain its shape (but before it fully solidifies), use a sanding block with 36-grit sandpaper or a cheese-grater file to knock off the high spots from the filler. It may take some time to figure out this sweet spot, but when you do, you will know exactly what it is.

When your timing is correct, the excess filler comes off as powder (when sanding) or as little strips (when using a cheese-grater file). With practice, you become more proficient with the application of the plastic filler and negate the need for coarser grits to begin sanding. With the price of quality fillers reaching $100 a gallon, the less that ends up on the floor, the better for your budget. As you gain experience, using 80 to 120 grit to begin sanding filler is not uncommon. This saves time and requires less wear and tear on your shoulders and arms.

You will no doubt have more sanding to do between now and paint application, but for now, we will move on to other steps that may be necessary to get the body up to par. When we get to Chapter 3, we will take the overall project to the point of getting ready to spray paint.

Panel Replacement

When collision damage is more than merely hammering out and/or filling some dents, you may need to replace the panel. Of course, this can apply to a panel that is rusted beyond repair as well. This is where it is useful to know which vehicles share the same body components.

Sources

Depending on the make and model that you are working on, replacement body panels may be surprisingly simple or all but impossible to find. Popular and common vehicles, especially ones that have the same body lines for multiple years, are easier to find than a rare, one-year-only specialty vehicle. Fortunately, the automotive aftermarket is at its strongest, with more parts available than ever.

Years ago, one had to search in *Hemmings Motor News* or the local salvage yards in hopes of finding a replacement body panel. Those were some of the only choices unless you knew someone with a stockpile stashed away. With the internet, type what you are looking for into a search engine, and several results will quickly appear. However, you need to know exactly what you are looking for and be willing to do a bit of research to find what you are really want.

In many cases, the internet search results include brand-new reproduction parts, new old stock (NOS) parts, and used parts at various prices that sometimes do not make any sense. Most of the ads include some bit of contact info and allow you to contact the seller to find more accurate information.

Typically, reproduction parts and NOS are the most expensive. Body panels are usually more expensive to ship, due to their size. When you are building a frame-off rebuild, you might be able to justify the additional expense.

However, when you are trying to resurrect a daily driver, buying local will most likely be less expensive. Chances are good that you will not be able to find a fender or hood the same color as the vehicle on which you want to install it. However, if you are repainting anyway, that is not an issue. In this case, shop for a better panel that requires less work than one that is the same color. Even if it is the same color, it probably will not match the new paint if you do not paint the replacement.

Regardless of where you buy, check to see what types of fasteners are used to secure the panel and purchase those too when available. When you have a body panel shipped, the additional price of a few bolts is not going to break the bank. If you do not order them and then cannot find them locally, it will often be more expensive to have them shipped. When you are buying a body panel from a salvage yard, the fasteners may not cost you anything. You must request the hardware when ordering the used panel because the person removing the panel from the donor car will often drop the hardware on the ground or leave them scattered around the car while disassembling. If this happens before you make the request to save the hardware, you will be stuck purchasing new hardware somewhere else.

Installation

Regardless of the source of new body panels, the first thing you should do is bolt them in place to ensure they fit as desired. If you have sanded or sprayed primer on them, you will not be able to return them. Realize they might not simply bolt

right up and have a perfect fit. It is quite possible that mounting holes may need to be slotted a bit to fit properly. To make panel gaps consistent, it may be necessary to slice the panel in two and add or remove metal. It does not seem like that should be the case, but it is a reality with many manufacturers of body panels. Whether or not that is an industry-wide standard is difficult to determine.

When working on a newer-model vehicle, you have another option with Certified Automotive Parts Association (CAPA)-certified parts. This is an independent company that certifies fit and finish for aftermarket parts. While these parts cost more than non-CAPA certified parts, they are generally worth the added expense due to their fitment and overall quality.

Rust Removal

Regarding rust, first assess the scope of the rust to best determine the most feasible method of removing it. If you are dealing with one removable panel that has been damaged by rust, a replacement panel may be in order. When rust extends to multiple

panels that can't be removed from the main body, media blasting may be a prudent choice.

However, when there are multiple areas of rust throughout the vehicle, chemical dipping is perhaps the best method of removing rust. Regardless of which method you choose to remove rust, the parts to be cleaned should be removed from the rest of the vehicle with all trim or rubber moldings removed for the best results.

Chemical Strippers

Chemical stripping can be done by a commercial vendor or as a do-it-yourself project. When you need to strip just a few small parts, you can do this easily in your own garage or driveway in a few hours with a gallon or two of aircraft stripper. When going this route, know that all tools that you use should be considered disposable. This is a messy operation, so to facilitate cleanup, consider spreading a large piece of plastic drop cloth on the floor where you will be working. When finished, this drop cloth can then be folded or rolled up and disposed.

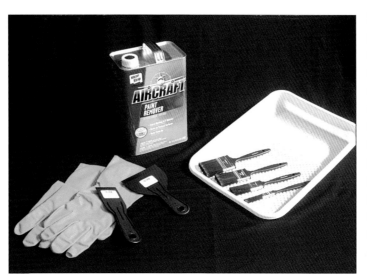

When using paint stripper, use disposable containers, brushes, and scrapers. Gloves to protect your hands are necessary, as getting even a little bit of the stripper on your skin is extremely uncomfortable.

Cover as much of your skin as possible and consider wearing a respirator. Paint stripper will not cut off your hand or fingers, but it does take a long time to quit burning when you get some on your skin. There is no doubt that it cannot be good for your sinuses, throat, or lungs. Only use paint stripper in a well-ventilated area. In addition to damaging your body, the fumes can linger in an area, and the caustic nature can attack finishes, such as paint or chrome pieces on other vehicles.

Paint stripper works best when it can easily soak into the painted surface. Scuffing the surface first with 100-grit sandpaper provides the best results. Pour some paint stripper into a disposable tray or bucket. Use a cheap, disposable paintbrush and spread paint stripper onto the surface. Be sure to coat the entire surface thoroughly and then allow the paint stripper time to work.

The paint will begin to bubble and wrinkle. As long as the top coats still do this, continue to let it work. As the process slows down, use a putty knife or some sort of flexible scraper to scrape off the loose paint. In areas where there is no paint or primer, the area is done. When substrates of paint or primer still exist, apply more stripper and let it soak into the paint and primer, then scrape it off. Continue this process until the entire panel is free of paint and primer.

When the entire surface is free of paint and primer, wash the metal with plenty of water to neutralize the stripper. Do not skimp on this process, as any remaining stripper will have a catastrophic effect on any primer or paint that is applied onto it. When all paint stripper has been neutralized and rinsed away, completely dry the surface. Then, clean it with wax and grease remover and apply two coats of epoxy primer to prevent rust from forming on the shiny, bare metal.

Paint Stripping

While applying paint stripper by hand takes some time, it makes sense for smaller parts. For an entire body, having the body shell dipped makes more sense. However, finding a facility that still dips entire car bodies may be difficult to find. Whether you are stripping just a fender or an entire body by hand, the process is the same. To help the paint stripper do its job, go over the painted surface with some coarse sandpaper to break the seal on the painted surface before applying any paint stripper.

Remember, any containers or brushes used to spread the paint stripper should be disposable. Cover any exposed skin, as any paint stripper that lands on your skin will burn for a while. You may choose to cover the floor with a disposable plastic drop cloth to catch the paint as it is scraped off the body panel. The drop cloth can then be rolled up and disposed of when the task is completed.

How to Strip Paint

1 *Using a disposable paintbrush, liberally apply the paint stripper to the surface to be stripped. Rather than doing a small area at a time, brush the paint stripper onto the entire panel to be stripped.*

2 *The paint will begin to wrinkle. If the paint has not yet begun to wrinkle after about 5 minutes, apply more paint stripper. As the paint continues to wrinkle, sit back and let the stripper do its job.*

How to Strip Paint *continued*

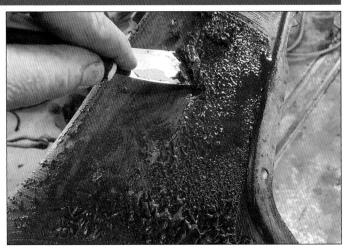

3 After the paint has wrinkled substantially, scrape the area with a putty knife or paint scraper. When the paint is difficult to remove, let the paint stripper continue to work and apply more if necessary.

4 When the paint stripper has worked sufficiently, the paint should scrape off quite easily.

5 While most of the loosened paint has been scraped off, some paint might remain. Apply more paint stripper, let it work, and then scrape off the rest of the paint. Thin coats of paint come off easily, and thicker coats require more stripper and take longer.

6 The more the paint wrinkles, the easier it is to scrape off. For stubborn areas, apply more paint stripper to speed up the process.

How to Strip Paint *continued*

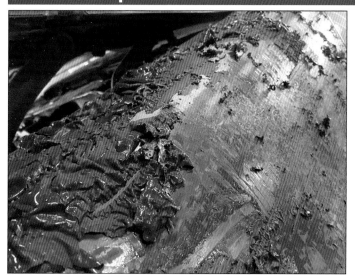

7 In areas where the paint has wrinkled the most, the paint stripper has done a more thorough job of removing the paint. All the paint must come off once the stripping process has started.

8 On this door panel that is in a vertical orientation, the paint stripper appears to have run down the middle of the panel, rather than soaking into the panel. When possible, have the panel to be stripped lie flat to help the stripper soak in.

9 When the paint stripper has done its job and all the loose paint has been scraped away, neutralize any remaining paint stripper by rinsing the part with plenty of running water. To provide superior adhesion for epoxy primer, use a palm sander with 80- to 100-grit sandpaper to condition the entire panel.

10 When finished with the paint stripping process, the sheet metal should look like this: clean metal with a semi-satin finish with a bit of texture. To prevent rust from forming, all bare-metal sheet metal should be protected with epoxy primer.

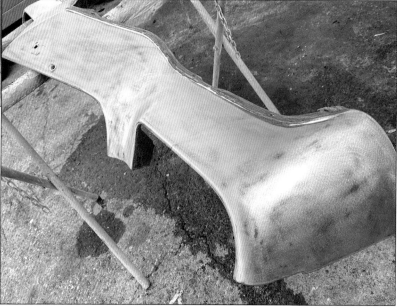

Chemical Dipping

If your vehicle sat in the outside elements for a while, or you simply do not know what condition the sheet metal is in throughout the vehicle, the only way to be sure of the condition is to strip all the paint primer off of it. While this is an additional expense, getting a clear view of your project's condition is often worth it. The best way to do this is to have the vehicle dipped to have all the paint, prime, and rust removed. When you pick up your dipped sheet metal, it will be solid and shiny. If there were any areas of rust, the rust will now be gone. However, if rust was all that was holding the carcass together, it will be in several pieces. But knowing that up front is much better than doing all the work to apply a great paint job, only to have it quickly fall apart.

When a vehicle or parts are dipped, everything (paint, primer, wax, grease, and rust) is removed from the sheet metal. There is no warping or pitting that can be caused by an inexperienced operator of a media blaster. However, after being immersed in liquid rust remover, all the sheet metal will be exposed to the elements, so it is essential to spray all surfaces with epoxy primer as soon as possible afterward.

Another good alternative to epoxy primer after dipping is powder coating. This process uses an electrically charged powder that is attracted like a magnet to the bare metal. This enables it to get into areas where a spray gun cannot reach. Many powder coaters can coat entire bodies with a quality primer that protects the body by sealing it. As a bonus, it provides a great substrate for doing bodywork.

Companies that specialize in this kind of work are not as common as in the past. When you find one, it will be worth your time to call ahead to see if you need to make an appointment to drop off parts. In the meantime, disassemble the parts of the vehicle to be dipped as completely as possible. Remove fenders, doors, and any other removable sheet-metal parts from the body, as they will be easier to manage. Remove all trim, rubber molding, upholstery, and electrical components.

If there is body filler on a part that is dipped, the chemical process will remove it if the filler is thin. When the filler is thicker than 1/8 inch, the stripper will not be able to remove it completely and the filler will lose its integrity. It will need to be removed, and it is easier to remove with a sander prior to going into the dipping tank. If you suspect there is some body filler in your vehicle, lay a magnet on the metal surface. If it sticks, the filler is not very thick (if present at all). When the magnet does not stick, body filler is present.

The dipping process of paint stripping is a multistep process that can take a week or two, depending on how much paint and primer is on the parts. Contrary to popular belief, the sheet metal is not dipped in acid. It is fully immersed in what is known as a hot tank to remove paint, primer, wax, and grease from the metal. The metal is submerged in this caustic solution for up to a day. The metal parts are then rinsed in plain water for up to four hours to fully neutralize the stripping solution.

Next comes the de-rusting process. The metal parts are submerged into a de-rusting solution and connected to an electrical charge, and the rust is pulled away from the metal. This may take a few days or up to a week. The parts are rinsed with plain water which leaves a phosphate coating on the metal. The metal should then be coated with epoxy primer after a thorough cleaning as is recommended by the manufacturer of the epoxy primer that was used.

Media Blasting

Media blasting is a common method of removing paint. While it is perfectly acceptable for removing paint from heavier metal (such as vehicle frames, wheels, rear axle housings, and other suspension components), it is losing favor for removing paint from thin sheet metal. This is due to the great possibility of warping the sheet metal by either too much air pressure or by creating too much heat as the blasting media is blown across the sheet metal. When the sheet metal is warped, it is difficult, if not impossible, to correct. Another downfall of media blasting is that the blasting material can be difficult to remove from a vehicle body.

However, when done correctly, media blasting can be a quick and efficient method of paint removal. As the consumer, be aware of the risks and do not be afraid to ask for references.

Hand-Held Rotary Sanders

For removing relatively small areas of old body filler or surface rust, a hand-held sander equipped with a 36- or 80-grit sanding disc will work wonders and will not break the bank. The operator must be prudent and avoid applying too much pressure or building up too much heat because this could warp the sheet metal just as media blasting.

When a thin layer of surface rust appears in an area of otherwise-solid sheet metal, it can usually be removed by block sanding with 80- or 100-grit sandpaper on your favorite sanding block. When all the rust is gone, clean the sheet metal with wax and grease remover and then apply two coats of epoxy primer. Sanding scratches from this grit of sandpaper provides an excellent surface for epoxy primer to stick to.

Scotch-Brite Pads

Any time a primered surface has been sitting around for more than a few days, it should be scuffed lightly with a Scotch-Brite pad before applying any additional coats of primer or sealer. This is done to provide better adhesion for subsequent top coats.

Metal Replacement

There may be times when a portion of a larger panel has been eaten up by rust or heavily damaged in a relatively localized area. In this case, it may be more prudent to weld in a patch panel rather than completely replace a panel. Much like body-panel replacement, the same options are available when it comes to a source for patch panels: use reproduction patch panels, find panels at the salvage yard, or roll your own.

Reproduction metal patch panels are theoretically smaller portions of a full-replacement body panel. For many makes and models, rust happens in typical places, so the manufacturers of patch panels may offer multiple sizes of patches. Instead of "good," "better," or "best," these patches may be thought of as "you caught it early," "you caught it in time," or "it can still be fixed." Provided the panel is large enough to adequately cover the

damaged area, the patch panel can be welded in to replace the damaged area that is cut out.

Do some investigative work with an ice pick or a small-blade screwdriver to determine the extent of the area to be replaced if the replacement is being done to eliminate rust. This provides a better idea of which patch panel to purchase when multiples are available. If you can easily push either of these fine-tipped tools into the sheet metal, it is cancerous and should be replaced. It is always better to purchase a larger patch panel than what is required. You can always cut the new panel down if necessary or to make a more convenient weld location.

When you have the new patch panel in hand, position it in place and trace around it to indicate the area of sheet metal to be cut out. Using a plasma cutter, cutoff wheel, or pneumatic saw, remove the old sheet metal and weld the new patch in its place.

As an alternative to purchasing a reproduction patch panel, if you have or can find an expendable body panel that includes the area you need to replace, cut a patch from it. Then, install it just like a factory patch panel.

Simple Patch Panel

Sometimes the majority of a body panel is still solid but may show some signs of rust (usually in lower areas), but that is not always the case. Instead of painting over the beginnings of rust only to have rust develop in the new paint, cut out the rust and replace it with a new patch panel. A patch panel may be available for the area that you need, but that is not a guarantee. When the contour is not complicated, you can make your own patch panel.

Scotch-Brite pads are great for scuffing a small surface to prep it for paint or remove minor surface rust. These pads are available in red, which is more coarse than the gray, but they both are finer than most sandpaper.

44   CUSTOM CAR PAINTING ON A BUDGET

Creating a Simple Patch Panel

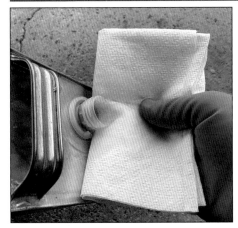

1 Clean the area by pouring some enamel reducer or lacquer thinner on a clean paper towel and wipe down the area where the patch panel is needed. This removes wax, grease, and other grime that is detrimental to a good repair.

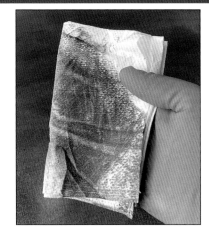

2 While the sheet metal may look clean, the paper towel shows how much contaminating stuff was still on it. When it comes to welding and/or painting, the surface can never be too clean.

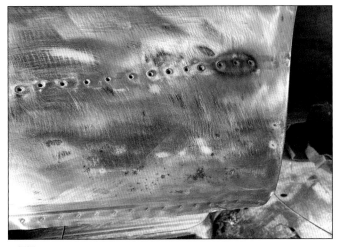

3 The small holes in a line can be filled with a MIG welder. However, the area below these holes is showing signs of the formation of rust. A new patch panel will be made, the rusted area cut out, and the patch panel welded in place.

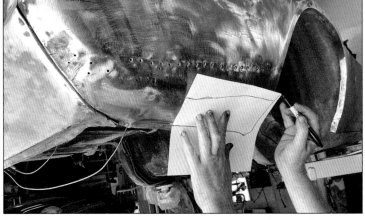

4 When the area is small enough, hold a piece of paper against the panel to be repaired and use a permanent marker to draw the outline of a patch panel. Make the patch large enough to cover all rust in the area but not so large that the patch is overly complicated to make.

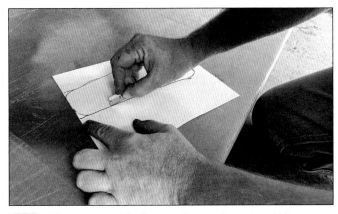

5 Use a razor blade or scissors to cut out the paper patch. Ensure the pattern is larger than it needs to be since it can always be trimmed down.

6 Hold the pattern against the area that you plan to patch. Ensure that it is large enough to allow you to remove all the rust from the area. Also determine the general contour to which the patch will need to conform.

Creating a Simple Patch Panel *continued*

7 When you have a stockpile of expendable doors and fenders, you may be able to find sheet metal that already has the correct contour. If it is not exact, it still might be better than starting with a piece of flat stock.

8 After finding a suitable donor for the sheet metal, position the pattern on the donor metal to obtain the best fit.

9 Use some spray paint of a contrasting color to transfer the shape of the pattern onto the donor sheet metal. Be sure to hold the pattern steady while spraying the paint onto it.

10 The inside of the orange paint is the desired shape of the pattern transferred to the donor sheet metal.

11 Use a cutoff wheel, air saw, or plasma cutter to cut out the new patch.

12 When using a cutoff wheel, you are limited to straight cuts. When this is the case, be sure to cut the patch large. Then, trim it to the desired size.

13 To help minimize the possibility of cracking, avoid angular corners on the patch panel and opt for rounded corners. Round off the corners of the patch with a die grinder.

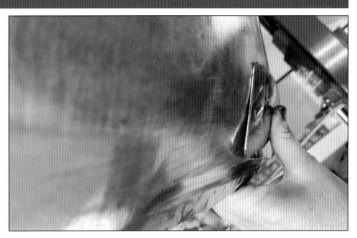

14 With the patch cut to size and shape, check it against the panel to be repaired to determine how to match the contour.

15 Use a metal-shaping mallet to slightly increase the curve of the contour in the patch panel. If you have access to an English wheel, it is a relatively straightforward process. When using a mallet, it may take a few tries to get it the way you want it.

16 The final size, shape, and contour have now been achieved.

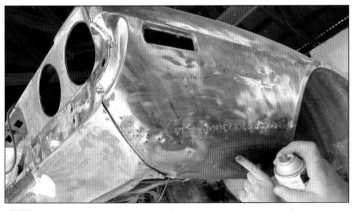

17 Much like when transferring the shape of the pattern onto the donor sheet metal, hold the new patch panel against the original panel and paint around the edges with spray paint.

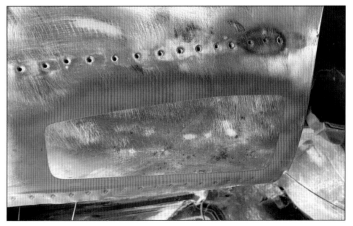

18 Use a cutoff wheel, air saw, or plasma cutter to cut out the inside of the painted ring.

Creating a Simple Patch Panel *continued*

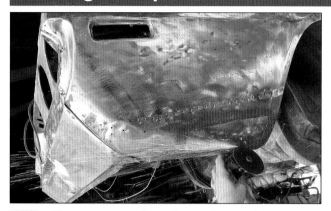

19 Always use caution when using cutting tools or tools that make sparks.

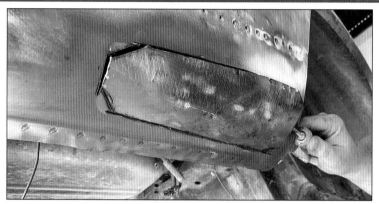

20 After cutting out the old metal, it may be necessary to pry it out from the vehicle. It may be hot, so handle with caution.

21 Use a die grinder, plasma cutter, or file as required to make the opening the same shape as the patch that will replace it. When there is rust on an exterior panel, there is most likely rust on the interior panel.

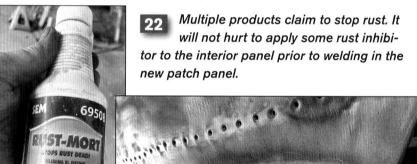

22 Multiple products claim to stop rust. It will not hurt to apply some rust inhibitor to the interior panel prior to welding in the new patch panel.

23 Make any final adjustments to make the patch panel fit as well as possible. Then, hold it in place with some welding magnets. Tack weld the patch panel in a few places to secure it.

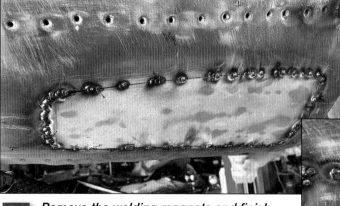

24 Remove the welding magnets and finish welding the patch panel into place. Skip around from one side to another to minimize any heat buildup in any one place.

25 Finish welding the patch panel in place, along with any small holes that should be filled. Use a grinder to smooth out the welds.

When all else fails, create your own patch panel from a piece of 20-gauge sheet metal. Depending on the area that you are trying to recreate, this may be as easy as cutting out a piece of sheet metal and rolling it over a welding tank or something to match a curved surface. Conversely, it may require using an English wheel and a planishing hammer to get what you need. Still, a new piece of metal welded in is better than a rusty hole.

More Complex Patch Panel

Making a relatively flat patch panel is easy, even when the panel has some curve to it. However, sometimes it may be necessary to replace a panel that has a complex shape. When you can find a commercially available panel, using that may be the simpler method if you are not experienced with metalwork. But it will cost some money for the replacement panel along with the time to have it shipped to you.

In the rear fascia of this Camaro, some bodywork has already been done, but it still requires some straightening. With the contour of this area, it may be easier to make a custom patch.

Creating a Complex Patch Panel

1 Begin by marking out the area that must be removed to make room for the new custom patch panel. Attempting to recreate the rounded edge of the fascia panel takes a lot of work to properly recreate with body filler.

2 Using a die grinder, pneumatic saw, or plasma cutter, cut out the sheet metal that will be replaced.

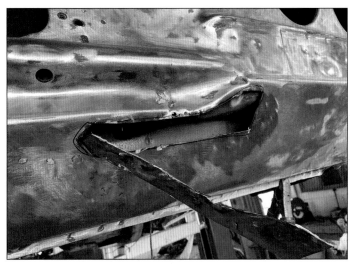

3 There are plenty of sharp edges and the metal might be hot, so remove it carefully with a pair of pliers.

4 Make a pattern out of paper or thin cardboard, check it for fitment, adjust it as necessary, and transfer the pattern to sheet metal.

Creating a Complex Patch Panel *continued*

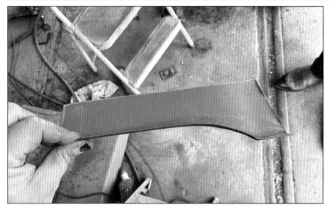

5 Cut and shape the patch panel to fit the area as closely as possible.

6 This custom patch panel is a much better repair than trying to weld the rust holes shut and cover it with body filler.

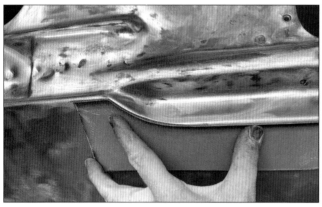

7 The patch panel appears to fit very well. To check for fitment, it can be judged against the opposite side of the repair for some final tweaks.

8 Checking against the opposite side, the custom patch requires a bit of flattening on the top outside.

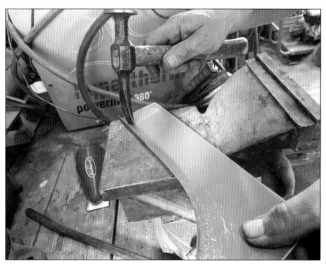

9 It also required a bit more crease, which is put in by the straight edge of a body hammer on the inside.

10 Just a bit more hammer work is needed on the outside until it is perfect.

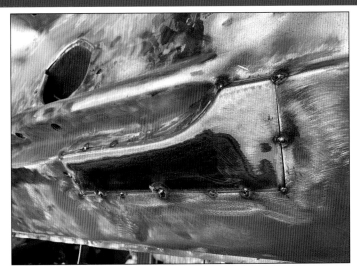

11 *Grind the edges to remove any paint so that the panel can be welded correctly. Clamp the panel in place. Then, tack weld it in place.*

12 *Finish welding the custom patch completely. Then, grind the welds smooth.*

13 *Mix another batch of plastic body filler to cover the patch. Sand smooth and prep for paint.*

Body Filler on Bare Metal

Some true craftsmen have been able to metal finish bodywork without using any body filler, but those talented people are becoming exceedingly rare. There is no shame in using plastic body filler, but it has its limitations, so learn to use it correctly.

Two important rules when using plastic body filler are: 1) the surface must be clean, and 2) apply the filler no more than 1/8-inch thick.

Fill Small Holes

Depending on the vehicle being repainted, some small holes may need to be filled. Resist the urge to fill them with body filler. Sure, you

can make it look good for a while, but the filler will quickly fail when the vehicle is put back into service. With the popularity and affordability of MIG welders, small holes can be welded shut quite easily. Even if you do not own a welder, find someone to weld the holes for you, as that is the only way to do the work correctly.

Using Body Filler

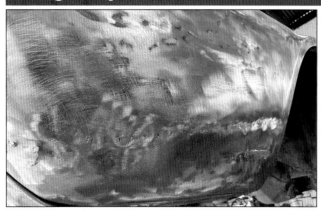

1 After any necessary patch panels have been installed, the holes have been welded shut, and the hammer-and-dolly work has been completed, there is still more work to do. The quarter panel does look better, but it is far from perfect.

2 To clean the sheet-metal surface, use a Roloc disc on an angle-head grinder to properly scuff the surface. When that is completed, the surface should be cleaned once again with wax and grease remover.

3 When applying body filler directly to bare metal, galvanized steel, aluminum, or fiberglass, use a filler, such as Evercoat Z-Grip. This product was designed to provide excellent adhesion to these surfaces and is quite easy to sand. Approximate setting time is 3 to 5 minutes, which allows you to begin sanding soon after application.

4 As with most body fillers, scoop a glob of body filler out of the bucket and put it on a flat mixing surface. Squirt some cream hardener onto the filler. Using a body-filler spreader, mix both components until there are no streaks of color in the filler.

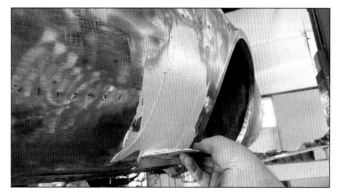

5 Use a clean spreader to trowel the body filler onto the area to be covered. Use a slight bit of pressure on the spreader to minimize air bubbles. Experience will be your guide as to how much filler to mix with hardener at any one time.

6 Ideally, you will spread the filler like this before it begins to set. If it starts setting up before you get the mixture spread, it was mixed a bit too hot with too much hardener. If it takes too long to set up, it was mixed too cool with not enough hardener.

8 When there are any low spots, use an air hose to blow away any sanding dust. Then, mix up some additional body filler and apply it to the low areas as before.

7 After about 3 minutes, the body filler should be set enough to hold its shape. At this point, begin sanding it with 40- to 80-grit sandpaper to knock off any high spots. Sand the surface smooth with 80- to 100-grit sandpaper. The orange masking tape is used as a guide to prevent any body filler from getting into the edge of the wheel well.

9 After waiting the appropriate time for the filler to set up, knock off the high spots with 80-grit sandpaper. Then, switch to 100- or 120-grit sandpaper to get the area as smooth as possible.

10 If any low spots are still detectable, fill them now, just as before. After each layer of body filler, use finer sandpaper before adding more body filler.

11 After applying a few coats of epoxy primer to the repaired area, the quarter panel is looking rather good. Good lighting helps to reveal any low spots or other surface imperfections.

12 With the bodywork repair done to the right rear quarter panel, all that needs to be done prior to paint is surface preparation.

Using Body Filler to Fill Small Holes

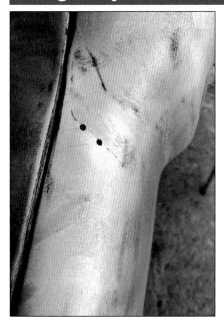

1 *Begin by removing any paint and primer from the area to allow for good weld penetration. This panel has already been stripped, so that is not an issue. If there is any possibility that the edges of the holes have any rust, run the next-size-larger drill bit through the holes to clean those edges.*

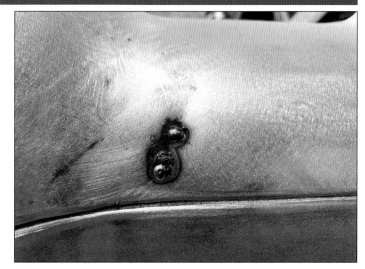

2 *With a few squeezes of the trigger and a few sparks, the holes are now closed. No need to worry about how soon body filler may have fallen out.*

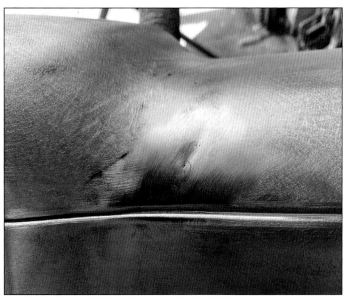

3 *Grind the weld smooth, and it looks better already.*

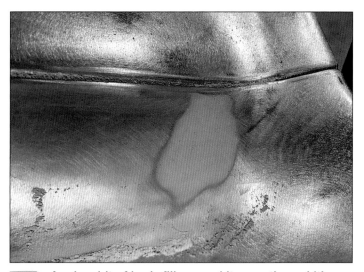

4 *Apply a bit of body filler, sand it smooth, and it's like the hole never existed. Other recesses and imperfections seen in this photo will be filled later with high-build primer.*

Custom Bodywork and Modifications

When there is any custom bodywork or modifications in your plan for a vehicle, now is the time to address those before doing any surface preparation prior to paint. This may include a hood scoop or hood opening for a blower motor, chopped top or filled roof, or any other modifications. Having an overall plan for your vehicle prior to doing any work helps you from doing work twice.

Cut the Hood for a Blower Motor

While it is no great custom feat, modifying a hood to allow for a blower motor to protrude from it takes some work to do correctly. The hole in the hood must provide enough clearance for the entire duration of the open-and-close motion, but you do not want the hole to be too large. Taking careful measurements and sneaking up on the final size is the key to success in the modification.

Cutting a Hole in the Hood

1 With the engine in the car and the hood off, the key to locating a hole in the hood is to measure from similar points on the hood and the car. In this case, there is a common line front to back, but the engine is in the way.

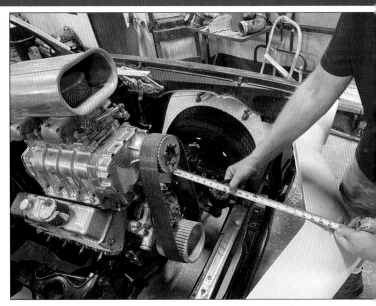

2 As a starting point, measure from the front center opening back to the front of the blower pulley. Other than the gap between the fascia and the hood, this measurement is fairly accurate.

3 Since the hood is reasonably square, a reference line can be duplicated easily by measuring back from the front corner of the hood opening. Place a mark on the fender at a convenient distance. Then, measure back the same distance on the opposite side and mark the fender.

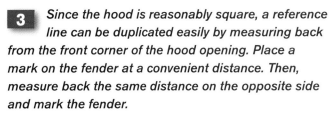

4 Duplicate those marks on the hood. You can stretch a piece of masking tape across the hood to mark it. Just be sure to measure from the correct side of the tape.

5 When the hood is square with the fenders (the same distance side to side regardless of the front-to-back location), this measurement works. However, if the side openings taper one way or another front to back, this type of measurement is incorrect.

Cutting a Hole in the Hood *continued*

6 Since the blower is not symmetrical, the opening for the pulleys needs to be measured from both sides.

7 Only one reference line was used in this modification, but having two reference lines running front to back (left and right) and two running side to side (one in front and another behind the engine) would have made this an easier task.

8 After taking your measurements from the engine location and transferring them to the hood, use a straight edge of some sort to connect the dots. When the lines are drawn, add up your front-to-back measurements on one side and compare them to the total for the other side. Do this for the side-to-side measurements. If the totals match, the opening is square. However, that does not mean that it is on-the-hood square. Measure twice; cut once.

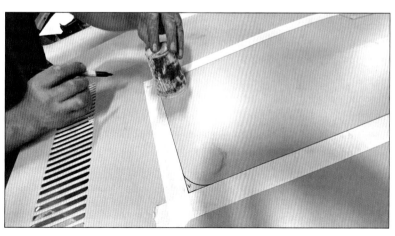

9 Outline the proposed hole with masking tape. To retain structural integrity, the hole in the hood should have round rather than square corners. Within reason, it does not matter what radius the opening is, so find something around the shop, such as a paint-mixing cup to trace around.

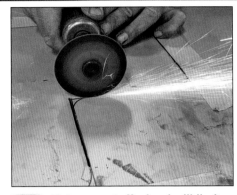

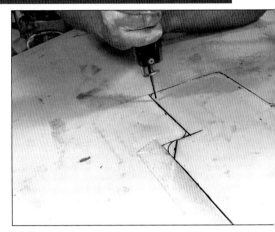

10 *Use a cutoff wheel, pneumatic saw, or plasma cutter to cut along the inside of the masking tape. Take your time and concentrate on being precise while cutting the hood. An error at this point could call for a replacement hood.*

11 *Using a cutoff wheel will limit you to straight cuts, but go ahead and make the straight cuts for now.*

12 *Use a pneumatic saw to make the curved cuts.*

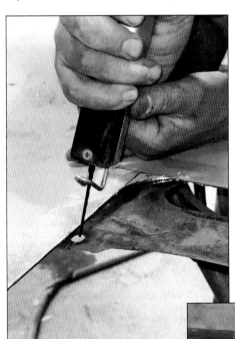

14 *Use a deburring bit on a die grinder to smooth the cut edges.*

13 *After removing the exterior layer of the hood, there is most likely some substructure that needs to be removed. It can be removed with a pneumatic saw as well.*

15 *With the necessary inner and outer portions of the hood removed, place the hood back on the car and check for clearance. At this point, the clearance between the back portion of the opening and the engine is insufficient. The hood will also not clear the scoop.*

Cutting a Hole in the Hood *continued*

16 *Approximately another inch was removed from the back side of the hood opening using the same procedure as before.*

17 *The opening does not allow for enough clearance around the blower pulley, so it must be made a bit wider. Gaping holes do not look good, but there must be sufficient operating clearance.*

18 *After a bit more work with a cutoff wheel and pneumatic saw, the blower pulley and belt will fit quite nicely.*

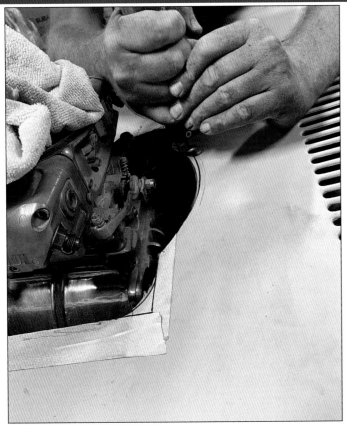

19 With a bit of work using the pneumatic saw at the back end of the hood opening, it will not be necessary to remove the scoop to open or close the hood.

20 Remove the masking tape and deburr the edges. Now, the hood is ready for paint preparation.

21 All good vintage muscle cars need a blower motor, and now you know how to make it fit.

SURFACE PREPARATION

Regardless of how good your painting ability is or how flashy the paint scheme might be, these things can not hide improper fit and alignment of the painted panels. True automotive craftspeople will prefer a detailed vehicle with great panel alignment and consistent gaps in primer over the flashiest of paint jobs over poor-fitting sheet metal.

There are many variables to consider regarding proper panel alignment, including the make and model of the vehicle being painted, unknown vehicle damage, and the overall collection of parts being assembled.

The make, model, and vintage are perhaps the most prominent variables, as they set the bar for how good is "good enough." Regardless of the vehicle manufacturer, any vehicle built in the last 10 years undoubtedly has tighter and more consistent panel gaps than one that rolled off the assembly line 90 years ago. Automotive manufacturing has improved exponentially during that period. In the mid-1930s and earlier, auto manufacturers were not yet able to stamp a one-piece roof exterior. Although they were beautiful automobiles, factory tolerances were not as tight at

that time compared to what they are now.

Additionally, the intended purpose of the vehicle played a part in what those tolerances were and how well they were maintained. Tolerances for passenger cars were probably consistent but not tight during the middle of the 20th century. Pickup trucks and commercial vehicles were intended for work, not for showing off at the family reunion,

so their tolerances were not as tight. With the high demand for vehicles during that period, it is a safe bet that some inspectors may have overlooked minor discrepancies during times of high production.

Unless you know the absolute complete history of a specific vehicle, you do not know any history regarding past collisions or other hidden damage. The more owners a vehicle has had, the more questionable the

This in-progress photo shows the driver-side door and quarter panel. While the gap between the two is not bad, the door is hanging a bit low, as evidenced by the body line. Body lines from one panel to another must be made to match. However, when the body line runs from front to back, it must be made straight and not just match at the panels.

This pickup was purchased on the internet, so its history is questionable, which makes it difficult to determine if this door is original to this truck. Regardless, the door does not fit very well.

history becomes. Any past accidents may have been repaired accurately and completely (or not). Body filler may be very thick in some places and painted over. There have been instances when it was not even body filler that was used to straighten a panel to make it look good.

Were all the panels in place and fit correctly when you first began working on this vehicle? If they were, you can probably get them to all fit again. However, it will require some work and may be a challenge. As the vehicle is disassembled, taking notes and photos are important during reassembly. Knowing that there were three shims on one bolt and only one on another can eliminate lots of head scratching and donations to the swear jar.

When all the panels are not installed and/or fit correctly when you begin, they may never fit without lots of work. This may be the reason they are not on the vehicle at this time. Disassembly is easy, yet reassembly can be tough, which often separates those who can finish

a task from those who give up. On some vehicles, even a slight tweak of the frame may cause fitment issues. When this is the situation, a collision repair shop that specializes in frame straightening may need to be consulted. They have chassis alignment systems that can take precise measurements and then pull and tug on the frame to correct any misalignment.

The sheet-metal parts being used may be part of the problem. When they are all original to the vehicle, they should be able to fit properly. To obtain consistent gaps on a 50-year-old vehicle may require some metal surgery to cut here and add there. How far you deem necessary is purely up to you and/or your customer. Consistent gaps win out over tighter gaps. The thickness of a paint stir stick (roughly 1/8 inch) is a contemporary standard but it is not always obtainable without a lot of work, which is beyond the scope of this book.

When there are sheet-metal parts that are not original to the vehicle,

they can cause inconsistencies. It might be that the front fender on a coupe is slightly different from the same fender on a convertible or sedan for that vehicle. Or perhaps the door from a 1953 is slightly different from 1954.

When you are dealing with aftermarket parts, especially those made for older vehicles that had looser tolerances, what might fit perfect on one vehicle may not fit great on yours.

Aligning Panels and Fitting Gaps

It is relatively easy to refinish a single door, fender, or any other sheet-metal panel and make it look great. Of course, that depends on what you start with. However, the real testimony for your bodywork is how well the panels fit together when they are assembled on the vehicle. Ideally, all the gaps between sheet-metal panels are the same. Not only should the panels have consistent gaps front to back but there should also be no misalignments in or out. The open road is your wind tunnel, so any misalignment in this direction can ultimately become a source for wind and road noise (not to mention it will look bad).

Doors, hoods, and decklids should all be able to open and close properly without binding. If any of them chip or scrape the primer, the fit should be reworked, as paint will make the situation worse. Movable panels typically have some amount of adjustability, but finding the sweet spot might be a challenge. Depending on how the hinge articulates, proper placement may seem counterintuitive.

When gaps are too tight and

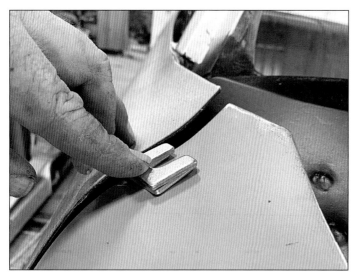

There is obviously a very large gap here. It is not a body-work issue and additional body filler is not the correct method to fix this. The best fix is to shim the rear part of the front fender to bring it in line with the door. This type of alignment repair may take one or multiple shims. Shims are readily available at your favorite parts store.

Shims are not uncommon on automobiles, so do not be ashamed to use them to perfect your panel alignment. They are commonly in a U-shape, so installing one or more shims is as easy as loosening the appropriate mounting bolt enough to insert the shim between the two panels and then tightening it down.

body filler has been used, the panel that has the filler is most likely the panel that is wrong. This commonly happens when a portion of the sheet metal is too high, and the surrounding area is filled to meet it. The high spot should have been knocked down correctly, requiring less filler to properly make the repair.

Not only is it important to maintain consistent gaps but body lines should also align. This also means the overall line should be straight. Imagine looking at the profile of a four-door sedan that has a distinct body line running from the front fender all the way to the rear quarter panel. Even though this line may match between the front fender and front door, front and rear door, and rear door and quarter panel, it looks really bad when this overall line is not straight across the vehicle.

There are two methods to align body panels, with both being common on any one vehicle: 1) use shims and 2) modify the body panel itself. If the vehicle left the factory with shims in it, they most likely need to be reinstalled. Being able to refer to notes and photos from the disassembly steps is of immense help during reassembly. It should be obvious that installing a shim or two is the easiest method and is what is common at the factory.

Modifying the sheet-metal body panel is often necessary when non-original body panels are used. The automotive aftermarket has made great strides over the last 50 years to allow for resurrection, restoration, and creation of more vintage automobiles than anyone can imagine. However, not all those reproduction body panels are as exact as they could be, or even as exact as we believe them to be.

For some desirable vehicles, all of the sheet metal necessary to build it is available in reproduction form. Presumably, all these parts fit together properly. However, it is quite common to run into fitment problems when reproduction body panels are used with some stock body panels. This becomes evident when the distance between two body lines is not the same or when a contour line is rounded on one panel and a bit more pointed on the other.

In the case of the body lines being different distances apart, it may be necessary to slice one panel and insert or remove material. It can be a lot of work, especially considering the cost of a reproduction panel. Yet, it might be a more economical solution than repairing the original panel or finding another original from a donor vehicle. Can you reproduce the panel yourself?

Sanding Blocks and Paper

With all the rust removed, any collision damage repaired, and all the sheet metal back on the vehicle, you should be ready to start spraying paint, right? Sorry, but no. Thus far, you have merely been doing bodywork and this is not even a bodywork book. Now, the surface preparation for painting can begin. You will become intimately familiar with your favorite sanding blocks. On the bright side, however, these next steps and how well you perform them will have a major impact (good or bad) on the overall outcome of your painting project.

Simply put, getting the surface as straight and flat as possible has a direct correlation to how shiny the paint can be when the job is done. When you want to obtain that smooth-as-glass and reflective-as-a-mirror finish, here is where that happens.

All efforts of sanding help to smooth a surface, but it does not necessarily help make the surface flat. On occasion, well-intentioned family or friends might offer to help sand your vehicle, insisting that they may not be able to do anything else, but they can sand. As much as anyone may want to help, there is more to it than just moving sandpaper back and forth. Whenever you see a sheet-metal panel that is very wavy, it is a good example of someone sanding in one area for too long and not as long in another area.

Long Boards

Mirror glass or a perfectly still pool of water provides a perfect reflection because their surface is optically flat. To achieve this optically flat surface, use the longest available sanding board or block that will fit into the area being sanded. Just like a vehicle with a longer wheelbase provides a smoother ride, the longer sanding board spans multiple ridges at a time, minimizing the high spots in the process. When a short sanding block is used, it runs up and over, and up and over again. This smooths the surface but does not make it flat.

It should not be your intention to eliminate any body lines by sanding, but rather minimize waves in any areas that should be flat. For example, when you tear a piece of aluminum foil off the roll, one side of it will be very shiny. However, when you crumple the foil into a ball and flatten it out again, the shiny surface is now gone. This is because light reflects off it in many different directions. Only when light is reflecting in only one direction is the surface optically flat.

For this same reason, sanding in only one direction should be avoided. Sanding on any one panel should be done in as many different directions as possible. For instance, when sanding the large, flat surface of a hood, move the sanding board in the front to back direction across

Just like body hammers, sanding blocks come in a wide variety of shapes and sizes, and most of them have specific purposes. There are a variety meant for use in large flat areas, gentle curves, small areas, and intricate areas.

Unlike a rotary sander that spins about an axis, a DA sander spins but also has an eccentric motion. This gives the sandpaper the ability to create a more even finish in a more controllable manner. DA sanders are available in sizes from 2 to 8 inches in diameter and with an orbit range from 3/16 to 5/16 inch. The smaller orbits are designed to cut slower and leave a smoother finish. The larger orbits remove material faster at the expense of the final surface's smoothness.

one portion. Then, come back across that same area moving side to side. Gradually move to another area with about 50-percent overlap. This takes a long time, but it makes a difference.

Flat or straight areas should be like a laser. Curved areas should be smooth curves. It has often been said that a blind person can determine more about the surface finish than someone with perfect sight due to

their sense of touch. As your sanding experience increases, you will become more aware of the sense of touch.

Sandpaper for long boards is typically available in coarser grades, as the desire is to get the body panels flat sooner than later. After you get the surface flat, it will stay flat if you continue to sand in various directions and overlap from one area to another.

Sanding Blocks

Not all body panels have enough room for using a long board sander, which makes a much smaller sanding block a necessity. As you get the overall surface flat and use a smaller sanding block everywhere, finer grades of sandpaper are more appropriate to create a smooth surface.

When the entire surface is considered flat, begin sanding with 180- to

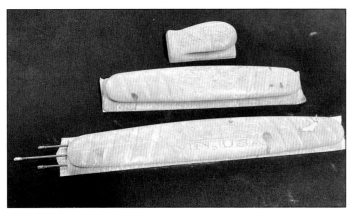

The three sanding blocks shown are used for different purposes. The small one at the top can be used anywhere and gets the surface smooth. The larger one in the middle is better suited in a larger flat area. With its longer length and rigidity, it helps make the surface flat and smooth. The largest one at the bottom is suited more to a large area or gentle curve, such as a door skin or roof top. Depending on the positioning of the internal rods, it flexes different amounts.

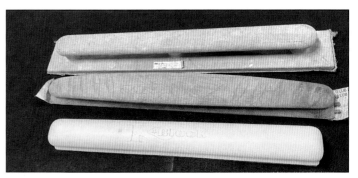

Although these three long boards are all about the same length, they still have distinct characteristics, and therefore different uses. The one at the top with the backbone is undoubtedly more rigid than the others for a large, flat surface. The one in the middle allows for some flex but is probably not as flexible as the one on the bottom.

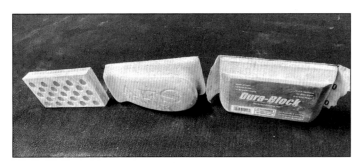

Sometimes, space limitations require the use of a small sanding block. The one on the left has dimples on the back for your fingertips to help prevent applying too much pressure. It is used when color sanding a painted surface. The middle block has a backbone to make it rigid, which helps make the surface flat. The one on the right flexes slightly to conform to the surface.

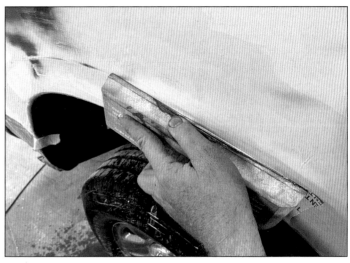

When sanding, it is critical that the sandpaper maintains even contact pressure with the surface. When that does not happen, waves develop. It is not necessary to push the sandpaper into the surface. Just slide it across the surface. Using the correct grit for the surface is significantly more important than the pressure applied to the sanding block.

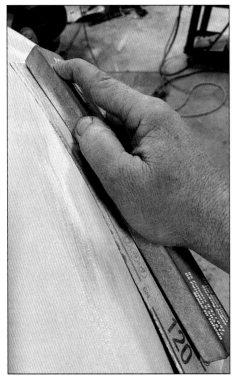

While a sanding block is essential to eliminate wavy bodywork, the different shapes of the body sheet metal require different sanding blocks. When the sheet metal is flat or has very little curve, a rigid block is required. When the sheet metal has curve to it, the correct sanding block must also curve. Remember, the sanding block is used to ensure the sandpaper remains in full contact with the surface being sanded.

220-grit sandpaper to work toward making the surface smooth. To your untrained eye, the surface may look and feel smooth, but it can be made much better. Any imperfections in the surface would be magnified tremendously if paint was applied now.

By now, any localized pits and divots should be apparent and filled. Apply glazing putty with a rubber squeegee, allow it to dry, and sand the immediate area with 180-grit sandpaper. Feather out the area with 220-grit sandpaper.

Specialty Blocks

Sanding blocks can be purchased at your local auto-parts store, through your paint supplier, or through countless vendors via the internet. They range from small rubber blocks that fit in one hand to hard maple long boards of various lengths that require two hands. There are also several styles and various lengths that have different amounts of flexibility.

When sanding an area that is large and flat, a longer and stiffer sanding block or board is more appropriate. Likewise, when the area is small and has various contours, a smaller flexible block is ideal. However, when sanding a large area that is curved, a longer and flexible sanding block is what you really need. The length will help get the area flat, but the sanding device must be flexible to do this.

The key to sanding properly is applying uniform pressure to the surface while moving the appropriate grit of sandpaper across that surface. Sanding with a piece of sandpaper in your hand does not provide this.

While vehicles have many areas that are flat and therefore easy to sand, there are lots of contour lines, some more intricate than others. These areas deserve to be as smooth as any other area, so it may be necessary to be creative with sanding blocks. For concave areas, a piece of rubber hose of similar radius works great as a sanding block. Local auto-parts stores have a variety of radiator hoses and heater hoses that can be used. Not that you want to spend a lot of money for a radiator hose, but depending on the amount of sanding you need to do, it might be worth it. An alternative is to check with a local auto-repair shop to see if it has any radiator hoses or pieces thereof in their trash bin that will meet your needs.

When all else fails, look around the shop to see if there is anything laying around that matches the contour of what you are sanding. It might be necessary to cut up a block of wood and shape it into the required shape. Anything you can wrap a piece of sandpaper around and move back and forth over the surface will suffice.

This sponge-type sanding block is designed to fit into a variety of intricate body contours. The secret of proper sanding is using the correct grit of sandpaper while maintaining full contact with even pressure.

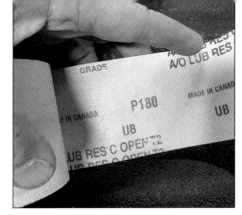

Sandpaper is available in a variety of forms to be used with different sanding blocks. Some sanding blocks are designed to be used with sandpaper that is dispensed on a roll. Simply tear the sandpaper off the roll for the length of the sanding block you are using.

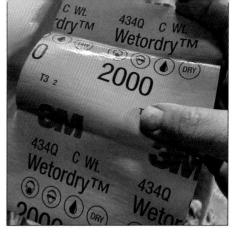

When you plan to wet sand, verify that the sandpaper you are using can be used with water. When it is, it says so on the back. In this case, the sandpaper is 2,000 grit and can be used wet or dry.

Sanding Grits

The entire purpose of sandpaper is to use a grit that is coarse enough to knock off the rough edges of the surface being sanded, and through multiple steps, remove any of the scratches left by the sandpaper. Coarse paper removes material in a hurry but leaves deeper scratches. Therefore, it is common to use 36- to 50-grit sandpaper for removing rust. When roughing in plastic body filler, the body filler is still somewhat soft and you will knock off the very roughest area, so 80- to 120-grit sandpaper is appropriate. As you get closer to the final contour, finer grits (such as 180 through 400) with multiple steps in between is appropriate.

Most sandpaper designed for use with automotive paint that is made in the United States carries the wet-or-dry designation. Both the grit and the paper to which it adheres are designed to hold up when used with water. Sandpaper used for a woodworking project does not carry this wet-or-dry designation, nor is it suitable for using with water.

Creating a Smooth Surface

When prepping the surface for a daily driver vehicle, it will not be necessary to do as much sanding as if it was for an over-the-top show car or a full restoration. In most cases, sanding the entire surface with 400-grit sandpaper is sufficient for a daily driver. However, that does not mean you can go directly from using 80-grit sandpaper on some body filler to 400-grit sandpaper and call it good.

The 400-grit sandpaper will never be able to remove the scratches incurred by the 80-grit sandpaper. To eliminate scratches, there must be a gradual succession from coarse to fine sandpaper. As a rule of thumb, it is good to not change more than 50 to 60 grits at a time, at least in the 80- to 400-grit range. A logical progression of sandpaper is 80-, 120-, 180-, 240-, 280-, 320-, and 400-grit sandpaper. ∎

Sanding a Surface Smooth

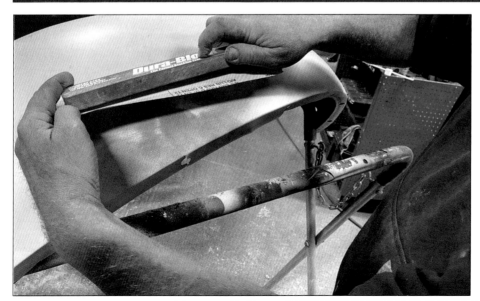

1 *Bodywork stands are handy to have, as you will not always have fenders and doors mounted on the vehicle while sanding, priming, and painting. These adjustable sawhorses allow for a narrow span to a wider span, which makes them useful for fenders as well as doors and hoods.*

Sanding a Surface Smooth *continued*

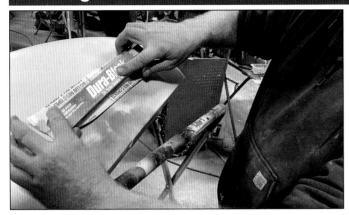

2 It is not necessary to apply lots of downward force to the sandpaper. Merely hold each end of the sanding block down with your fingertips, especially with the finer grits of sandpaper.

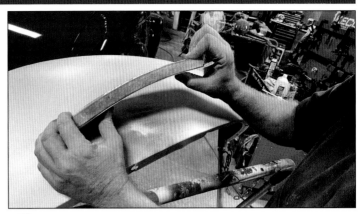

3 Sanding blocks have a certain amount of flexibility. Therefore, holding both ends of the sanding block down against the surface allows it to conform to the vehicle's surface and provide a flat surface.

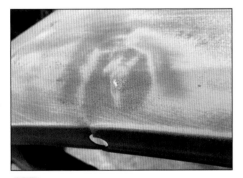

4 When block sanding, primer or paint will come off high spots quickly and result in shiny spots. The light gray area is close to the correct height, as it is matching the bulk or the area. The darker gray area is lower than the other areas, as evidenced by the primer not coming off it.

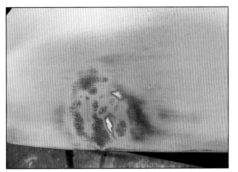

5 After sanding a little more in the same area, a more detailed assessment of the area can be made. Decide where to split the difference between the high and low spots. In some cases, a few light taps with a hammer are necessary, while sometimes covering the entire area with a bit of filler is sufficient.

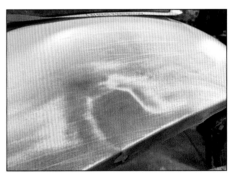

6 The big dark gray area is lower than the whiter areas where the primer is coming off faster. A guide coat of contrasting colors shows this quite visually, whereas using the same color primer throughout the block sanding process is not so telling.

7 Filling the low spots is as easy as mixing some of your favorite body filler on a mixing board. Some body fillers are more suitable for roughing in areas of bodywork, while others like this are more suitable for small areas of final bodywork.

8 Mixing boards are available in a variety of types. Rather than a solid-yet-flexible board, this photo shows a tablet of disposable, tear-off paper sheets. Mix the filler on one sheet, tear it off, and use the next sheet for the next batch.

Sanding a Surface Smooth *continued*

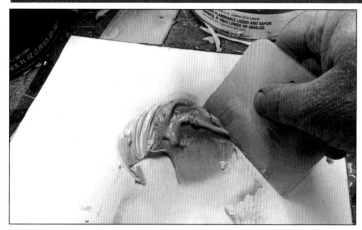

9 After adding the appropriate amount of hardener, use a spreader (squeegee) to mix the two components together. Slide the squeegee under the mix. Then, flip it over. Continue this until all the streaks of color are gone.

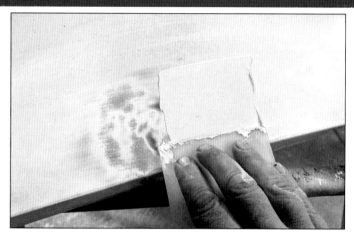

10 Scoop some body filler onto the squeegee and gently spread the filler onto the area to be filled. Move the squeegee in one direction to fill the area.

11 Wipe off the excess filler by moving the squeegee across the surface at approximately 90 degrees from the first direction. This helps compact the filler into the low spots as well as knock off some of the ridges.

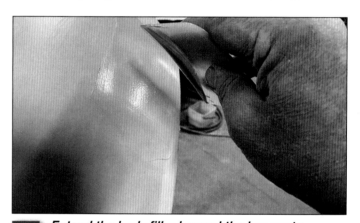

12 Extend the body filler beyond the low spots enough to feather it out to the surrounding area. When just the low spots are filled, the bodywork will more likely show up in the paint later. When the filler is feathered out, it blends in much better to the surrounding area.

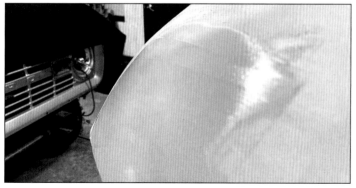

13 Allow the filler to dry sufficiently so that the sandpaper will not gouge scratches in it. Doing so is counter-productive at this point.

14 Using a sanding block that will conform to the surface profile being sanded with 120-grit sandpaper will have this bit of body filler sanded smooth in no time.

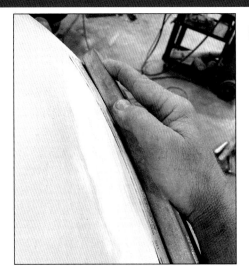

15 Maintain even pressure on the sandpaper by using a sanding block that conforms to the shape of the surface and move the sandpaper in various directions to get the surface smooth and flat.

17 While the filler area can still be seen, the edge is becoming more obscure. It is better near the bottom of the photo but still clearly recognizable near the middle.

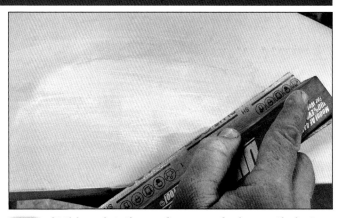

16 At this point, the surface may feel smooth, but a distinctive line still appears at the edge of the filler material. If paint was applied at this time, this line would still appear. Any areas where filler has been added must be feathered out by sanding out past the edge of the filler material.

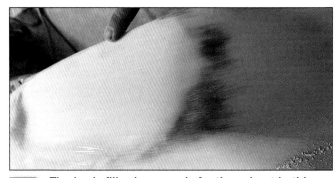

18 The body filler is properly feathered out in this photo. However, the slightly darker area at the end of the finger indicates a low spot. It is not a lot lower than the surrounding area, but it is lower. This can be filled with some spot putty, allowed to dry, and then sanded smooth.

Removing Scratches

When a smoother surface finish is desired or required, such as when applying paint that utilizes high metallics, using 600- and then 800-grit sandpaper prior to applying paint may be in order. Another method to achieve a very smooth surface is to wet sand. Something especially important to remember when considering this is that wet sanding should be done only over a catalyzed surface, which means a primer or paint that had a hardener added before application.

Common filler primer or high-build primer is extremely porous. Applying water to it would be soaked up by the primer and quickly begin the corrosion process. To avoid ruining your arduous work, verify with your paint and primer supplier if the product can be wet sanded.

When the material being sanded can be wet sanded, you must use sandpaper that is suited to wet sanding. Begin by filling a clean bucket with water and let it sit for about 15 minutes to allow any minerals in the water to settle to the bottom of the bucket. When using a rubber sanding block, dip the sanding block and sandpaper into the water bucket and then begin sanding. The water helps move any dry material that can cause additional scratches away from the

When wet sanding, the sanding block with sandpaper attached can be dipped into a bucket of water as needed to keep it wet. This works well when the sanding block is smaller than the bucket. When using a long board, soak a towel in the water bucket.

surface, so it will quickly become apparent when you need to dip the sandpaper in the water again.

When the sanding block will not fit into the water bucket, a cloth towel can be used. Soak the towel in the water, roll up the towel, and place it above the surface being sanded. The water running out of the towel lubricates the surface. This helps keep the sandpaper clean, which keeps the sanding consistent and extends the life of the paper.

Is Going to Bare Metal a Necessity?

Is it necessary to go to bare metal prior to painting a vehicle? When you want to know what is there, yes, it is. Going to bare metal on every piece of sheet metal is the only way you can be 100-percent positive of what lies below the surface. A previous owner may have told you that the vehicle has always sat in a garage and has never had any rust. How much do you trust what the previous owner said? There is only one way to know for sure.

What Lies Beneath?

Who knows what may lie beneath the current surface of any vehicle? The age of the vehicle and the part of the world in which it has spent most of its life has a significant impact. Sure, the metal may all be good with zero rust. If that is the case, and you went ahead and stripped it anyway, there is now a perfectly clean slate upon which to begin your masterpiece.

However, there may be rust, body filler of questionable integrity, or other questionable materials. Instead of welding in an appropriately shaped patch panel, perhaps a piece of traffic sign has been set in place and covered up with tar. Perhaps some rotted fiberglass is hiding beneath the multiple layers of body filler. Watching automotive reality shows on television will give you an idea of how bad a vehicle can be.

Do You Care What Lies Beneath?

What is the intent for this vehicle? Unless it is going to be used in a demolition derby, the bodywork and paint should be as good as you can make it. Unless you have been painting cars for a lifetime, there will be flaws, but you should try to do the work as well as possible. Paint products and your time are too valuable to waste on a vehicle that is hiding damage.

Position the wet towel so that the water will run out of it and onto the area being sanded. When necessary, put the towel back in the bucket to soak up more water. Then, repeat the process.

When repainting a vehicle, the only way you can find every potential problem is to remove all the existing paint. True, the vehicle may be flawless, but chances are good that it is not. When you get down to bare metal, get the sheet metal back into epoxy primer as soon as practical to prevent any rust from forming.

MASKING

There are always times during a painting project when something should not receive paint or primer. This might be glass, a piece of trim, or something that is going to be a different color. When these surfaces are small, they can be protected from paint with masking tape. When areas are larger, they can be covered with masking paper. When they are larger yet, roll masking film can be used.

Masking Tape

Masking tape in widths from 1/4-inch to 2 inches is available at most auto-body paint stores. While 3/4-inch-wide tape is the most used masking tape, having a roll or two of a wider size comes in handy when masking an entire vehicle.

Any time that masking tape is used for an automotive painting project, the masking tape must be designed specifically for use with automotive paint products. Ordinary masking tape will not withstand the chemicals used in automotive paint. Additionally, ordinary masking tape is not designed to easily break loose from the surface, which may result in adhesive residue remaining on

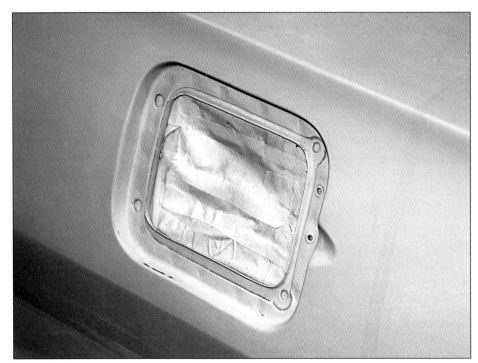

This is an example of a nice masking job. Going to the extra trouble of masking the gas-tank filler neck provides a more professional appearance than seeing overspray every time you fill up.

the surface. If left on too long, it can damage the new paint.

Masking for a Multicolored Panel

Masking panels prior to applying paint is a skill worth developing if you plan to do much painting. Whether masking is done to keep a piece of trim, glass, or something else from receiving paint or as part of a painting a multicolor paint scheme, doing it correctly is worthwhile. It will always take longer to remove paint from an unintended target than to prevent it from happening in the first place. Simply put, keeping paint off is easier than getting it off.

Masking a Multicolored Panel

1 *For masking any curved shape, it is always best to begin with 1/8- or 1/4-inch-wide fine-line tape. This tape is significantly more flexible than wider masking tape and provides a more definitive edge along the masked area.*

2 *With the tape firmly in place around the headlight bucket opening, bring it back along the rest of the fender. It is best to pull the tape taut with one hand to establish the desired line and then press the tape in place with the other hand. Trying to press the tape in place without pulling it taut results in a wavy line.*

3 *When possible, use one continuous piece of masking tape for the initial layout. However, when that is not possible, put down the first piece, ensure it is where you want it, and firmly press down on the surface. Align the next piece of tape with a bit of overlap and continue outlining.*

4 *This fender is being masked for a multicolor paint scheme, but the general process is the same for any type of masking. This photo shows just how flexible the fine-line tape can be. Be sure to firmly press the tape down onto the surface to provide a sharp paint edge.*

5 *Notice how the fine-line tape is positioned to closely match the body lines. The front portion is around the round headlight opening, while the lines running toward the back of the fender match the wheel opening and the edge of the fender. Paint layouts should accent the vehicle's bodylines, not fight them.*

6 Something to keep in mind when masking tapered lines is where the paint will come to a point. As the outlines converge upon one another, the tape overlaps. Keep in mind which side of the tape is defining the shape you are outlining. This is especially important when outlining multiple shapes that you want to be similar in appearance.

7 With the shape outlined with fine-line tape, the area to be masked off can be covered with wider automotive-paint-grade masking tape. On this fender, the entire piece has been painted with a metallic burnt orange top coat. Allow the proper time for the first paint to dry prior to applying any tape. The area within the outlined area will receive another color of paint.

8 Use a single-edge razor blade to trim any masking tape that extends past the outline.

9 Gently pull the excess masking tape away. If you look closely, the red fine-line tape is still the defining line at the edge of the paint scheme. After any necessary trimming is done, firmly press down the edges.

10 With the outline delineated by very narrow tape (red) and wider masking tape (yellow) attached to it, the rest of the area to be masked can be covered with masking tape and/or masking paper. The area between what will become two white stripes is still narrow so that it can be covered with some wider masking tape (green).

11 Continue masking the remaining area with appropriately sized masking tape, making sure to overlap each piece sufficiently to avoid any slivers where errant paint could fall. Trim any excess masking tape with a single-edge razor blade. Before spraying any paint or primer, verify that all masking tape edges are pressed down firmly.

Masking a Multicolored Panel *continued*

12 To mask the larger areas, use 3/4-inch-wide masking tape to secure masking paper to the outer pieces of masking tape that are already in place. Press the edges of the masking tape down firmly.

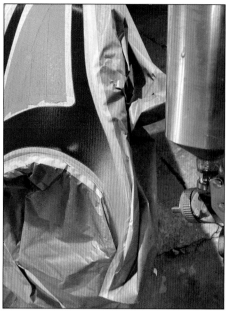

13 After securing all loose edges of the masking paper, the next coats of paint can be applied.

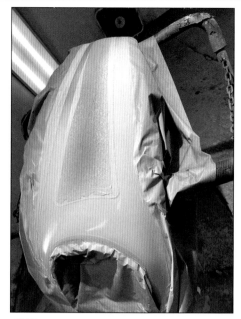

14 After applying the white paint, it is given the proper amount of time to flash between coats and before removing or applying any additional tape. The time between coats and tape time can be found on the instruction sheets for the product being sprayed.

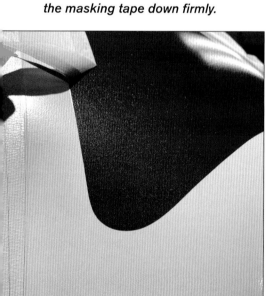

15 After awaiting the proper time, the masking tape can be removed by pulling it back on itself. When the process has been done correctly, there is a nice clean edge with no blow through where tape was not pushed down sufficiently.

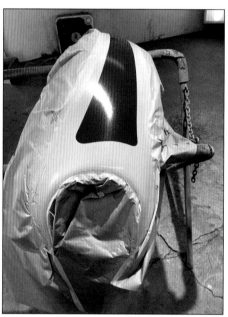

16 The top of the fender will be masked again for a third color to be applied to the area that is currently burnt orange and unmasked. As a reminder, the area beneath the masking paper will remain burnt orange when all is said and done.

17 Begin by outlining the area with narrow fine-line tape. The tape should cover the area where paint is not to be applied. In this case, it will be applied to the white area. Masking a multicolor paint scheme requires a fair amount of concentration.

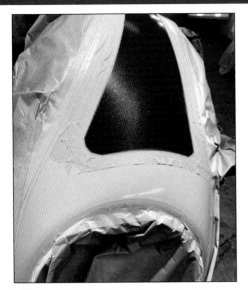

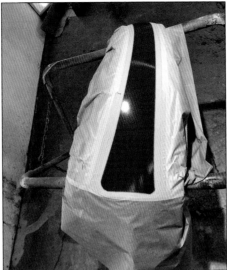

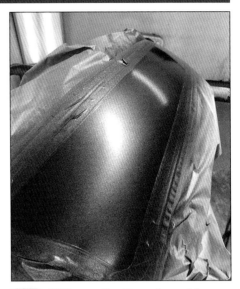

18 *Wider 3/4-inch masking tape is applied to the fine-line tape that outlines the area. This provides a surface to secure the masking paper.*

19 *Cover everything else that is not to be painted with masking paper. Secure it with masking tape as required.*

20 *With a collection of masking tape and masking paper covering everything that is not intended to receive the third color, the final coats of color can be applied.*

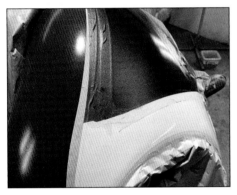

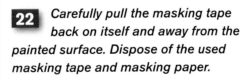

21 *While masking materials should not be allowed to remain on the surface for extended periods of time (no more than a day), allow adequate time for the paint to dry sufficiently before removing any masking. With the multiple layers of paint that may have been applied, edges of masking tape and masking paper can damage fresh paint, so take your time and be careful.*

22 *Carefully pull the masking tape back on itself and away from the painted surface. Dispose of the used masking tape and masking paper.*

23 *After all the masking material has been removed, carefully inspect the freshly painted surfaces to ensure that no touch-up is required. When all is as planned, allow the proper amount of time for the paint to cure. Then, apply clear. Except for a possible rare occasion, multicolor paint schemes should always be finished with clear to provide an even overall surface.*

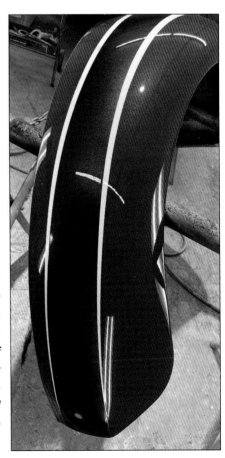

Masking Paper

Masking paper is the ideal product to use when masking areas that are larger than 2 inches wide. Masking paper comes in assorted sizes, typically in 2-inch increments ranging from 6 to 36 inches wide. Twelve-, 18-, and 36-inch widths are common, but the other sizes are available from various sources. Like the masking tape used to hold it in place, the masking paper must be designed for use with automotive paint products.

Don't Use Newspaper

Regardless of what anyone may suggest, avoid using newspaper as masking paper. Newsprint is porous, which allows paint to soak through and potentially threaten the surface that you are trying to protect. Newsprint will turn to lint when it gets wet, whether from water or paint. This lint will spread everywhere and can ruin a paint job as it is too small to easily pick out of the paint. Even though newspaper is cheap, it is not a suitable product for use with automotive paint products. Masking material is certainly not a place where you should attempt to save money during a painting project.

Coverage

Masking paper is required in multiple places during a paint job, even when everything is going to be the same color. The most common use is to protect the windshield, back glass, and any other glass in the vehicle, presuming that you are not doing a complete frame-off repaint. The glass is typically removed when doing a frame-off repaint. When doing a frame-off paint job, painters usually paint the inside of the passenger compartment at a different time from the exterior to avoid dragging an air hose through wet paint at the doorjamb. This opened door is masked off with masking paper. Note that whenever the interior is a different color or different level of gloss, the break is usually made at the inner edge of the doorjamb. This allows the rubber molding and/or garnish moldings to hide the exact line where the finish is different.

Whenever you use masking tape, press it firmly to ensure that the tape sticks to the surface. When the edge of the masking tape is not pressed down firmly and lifts slightly, paint can (and will) find its way beneath this loose edge.

Small Area

Masking a vehicle for painting may sound like a simple task, but it is a tedious task that will have a significant impact on the final results of your paint job. Thin slivers of paint on a surface that should not have paint, or previous paint or primer where there should be new paint are telltale signs of a new paint job. To some, this indiscretion does not matter, but to car-show judges or potential buyers, it can make or break the deal. Whether spraying primer, paint, or clear, any surface that should not receive it must be masked off. It is much easier, and it

Interiors are often painted the same color as the exterior of the vehicle but with a paint with less gloss. To prevent getting glossy paint inside this 1934 Ford coupe, the door and window openings have been covered with masking paper.

Whether spraying primer or top coats, any areas that should not be covered must be masked properly. An indicator of a professional-quality paint job is not having any traces of bad masking. Errant primer or paint is a quick indicator of a repaint.

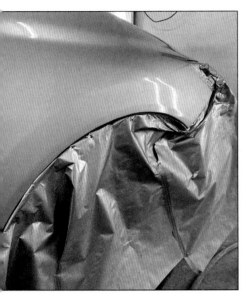

Even the inside of wheel wells and fenders should be protected from primer or paint overspray. Begin masking by defining the edge of the painted surface with 3/4-inch-wide masking tape. Then, tape masking paper to the first layer of masking tape.

is time well spent to mask rather than clean up afterward.

When the area to mask is too large to cover with masking tape, it is best to start by using 3/4-inch-wide masking tape to outline the entire area to be masked (unless the area to be masked is an intricate shape). For intricate shapes, begin with 1/4-inch-wide fine-line tape for the outline, as it is much more flexible.

With the outline masked, cut a piece of masking paper that is slightly longer than the area being covered. Professional shops use a masking-paper dispenser that applies masking tape to one edge of the masking paper as it is pulled from the roll. A blade on the device cuts both the tape and paper at the same time. This taped edge makes it easy for one person to apply masking paper without requesting the help of an assistant. A masking-tape dispenser may be too expensive for the hobbyist auto painter.

Spread out the masking paper and position one edge so that it overlaps the masking tape encircling the area to be masked. Use masking tape to secure the edge of the masking paper to the masking tape outline. Continue along this first edge and press the masking tape down firmly on the outline tape.

After you finish taping the first edge, press out any wrinkles in the masking paper toward the opposite edge. When it extends past the opposite side, trim as necessary or fold it back over, and then tape down the edge the same as with the first edge. On the two remaining edges, trim or fold the masking paper as necessary so that it ends on the outline tape. Secure the masking paper to the outline tape with more masking tape.

At this point, all edges of the masking paper should be secured to the outline masking tape. Where multiple pieces of masking paper are required to cover one area, tape the open edge down along the entire edge. Overlap the first piece with the second slightly and tape the second piece of masking paper to the first. When there are exposed edges of masking paper, they should be

To cover any area that requires masking, begin by applying masking tape to the perimeter of the area to be protected from paint. Rub your hand or fingers over the edges of the masking tape to ensure the tape is stuck to the surface.

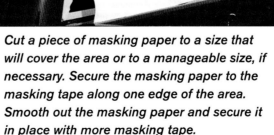

Cut a piece of masking paper to a size that will cover the area or to a manageable size, if necessary. Secure the masking paper to the masking tape along one edge of the area. Smooth out the masking paper and secure it in place with more masking tape.

Trim or fold the edges as necessary. Then, secure it in place with masking tape. Verify that all edges of the masking paper are pressed flat and taped down. Ensure the masking paper or tape covers the entire area that it is intended to cover.

covered with masking tape. Do not have any openings where the sprayed material can find its way to the area being masked.

Roll Masking Film

Roll masking film comes in rolls approximately 36 inches wide, but the film folds out to various widths in 14 feet, 20 feet, or even wider depending on what it is designed to cover. It is a very thin and lightweight plastic material that is meant to cover large areas such as a complete vehicle or other parts that must be stored in areas where paint is being sprayed. It is significantly lighter than a plastic drop cloth designed to place on the floor or over furniture when painting inside a home. You must pay attention to the "paint this side out" printed on the material. This surface is treated with a coating that will allow paint overspray to adhere to the plastic and not blow off and land back in your paint. If you accidently put it on a vehicle inside-out, it can leave a transfer of the coating onto the very surface it was meant to protect. A word of caution: do not use roll masking film on a painted surface that has not fully cured.

Large Area

When working in a cramped area, such as a two-car garage, it may be necessary to prime or paint some parts while part of the area is full of items that can be damaged by overspray. Roll masking film is a preferred method of covering these other parts while spraying nearby.

Begin by cutting a piece of the roll masking film that is long enough to cover the desired area. With help from an assistant, unfold the roll masking film to its maximum width. Drape it over the desired parts to be protected. Air pressure from a spray gun is powerful enough to blow the masking film around, so the edges must be taped to the floor or held in place with whatever you have available that will not be negatively affected if covered with overspray.

Work Area

To block off parts of the working area, plastic or canvas drop cloths can be hung temporarily by stapling the edges directly to roof rafters or to drywall. For an inexpensive but

semi-permanent room divider, suspend a piece of pipe (1/2-inch copper, electrical conduit, or something similar) from the ceiling and hang a canvas or plastic drop cloth from it with shower curtain hooks.

Drop Cloths

For covering anything else in the area where you are spraying paint to protect it from overspray, you have several choices. Disposable plastic drop cloths are economical, and slightly heavier plastic sheeting is a bit more expensive. Either of these can be held in place with masking tape and/or staples. Roll masking film can also be used to cover a large area. It is designed to be used as a covering for automotive parts, but it can certainly be used to cover anything else in the area.

Regardless of what you use, just be sure that you cover anything and everything in the area where you are spraying, as paint overspray will find it. On some things, it may not matter, but there will always be something that does not need to have overspray on it.

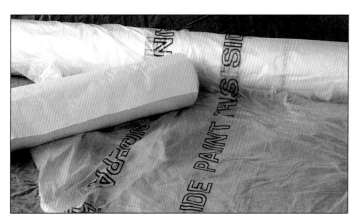

Masking film is great for protecting large areas of a vehicle that is not being painted. It comes in rolls about 3 feet wide but unfolds to about 10 feet wide. It is exceptionally light and designed to not damage painted surfaces.

Masking film is being used to cover the truck bed and other components of a painting project that will be painted later. Lack of storage room makes masking film one of your best friends during a painting project.

PRIMERS AND OTHER SUBSTRATES

Substrates, also known as under-coats, are paint-related products that are applied prior to the color coats of paint. This includes etching primers, filler primers, and sealers. Although no one sees these products after the vehicle is painted, they are particularly important in the overall paint job. These substrates work together to properly prepare the sheet metal, fiberglass, or carbon fiber for the application of paint.

Some things that the primer does not do is hide dents and scratches or eliminate rust. In all actuality, a good coat of filler primer usually reveals bodywork that is not ready for paint. Filler primer is porous, so it is not going to stop or eliminate rust. When a surface is covered only with filler primer, it will quickly rust when moisture reaches it.

All undercoats and top coats are designed for specific uses to be compatible with certain undercoats beneath them and certain overcoats to be applied to them. All this product specific information is available from the manufacturer through retail outlets or the manufacturer's website. These information sheets list especially vital information, such as compatible surfaces, required products, surface preparation, mixing ratio, air-pressure and spray-gun setup, application, drying times, and compatible top coats. Always verify the instructions for the specific product being used for the best results.

Epoxy Primer

Epoxy primer, or etching primer, is commonly used directly over properly prepared steel, aluminum, stainless steel, or galvanized metal. Not all etching primers are designed for use over all materials. A product that works well on steel and aluminum might not work well on fiberglass. Prior to purchasing any epoxy primer, verify its compatibility with what you will be working on, especially if it is a Corvette or any fiberglass reproduction. There is an appropriate epoxy primer, and you must find the right one.

In general, epoxy primer is mixed with its specific catalyst in a 2:1 ratio. Each brand of epoxy primer usually comes in a few distinct colors. Some epoxy primers can be tinted, while others cannot. However, epoxy primer can be blended with similar products of a different color when a unique color is desired. This may be desired (especially when the epoxy primer is used as a sealer) to create a color similar or contrasting to the

Epoxy primer consists of a primer that must be mixed with an appropriate hardener or catalyst. This catalyzed primer protects the surface from corrosion and promotes adhesion of subsequent primers and top coats. It also allows for wet sanding without fear of moisture penetrating the surface metal and causing rust issues. This brand calls for a 1:1 mixing ratio.

top-coat color. A similar color may be desired to help disguise minor rock chips or scratches in a vehicle that will be driven often. A contrasting color may be desired to assist the painter in knowing when full coverage is achieved.

Since epoxy primer is thick, it requires a relatively large paint tip (1.3 to 1.6 mm or equivalent). It also requires close to 40 psi of air pressure at the gun for a siphon-feed sprayer or around 10 psi for an HVLP spray gun.

Typical applications are one to two wet coats with 10 to 15 minutes of flash time between coats. Drying time before the top coat is about 60 to 90 minutes. Drying time before applying body filler can range from 60 minutes to overnight.

To Prevent Rust and Corrosion

Epoxy primer requires a catalyst, which provides excellent corrosion-protection and excellent adhesion when applied to properly prepared surfaces. These are the two main reasons for using epoxy primer. Uncatalyzed filler primer (lacquer primer) does not provide these two benefits.

Apply over Bare Metal

"Properly prepared" means "cleaned and sanded," which can vary somewhat for each type of material. Typically, cleaning includes soap and water, followed by wax and grease remover prior to application of the etching primer. On harder surfaces, such as stainless or galvanized steel, scuffing the surface first with 180- to 240-grit sandpaper is required. All surfaces should be primed immediately after cleaning. Just as primers vary, cleaning instructions vary also.

Apply over Primer or Painted Surfaces That Have Been Scuffed

Epoxy primer can be applied over primed or painted surfaces, but the surface must be cleaned according to its instructions. For painted surfaces, this usually includes sanding with 320- to 400-grit dry sandpaper or 600-grit wet sandpaper and then cleaning again.

Additional coats of epoxy can be applied at any time for up to a week. However, after a week, the surface must be cleaned, sanded, and cleaned again prior to additional coats.

High-Build Filler Primer

High-build filler primer (primer-surfacer) is commonly used during bodywork. It must be compatible with whatever is already on the surface, as well as whatever you intend to apply afterward. Before you get deep into a bodywork/painting project, it is always a promising idea to check with your paint and bodywork supplier to verify availability and compatibility of the products that you intend to use.

Not so long ago, high-build primer was mixed with a specific ratio of reducer prior to application. When it dried for the appropriate amount of time, the sanding would begin. As paint-related products have evolved, many of these high-build primers can be mixed in different ratios for different results. The way you use the product depends largely on the surface condition, how much bodywork has been done, and how deep any sand scratches may be.

Either mixture can be sprayed at about 8 to 10 psi through an HVLP spray gun or 29 to 40 psi through a siphon-feed spray gun. As

High-build primer is intended for use during bodywork to cover areas of hammer and dolly work. While the sheet metal should be worked to bring it as close to its original contour as possible, the high-build primer serves to match the exact contour through sanding.

Not all primer products repel moisture. For direct-to-metal applications, verify that you are using an epoxy primer designed to be applied directly to the metal. If the primer used for that does not meet that requirement, sheet metal may quickly begin to rust, depending on the climate.

Primer-surfacer essentially serves the same purpose as high-build primer. Properties to look for are minimal shrinkage, quick dry time, and easy sanding.

a primer-surfacer, the spray gun tip should be between 1.6 to 1.8 mm but slightly larger for sprayable filler. The pot life for primer-surfacer is about 60 minutes, but it's a mere 30 minutes when mixed as a sprayable filler. In either case, your spray gun must be emptied and cleaned prior to that. Otherwise, you risk ruining your spray gun.

With contemporary high-build primers being much lighter than in years past, it is especially important to mask anything in the area that should not receive primer. However, since most primer-surfacer will be removed during the block-sanding process, it is not a requirement to spray the primer in a spray booth. Any clean, dust-free area will suffice.

Primers typically have a high solids content, therefore any masking used while spraying primer should be removed prior to spraying top coats. Apply fresh masking materials prior to spraying the top coats.

Apply Epoxy Primer or Body Filler

To use as a primer-surfacer, the filler is mixed with its catalyst and reducer in a 4:1:1 ratio. This can be applied as 2 to 3 wet coats, with 5 to 10 minutes between coats. The time advantage is that primer-surfacer can be sanded after 90 minutes, which makes it suitable when working areas

of bodywork to repair collision damage or remove rust.

After applying the primer-surfacer to just the areas where bodywork has been performed, block sand the surface with 150-grit sandpaper. Apply two more coats of primer-surfacer and then sand with 280- to 320-grit sandpaper.

When you are doing a budget paint job or a simple repaint to a daily driver vehicle, you can now move on to spraying a guide coat. When you want a top-notch paint job, finish sanding the bodywork areas with 400-grit sandpaper.

After Performing Bodywork

After performing all the necessary bodywork, minor flaws (including sanding scratches) may exist. These can usually be removed by applying a sprayable filler to the entire body, fenders, doors, hood, and decklid.

To use high-build primer as a sprayable filler, the filler is typically mixed with its catalyst in a 4:1 ratio without the addition of reducer. It can then be applied with up to four wet coats, with 5 to 10 minutes between coats. This covers most scratches, including those put in with 80-grit sandpaper. Prior to sanding, the sprayable filler should dry for 6 hours or more. It can then be sanded with 400- to 600-grit wet or

320- to 500-grit dry.

There are now two steps of undercoats left prior to applying paint: 1) applying a guide coat and 2) applying sealer. Filler primers are typically the last undercoat products to be sanded. For this reason, it is especially important that these layers of primer be applied correctly and sanded to a smooth surface prior to applying sealer.

Guide Coat

As the last chance to verify that the vehicle's sheet metal is as straight, flat, and as smooth as can be, professional painters spray a guide coat. Most any sandable primer can be used as a guide coat, but rattle can enamel will also work well.

Some paint companies manufacture specific guide coat products that are generally available in a spray can. Whether using a specific guide coat product or a spray can of hardware store grade spray paint, mist it onto the surface in a uniform coverage.

Uniform Coverage and Contrasting Color

The key to an effective guide coat is uniform coverage. It is not necessary or even desired to totally cover all the primered surface. A uniform, misted coat is all that is necessary. The color must also be a color that contrasts with whatever color the vehicle is now. Give the guide coat enough time to dry adequately.

High and Low Spots

Using a sanding block and the same grit or finer of the most recent sandpaper that was used, sand off the guide coat. Any areas where the guide coat comes off quickly is higher than the surrounding area. Any areas where the guide coat remains after sanding is a low spot. Any of these spots (high or low) should be small and localized.

For high spots, it may be necessary to use a hammer and dolly to gently tap the high spot down to the correct level. Low spots can typically be filled with spot putty. This is like body filler but is much finer and does not require any hardener. This is a lacquer-based product that is generally red in color and comes in a tube. Since it requires no activator, it is not as stable as a catalyzed product and should be used sparingly. Apply the spot putty with a squeegee to fill the area and allow it to dry. Using a sanding block, sand off any excess.

If there are many high or low spots, it may be desirable to apply a second guide coat and sand with a sanding block again. With the contrasting-color guide coat, it is quite easy to see any imperfections, whether they are spots or scratches.

Utilize Guide Coat

When you get to the point of using a guide coat, the basic work is the same as done before, except the materials used are finer.

Prepping with a Guide Coat and Filling Low Spots

1 Spray the guide coat onto the surface with a mist coat so there is uniform coverage. Do not try to completely cover the surface below but cover it completely with a mist. This entire coat will be sanded off, so do not worry about any runs or drips.

2 Use a sanding block with 400-grit-or-finer sandpaper to sand off the guide coat. If you are using a catalyzed primer, wet sandpaper can be used. This photo shows an appropriate application of the guide coat.

3 Using a light pressure on the sanding block, remove the guide coat by sanding in various directions. Any high spots are revealed by the guide coat quickly being removed. You should not have any of those at this point. Any low spots are revealed by localized areas of guide coat remaining.

Prepping with a Guide Coat and Filling Low Spots *continued*

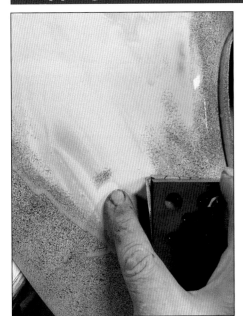

4 While much of this fender still requires sanding, this one area still shows a low spot. Some people may try to remove this area of guide coat by sanding only in this area, but that defeats the purpose of using a guide coat. It is obviously lower than the surrounding area, so it should be filled.

5 After finishing sanding all the guide coat, fill any low areas with glazing compound. This is an exceptionally fine body filler designed for this very purpose. Note that some glazing compounds require hardener, while some others do not.

6 This brand of glazing compound requires hardener. Therefore, it is mixed with a proportionate amount of hardener.

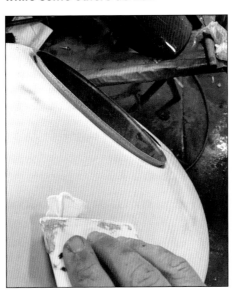

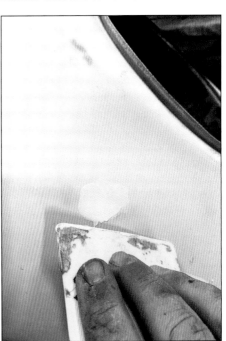

7 Using a squeegee, mix the glazing compound with the hardener until no streaks of color appear.

8 Apply the glazing compound into the low spot with a squeegee. While you want to fill the low spot entirely, you do not want to spread it all over the surface, which would require additional sanding.

9 With the relatively small amount of filler (glazing compound) being applied, you can get it pretty smooth simply with the squeegee.

Prepping with a Guide Coat and Filling Low Spots *continued*

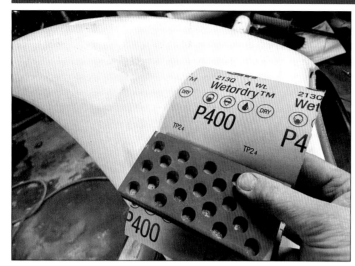

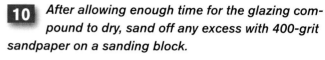

10 *After allowing enough time for the glazing compound to dry, sand off any excess with 400-grit sandpaper on a sanding block.*

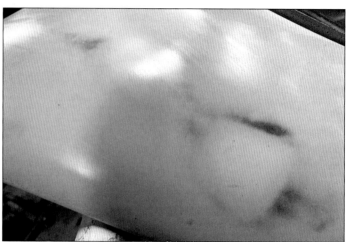

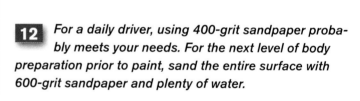

11 *Continue sanding the area until the glazing compound is feathered out completely. There should be absolutely no solid edges of filler visible, and you must not be able to feel any discrepancies in the surface.*

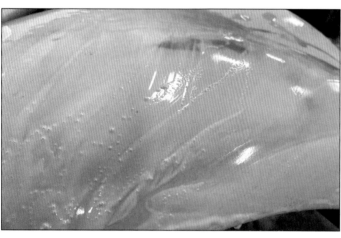

12 *For a daily driver, using 400-grit sandpaper probably meets your needs. For the next level of body preparation prior to paint, sand the entire surface with 600-grit sandpaper and plenty of water.*

Sealer

Sealer is applied as the last of the coats of undercoats prior to the application of paint. As such, extra care should be taken during the application process and inspection afterward to ensure that everything is as it should be. For someone new to painting, the application of sealer can serve as a great practice run for the actual paint application.

Sealer products can be standalone products used only as a sealer, while some primer products can be used as a sealer. With the latter, the mixing ratio is usually a bit different for a sealer than as a primer.

Providing a Uniform Surface for Paint Application

Whether lots of bodywork or no bodywork has been done, spraying two coats of sealer before applying paint is a good practice. The even coats of sealer provide a uniform surface on which to apply the paint. Therefore, the paint should consistently look the same color everywhere it is applied. It is common to see vehicles have a door or fender that does not match the rest of the vehicle. This is because that door or fender has been damaged and the repair was done only to that specific panel. While you cannot expect a body shop to paint an entire vehicle when only a door has been damaged, this illustrates the point of having a consistent surface and the general need to blend the color onto adjacent panels when doing a partial repair/paint.

Sealer also provides a layer of uniform solvent evaporation, which greatly decreases blotches, clouds, or bleed-through. These flaws may not appear when applying a dark color but can be quite noticeable when applying a light color over a dark color.

When applying paint over a factory finish, spraying sealer prior to applying paint is necessary. With the factory paint being baked on, it is difficult for new paint to achieve maximum adhesion. Without scuffing the surface and applying a few coats of sealer, the new paint job is prone to paint flaking randomly or coming off in large sheets—neither of which is good. If someone asks you to do a simple color change on a new vehicle, it will still require some scuffing and sealer. This also applies to adding graphics, flames, scallops, or a second color to a portion of a new vehicle.

Sealing in Substrates

The other important reason for using sealer is to seal in the substrates and their chemicals, preventing them from causing issues with the top coats. Even when there has been no bodywork, you most likely have no idea what brand or type of paint is currently on the vehicle. The sealer forms a barrier yet provides good adhesion between the old and new surface finishes.

Prior to Spraying Sealer

When spraying sealer, make every effort to ensure the surface is clean. You should have been doing that all along, but it's especially important now. The bodywork is done, so now is a wonderful time to thoroughly clean and vacuum the entire area where you will be spraying sealer and paint. Eliminate as much dust and dirt as possible. Do whatever you can to eliminate any flies, bugs, or anything that can potentially harm a fresh coat of paint.

Use an air hose with a nozzle to blow any dust and dirt away from the vehicle. Blow everything out of all the crevices and body seams where anything can be hiding. Clean the entire vehicle by wiping wax and grease remover on with a clean towel and wiping it off with another clean towel. If desired, the wax and grease remover can be sprayed on, but it must be wiped off with a clean towel and not allowed to dry on the surface. Refrain from using ordinary paper towels when cleaning an area prior to paint, as they can and will leave a lot of lint or paper fibers, which will likely end up in the paint. Lint-free towels are pricey, but you must use something that is low-lint or lint-free.

Using the methods of masking described in Chapter 4, do the best job of masking that you can. Take your time and get it correct. When you do it correctly, the masking techniques used when spraying sealer can be utilized throughout the rest of the paint job.

Mixing Sealer

Depending on the brand of sealer being used, there may be alternate methods of mixing the sealer that may be of interest. When being used purely as a sealer, it is typically mixed with a specific catalyst and a reducer in the ratio of 2:1:1. Just as with most primers, distinct colors of the same brand and type of sealer can be blended together for a unique color. These are still mixed in the same 2:1:1 ratio.

However, many sealers can be tinted with specific toners from the same manufacturer to provide custom colors. Many popular custom cars of the 1950s were painted with this process for a specific appearance. The colors were often of a lighter, pastel variety, but this purely depends on the toner used and mixing ratio. At least one manufacturer recommends a mixing ratio of four parts sealer, two parts catalyst, two parts reducer, and one part toner.

Tinting the sealer provides two distinct options. One is to tint the sealer to a shade comparable to the desired finished paint color. This provides more depth to the color and better coverage. When the sealer and paint are near the same color, you have a little more latitude when wet sanding. Along those same lines, even if a rock chip breaks through the paint, it will not be as noticeable when the primer is nearly the same color.

A second option is to use the tinted sealer as the final color. While this should not be a long-term choice, it is certainly a short-term option when you or a customer need to save up some money for final paint. It is also acceptable when it is desirable to get a new build out on the road for some break-in miles in order to avoid mechanical repairs that might take a toll on fresh paint.

Regardless of how the sealer is mixed, one to two wet coats are normally applied with a 1.3- to 1.6-mm spray-gun tip. Drying time will be around 10 to 15 minutes between coats.

Since we are getting ready to spray paint, be aware of a new time to watch: the drying time to top coat.

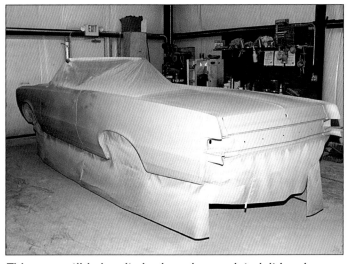

This convertible has its bodywork completed, it has been block sanded, it is in the final coats of sealer, and it is masked and ready to receive paint. A body dolly is great for moving a body, so the chassis, wheels, and tires do not require masking.

A custom trick that has been around since at least the 1950s is to tint the sealer with some toner in the color of your choice. The tinted sealer often takes on an eggshell appearance and provides some color and looks good until you save up enough money for a real paint job. Note that when doing this, the entire surface needs to be scuffed and a new coat of sealer applied prior to applying paint.

With one coat of sealer dry to top coat is about 15 minutes, with dry to top coat of two coats of sealer is about 30 minutes. There is a specific time window to apply paint. When that time window (usually about 72 hours) is exceeded, the sealer must be scuffed before applying any top coat.

Reducer

All paint manufacturers design their products under what they consider to be perfect climatic conditions, around 70°F and 30-percent humidity. It is unknown if this is an industry standard or simply what one or more companies chose to design to. However, unless one is spraying in a climate-controlled spray booth, temperature and humidity are beyond the control of the painter. To compensate for this, paint chemists design various reducers to be used with their products.

Reducers are rated according to their evaporation abilities: very slow, slow, medium, and fast. When spray-ing conditions are hot, a slow or very slow reducer should be used to evaporate more slowly so that the paint has more time to dry. When the spraying conditions are cool, a relatively faster reducer should be used to help the paint completely dry.

When the paint dries too quickly, it may suffer checking, crazing, or cracking issues. However, when a fast reducer is used to compensate for cooler temperatures, it can result in blushing (moisture trapped in the paint) if the humidity is high. When in doubt, opt for a medium reducer.

Fixing Errors

Look at every square inch of the sheet metal that received sealer. Look for and find all errors because they must be fixed now. For any pinholes that appear, fill them with spot putty,

Reducers for use in automotive paint products are designed with specific temperature ranges in mind. While the temperature ranges may vary from one manufacturer to another, they are rated as slow, medium, or fast.

A slow reducer is designed for use in warmer temperatures than a fast reducer, which is designed to be used in cooler temperatures.

let dry, and sand away the excess with 600-grit sandpaper used wet.

For any runs in the sealer, spread some spot putty over the entire run with a squeegee. Let it dry. Then, sand away the excess with 600-grit sandpaper used wet. For any of these areas, clean the area with wax and grease remover, then touch up the area with sealer using slightly less air pressure. Thoroughly clean your spray gun while the sealer is drying.

Before You Spray

Regardless of which brand of paint (PPG, BASF-Glasurit) or paint system (urethane, polyurethane, waterborne) you use, realize that the instructions for each type of product will vary. Being able to purchase products locally and in person will allow you the opportunity to build rapport with the experts in your area for that product. They will have access to the product information sheets and can also provide the necessary links to corporate websites so you can print your own copies for use in your shop.

Flash Time/Drying Time

Most all flash and drying times are based upon a certain temperature and sometimes a specific humidity range. These also vary from one manufacturer to another and from one product to another. This does not mean you can only use the product when the temperature is 70°F, but realize that it will dry quicker when the temperature is higher and will take longer when it is cooler. Whether you are able to spray in a professional spray booth or make do in a home garage, as a rule of thumb, you must have an ambient temperature of at least 55°F to use any automotive paint products.

Drying Time Term	Description
Between coats	The time to allow after spraying one coat before spraying another coat
Dust free	The amount of time the surface must be kept free of any dust
Tape time	The time to allow before applying any masking tape, such as for a multicolor paint scheme
To sand	The time to allow before sanding with the recommended sandpaper grit
To top coat	The time to allow before applying a top coat to the surface just sprayed

The Surface Must Be Clean

Information sheets for all paint products list compatible surfaces on which to apply the product as well as acceptable top coats to apply over it. Dust, dirt, grease, and wax are never listed in any of those acceptable surfaces. Automotive paint products do not adhere to these substances, so they must be removed from the surface to be painted.

Wax and Grease Remover

To remove most contaminants that you can't see, clean all surfaces to be painted with wax and grease remover. The wax and grease remover can be sprayed directly onto the surface or onto a clean cloth or paper towel and wiped onto the surface. Wipe the surface off with a second clean cloth or paper towel.

Be sure that the cleaning cloths are clean and free of any wax, polish, grease, or anything else. If desired, purchase a few yards of new flan-

Wax and grease remover is designed to remove contaminants that inhibit good paint adhesion from the surface. It can be sprayed or wiped onto the surface and then wiped off with a clean towel. After wiping the surface clean, attach an air nozzle to the air hose and blow air over the entire surface to ensure that no wax and grease remover remains on the surface.

nel material from a fabric store. Cut it into whatever size works best for you and wash the cloths in a washing machine after each use. If you choose this route, it is best to have a dedicated washing machine because chemicals from the rags can contaminate the washing machine, and those chemicals can transfer to clothing. To keep them clean, store them in a resealable bag.

Tack Cloths

Aside from wiping the surface clean with wax and grease remover, most painters wipe off the surface to be painted with a tack cloth that is made of a special material. Gently wipe (do not rub) a tack cloth over the area to be painted to pick up tiny particles of dust and lint. These cloths are relatively inexpensive

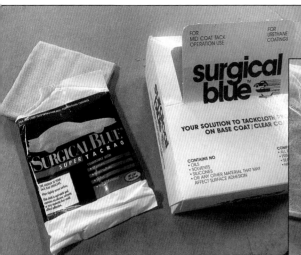

While wax and grease remover is used to remove wax, grease, oils, and solvents from the surface to be painted, you may still be forced to contend with dust and dirt on the surface. Tack cloths are designed to pick up miniscule particles of dust and lint.

When you take the tack cloth out of the packaging, unfold it completely. Then, fold it into a manageable size. Gently wipe the tack cloth over the surface prior to applying paint.

and available at most of the places where you will purchase your paint. There are two basic types of tack cloths: those designed for primer and those designed for base coat. Primer tack cloths are usually white and are thicker and stickier. The lighter-weight blue cloths are lower tack and designed for base coats. After you take the tack cloth out of the package, unfold it completely and lightly fold it back into a manageable size.

Removing Masking Material

Paint overspray and potentially any dust in your spray area can accumulate on the masking material and in any crevices that may exist. For these reasons, leave the masking material in place long enough for the recently sprayed material (primer, paint, or clear coat) to dry adequately to prevent dust from adhering to the latest coats. This time is referred to as "dust free" on information sheets for paint products.

After waiting the appropriate amount of time, exert some restraint when removing masking material. Now is not the time to relive your 4-year-old self opening a birthday present. Begin pulling a piece of masking tape back on itself and pull the tape away from the painted surface. Continue doing this until the masking paper is loose. Pull the masking paper away from the surface and avoid dragging it across the

freshly painted surface. Continue until all the masking tape and paper is off the vehicle.

Mixing and Application

Mixing automotive paint products to paint your classic car is not the time to play chemist. The paint manufacturers have gone to great lengths, spending time and money to create their products. Everything needed to know about mixing the products is included in their respective information sheets. For the product being used, the information sheets list compatible catalysts (hardeners), reducers or thinners, and any other compatible additives.

They will be listed as a ratio, which allows you to mix as much or as little as you need. While that translates to 1 gallon of product to 1 quart of reducer for a 4:1 ratio, you may not need 5 quarts of sprayable material for the project. Providing a ratio minimizes the math.

Mixing Components

Whether preparing primer or paint, some consumables are required for a painting project: mixing cups, stir sticks, strainers, and

When masking is done properly, it is relatively easy to remove, as it will come off in sheets. Start in a corner, then gently peel the masking paper and tape back onto itself. When a piece of masking is free from the vehicle, dispose of it in a trash can.

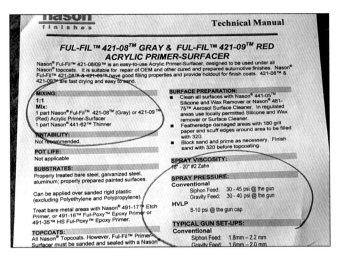

Information sheets for primer, paint, and clear products provide necessary information for mixing and spraying the product. These information sheets are available where you purchase the product and on the manufacturer's website.

spray-out cards. None of these are expensive and are often free when you purchase your paint and primer products. Some smaller outlets may charge you for these components, but the cost is negligible and is typically to keep track of inventory.

Mixing Cups

Mixing cups are the plastic measuring cups used for mixing the components together prior to pouring the mixture into the spray gun. They are available in pint, quart, and gallon sizes, with the quart size being the most common.

The cool thing about mixing cups is that they have a variety of common mixing ratios (along with equal units) printed on the side. Each component of the ratio has its own column marked with incremental horizontal lines. From the bottom of the mixing cup, the first number will be one, the next is two, three, etc. Each horizontal line in each column is in the correct location to obtain the proper mix.

For example, when mixing a primer product that has a 4:1:1 ratio, this requires four parts primer, one part catalyst, and one part reducer. When you need to mix just a little bit of the primer, pour the primer in the cup up to the first horizontal mark in the first column. Pour the catalyst in the cup up to the first horizontal mark in the second column. Pour the reducer up to the first horizontal mark in the third column. This provides the proper portions for the example primer.

When you require more product, pour each component into the mixing up to the desired horizontal line, whether that is one, nine, or somewhere in between. Just be sure that you fill each column to the same ratio number.

Mixing cups are reusable if they are cleaned thoroughly between different products. For instance, you can use the same mixing cup multiple times for primer if you can still see the lines. When finished mixing primer, you can use the cup again for paint, but you must clean it thoroughly prior to doing so.

When a mixing cup becomes too grungy to use for mixing, use it as a receptacle for whatever may be left in the spray gun when you are finished spraying. Allow the extra paint to air dry and become somewhat solid, and it can be disposed of.

Stir Sticks

Even though paint and primer products are mixed at the factory, they have no doubt sat quite a while

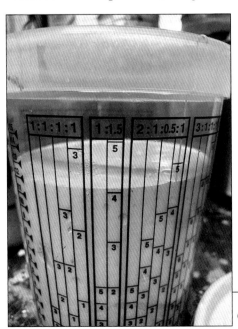

Mixing cups may look confusing, but they are easy to use and make mixing primer or paint significantly easier than trying to do so without them. In this example, the desired mixing ratio is 1:1.5. The primary component (primer, in this case) takes 1 part to 1.5 parts of reducer. To mix the required amount of primer, it is determined that using the 4 line will provide the necessary volume. Add primer to the 4 line in the first column and then add reducer to the 4 line in the second column.

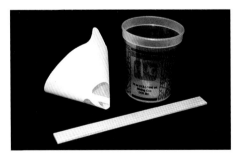

Mixing cups are necessary to ensure that your primer or paint is mixed in the correct ratio with reducer and hardener. Stir sticks are necessary to stir the mixture thoroughly. Strainers are essential to prevent stray objects from ruining your spray gun.

prior to you using them. For heavy primer products that have not yet been opened, consider setting the can upside down for a day or two prior to using it to allow the material to slightly mix itself. Still, when you do open it, it will require thorough stirring. While stirring, use the paint stick to scrape up any material that has collected at the bottom of the can.

Use a paint stick to thoroughly mix each component together prior to spraying. While you can use the paint stick that you used to stir the primer to mix the other components, do not use the mixing stick to stir the primer in its original container. Any residual catalyst or reducer will contaminate the unmixed primer.

Strainers

Paint strainers (filters) are essentially a paper funnel with two pieces of filter material in the bottom. It is not necessary to filter the materials as they are being poured into the mixing cup. However, the importance of straining the mixed primer or paint when pouring it into the spray gun cannot be ignored. Regardless of how miniscule it may be, any dust or dirt inside of the spray gun can be enough to render it useless. Having a paint strainer at the top of the spray cup when pouring product in prevents this from happening.

Spray-Out Cards

Spray-out cards are designed for two distinct purposes: 1) to determine how many coats of paint are required to cover and 2) to match paint color. These cards are black and white in color, have white and black text printed on them, and have a hole near the middle. The hole in the middle allows you to hold the

spray-out card against the existing paint and determine if you have a perfect match (or not).

For gauging coverage, spray the paint you are going to use to paint your vehicle onto the spray out-card. Using the same overlap, spray gun settings, and time between coats, apply enough coats of paint to cover the spray-out card entirely. No card or text should be visible. The number of coats required to obtain this coverage is the number of coats required on the vehicle.

Cleanup Thinner or Reducer

Most all sprayable automotive paint and primer products require a specific reducer or thinner to make them sprayable. These same materials can be used or clean your spray gun as well as general cleanup, but this can get expensive. Most paint suppliers can recommend a similar product, which is a bit more economical. Whatever you use, ensure there is always some available so that the spray gun can be cleaned up in less time than the product's pot life.

Application Process

In addition to great surface preparation and the proper mixing of components, the success of a paint job depends greatly on the application process. The obvious goal of this is to avoid any runs and achieve complete coverage.

This is a combination of having the spray gun set correctly for its contents and the painter's movement in relation to the object being painted. With every cup full of primer or paint that you spray, first spray a test panel to ensure the spray gun is set correctly.

Test Panel

As mentioned previously, information sheets for primer and paint products include recommendations for spray-gun setup: air pressure and the spray-gun-tip size. There is a bit of latitude on these, as whatever works best is what is best. For many primer products, 8 to 10 psi at the air cap is best for an HVLP spray gun. Realize that to achieve this pressure at the air cap, where the primer exits

After each application of primer, sealer, and paint, clean the spray gun. This will occur throughout a paint job. For this cleanup process, some economical no-name lacquer thinner will work as good as a similar product from one of the paint companies. Larger quantities at a more economical price can be found at your local auto-parts store.

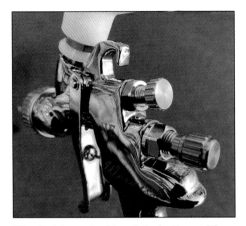

The fluid-control knob is in line with the paint tip and is the larger of the two knobs in this photo. Turning this knob inward provides less volume, and turning it outward provides more volume. The upper knob is the fan control, which controls the pattern.

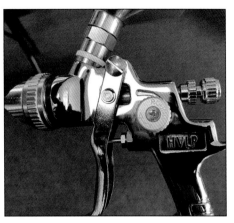

The fluid-control knob is in line with the paint tip. On this spray gun, the fan-control knob is on the side. Turning the knob clockwise (inward) provides a round spray pattern. Turning the knob counterclockwise (outward) provides an oval pattern.

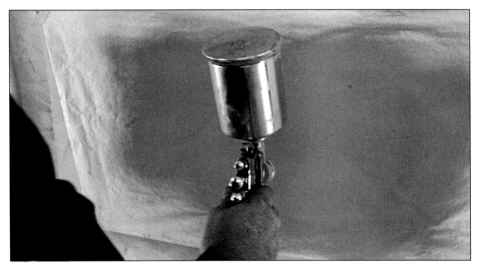

Prior to spraying primer or paint on your vehicle, spray a test pattern to verify that your spray gun controls are set correctly. Tape a piece of masking paper onto the wall of your spray booth for a target. Do this every time that you fill up your spray gun.

the gun, the air pressure coming out of the air compressor must be at 40 psi or higher, depending on the air hose diameter and length of hose.

The required 1.3- to 1.6-mm spray tip is simply the size of orifice required to efficiently pass the primer through the spray gun. Whenever you purchase a spray gun, it will either have tips of various sizes or the spray gun kit will include multiple spray guns, each with a different-size tip. In the latter case, each spray gun will have a distinct color-retaining ring to secure the spray tip and allow you to easily distinguish the primer gun from the top-coat gun.

Although the location may vary slightly, most spray guns have two control knobs. The volume of paint is controlled by one and the fan spray is controlled by the other. The fluid-control knob is always the knob in line with the spray nozzle. To allow full paint volume, turn this knob almost all the way out and fully squeeze the trigger. Turn the fluid-control knob inward until you feel pressure on the knob. In most situations, this is appropriate. However, lower volume may be required when blending colors. Turning the knob inward will achieve this.

The fan-control knob may be located near the fluid-control knob, or it may be located near where the air hose connects to the spray gun. With this knob all the way open, an elliptical pattern is achieved. Turning this knob all the way in results in a circle pattern. The larger elliptical pattern is desired for most situations.

A third adjustment found on some spray guns is an air micrometer used to fine-tune the amount of air entering the spray gun. When this adjustment exists, it is typically left wide open.

To spray a test pattern, tape a piece of masking paper or cardboard to the wall. Fill the spray gun cup with whatever you intend to spray next and connect it to the air supply. Hold the nozzle of the spray gun about 8 inches from the surface of the test pattern and squeeze the trigger to completely open and close in one motion. Adjust the knobs as previously explained and repeat as necessary to obtain the desired spray pattern.

Spray Tip-to-Surface Distance

The spray tip-to-surface distance should remain constant at about 8 inches. When the distance is greater, the paint or primer begins to dry in

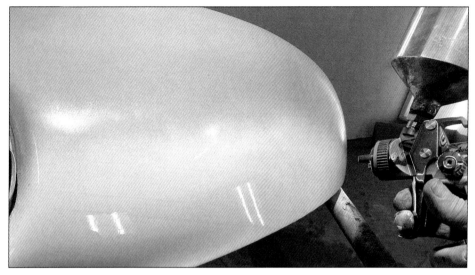

Obtaining a smooth application of primer or paint is a combination of air pressure, spray tip-to-surface distance, paint volume, and spray-gun movement. Air pressure must be adequate to move the paint through the air and onto the surface. The distance between the spray tip and the surface must be matched to the air pressure. The spray gun must be adjusted to spray enough paint through the nozzle. The spray gun must be moved adequately to prevent too much paint from reaching the surface and causing runs.

midair prior to reaching the intended surface, which results in dry spots. When the distance is less than this, the sprayed material will begin to run.

Paint Volume versus Spray-Gun Movement

All things being equal, when you move the spray gun slowly, the spray gun must be adjusted to spray less material. However, when the spray gun is moved faster, the spray gun must be adjusted to spray more material. Spraying a test pattern on a disposable surface, rather than on your vehicle, is the best method of determining what works best for you. Remember that primer products will spray differently than top coats, so it should be standard practice to spray a test pattern each time you fill the spray cup, regardless of the contents.

Overlap

With the spray gun adjusted as required and you are feeling con-fident in your application ability, begin by spraying the edges of the intended surface first. Then, spray the overall panels, overlapping each pass with the spray gun approximately 50 percent. Spray all surfaces using this technique, and then allow the proper flash time prior to spraying the next coat.

Sand out Runs

After allowing the surface to dry, inspect the finish for any runs, drips, or other errors. When any of these exist, use an appropriate grit of sandpaper to sand out the blemish. When the surface is smooth again, touch up the area with the appropriate primer or paint being applied at the time.

Drying

Solvent-based paints can dry via three basic procedures: air dry, force dry, and infrared. Obviously, the most common of these is air dry. The

working conditions you have may have some impact on which paint system works best for you. Always consult the information sheet for the products you are using.

Air drying acrylic urethane requires about 6 to 8 hours, while base-coat color requires only 20 to 40 minutes to air dry, depending on how many coats have been applied. However, the clear that is applied as part of the base coat/clear coat paint system requires about 16 hours to air dry.

Force drying acrylic urethane can be completed in about an hour, but this requires a heated spray booth. Clear applied atop base color can be force dried in about 30 minutes.

Infrared heating can cure acrylic urethane in about 15 minutes, but the heaters are better suited to small parts rather than a complete car body. Infrared heaters are ideal for motorcycles or other relatively small parts.

TOP COATS

When going to the time, trouble, and expense of painting an automobile, perhaps the worst thing you can do is to paint it a color that you or your customer will get tired of quickly. This is not so much of a problem when repairing collision damage to a relatively late-model vehicle, where the intent is to match the existing color. However, whether the vehicle is planned for use as a secondary family vehicle or is a fulfillment of a longtime dream, the intent should be to like it for a long time.

Matching an Existing Color

The vehicle has an identification tag that includes a color code that can be used by the paint supplier to determine the correct color. The original paint code can also be determined from the vehicle's VIN or color and options tag. This information reveals the vehicle's original color, which may not be what color it is now. If it is not the same color, it has been repainted, or the VIN has changed.

When you order paint based upon information from a VIN or options tag and it does not match, it may be that a variant formula is required. When the automobile manufacturers switched to robotic painting systems, the paint system does not stop during color changes. Toward the end of a run of vehicles

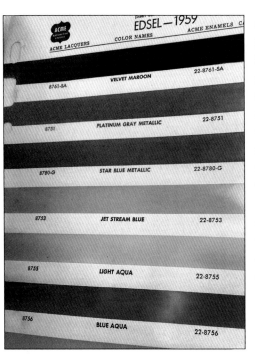

As long as a paint code that provides a paint formula is available, any factory color can be reproduced, regardless of age. For true classic and collector cars, this is important, as restoration to original condition is important at concours events.

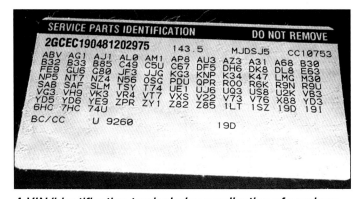

A VIN/identification tag includes a collection of numbers that does not make any sense to most people but provides plenty of information regarding equipment and options to those who know the codes. The counterperson at your favorite paint supplier will know which of these numbers to use. An educated guess for this is "BC/CC U 9260 19D" for base coat/clear coat. For the context of this book, it provides the paint code for the paint on the vehicle when it left the factory.

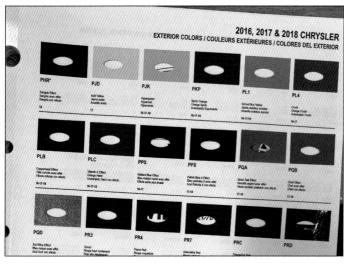

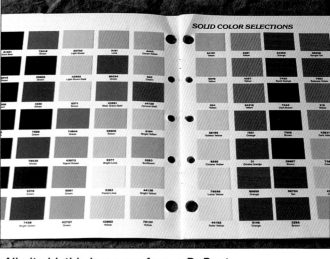

While many people cannot see the difference, others can easily distinguish 14 or 15 variations of red on this color chart. The oval-shaped holes allow you to lay the page from the color chart onto the body of your car to determine which color best matches.

Albeit old, this is a page from a DuPont commercial-vehicle color chart. Some color charts include names, while some do not. However, they always include a number that provides the formula for mixing that specific paint.

being painted one color, the next color is introduced to the system and provides a slightly different shade of the color as what was sprayed in the middle of the run. As this second color continues, it sprays the prime formula. Then, before this line is completed, the color being sprayed will reach another variant. This situation affects all robotic painting systems, so it is not limited to one manufacturer or color.

Whenever a paint code is entered into a paint-matching database, the prime formula is displayed, along with any known variants. The prime formula provides the recipe for mixing the paint to achieve the color that is seen in the color charts. A variant code will include properties or notes such as "less white, more yellow" or "less red, more black." In this case, to match the color correctly, compare color chips of these variant colors to the vehicle. When the correct variant is determined, the paint can be mixed from the formula provided for that variant.

Matching Any Color

There may be times when you desire to paint a vehicle to match a specific color that may or may not be a stock automotive color. This requires the use of a color spectrometer and requires something that is already the color to be matched. The existing color is scanned. Then, through the magic of computers, a paint formula is developed and printed. However, this process cannot be perfect. While it does work well on solid colors, it cannot determine the formula for tri-stage paints (candy, pearl, or metallic).

Selecting a New Color

When doing a complete repaint, it is important to choose a good color. Part of the process toward selecting a suitable color is to view the short list of possible colors under as many lighting conditions as possible. Unless you have a very specific color that you are trying to match,

such as a corporate color palette or other very specific color, selecting an existing color is a great choice.

It makes sense that OEM colors are chosen based on customer surveys and other marketing techniques. During the life of automobiles, there are more than enough from which to choose. We have all seen vehicles that are like a common OEM color but do not look as good. This often comes from seeing a color on a vehicle that really looks great but then taking the liberty to mix paint slightly darker, lighter, or with a little more or less of this or that color. When the custom color is mixed and applied to your vehicle, it does not look like it did on the new car you saw on the street or at the dealership. That is no surprise, as you have altered the mix.

From Toner to Paint

When you have selected a color, whether it is a match to an existing color or a custom blend that you dreamed up on your own, the actual

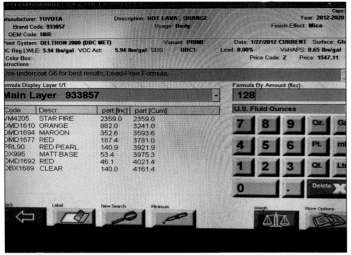

When you have determined a paint code, the formula (recipe) for mixing the paint and other information becomes available. The more complex the paint color, the more ingredients, and the higher the price.

paint is mixed from a selection of toners and additives when required. A true custom blend will result from someone adding a little bit of this to a bit more of that until they achieve the desired color.

Of course, this is difficult to duplicate unless the person mixing the paint keeps accurate notes. Auto-body shops that mix their own paint can document custom colors within their system. When you go to a paint distributor to have paint mixed, you can request them to print the formula for you. When it is a custom color, you can also request that they add your mix to their files. They will save the formula as perhaps the customer's name and a color, such as "Joe Doakes, Deep Red." The next time Joe needs paint for his fleet of trucks or next hot rod project, he can easily ask for this specific color if he goes to the same paint distributor.

However, when the formula is known, obtaining the desired color is simply a matter of adding precise amounts of each toner. The paint is typically mixed by weight, so you must know whether you want to mix a pint, a quart, or a gallon. For the desired amount of paint to be mixed, the formula will include the product

code for the toner, its description, the amount to be added, and the cumulative total of the parts.

While we know from elementary-school art class that equal parts of red and yellow make orange, automotive paint is not quite that easy. There are lots of colors of toner that you would not suspect in some paint colors. As metallic and pearl is added to the formula, it gets even more complicated.

For factory colors, the paint code also provides additional information that you may or may not care about. This includes the manufacturer, brand code, OEM code, color description, where it is used, what years it was used, and the finish effect. Other information is more technical in nature, such as the paint system, which safety data sheet (SDS) information pertains, the percentage of lead contained, the price code, and the price.

While speaking of toner, a method of requiring somewhat less paint for your project is to add an appropriate amount of toner to the sealer. You would not include all the toners that go into the paint but just the basic color. For instance, the Camaro being painted in this book

has been painted Hot Lava Orange, which for purposes of this discussion is basically a bronze color. The final paint includes various red toners, but orange is the primary color of toner. When orange toner is added to the sealer, the paint will cover more efficiently.

Additionally, the original color of the sealer also has some effect on the overall color. When the original sealer is dark gray or black, the color is naturally slightly darker. When the original sealer is white, the color is slightly brighter. Of course, all of this requires a sealer that can be tinted with toner.

VOCs

Chemical substances from paint overspray and solvent evaporation are known as volatile organic compounds (VOCs). When these rise into the atmosphere and unite with nitrous oxides, they produce ozone. For this book, VOCs are the automotive paint products that evaporate. The solids in paint (resins comprised of pigments and binders) do not evaporate, so they are not part of the problem. However, thinners and reducers used to make these solids are 100-percent solvents that evaporate.

The automotive paint manufacturers are bound by regulatory agencies to reduce VOCs within their products. Therefore, automotive paint manufacturers are very transparent of their disclosure of the amounts of VOCs in their products. Other than disposing of waste products properly, there is nothing the consumer can do to minimize VOCs in any specific paint product.

However, waterborne paint products, along with HVLP spray guns are two of the products that have

After the paint is mixed, the paint retailer adds a label to the container that identifies the color, color code, paint type, and additional information. In this case, the label provides the mixing ratio and the applicable reducers to use.

The paint retailer puts the mixed paint in a paint shaker to ensure that the various toners and any additives are thoroughly mixed. This provides the first opportunity to see how the paint will actually look.

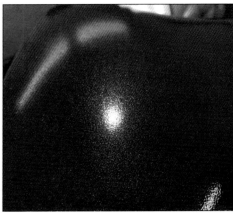

On this test panel, the mica finish in the paint stands out as intended. If you are using spray-out cards, apply the paint onto the spray-out card just as you would on the car. The number of coats required to cover the color and text on the card is what is required to properly paint the vehicle.

been developed to minimize the number of VOCs emitted into the atmosphere. Use of these products is something that can be done by the consumer. For hobbyists who already have spray guns for solvent-based automotive paint, painting a vehicle or two in your home garage each year is not a big problem. However, if you are new to automotive painting or have plans of starting your own commercial shop, using waterborne paint products from the beginning is a good thing.

When you do not have a preconceived idea of what color to paint the vehicle, check out several different new car lots. With so many dealerships selling vehicles from several different manufacturers, walking the lots of just a couple may display a full array of colors available for the current model year. When you see a color that you really like, look on the window sticker to see what color is listed. Consider pulling out your cell phone and taking a picture of the sticker to capture the name of the color and

any associated numbers and model identification. You can then take this information to your paint supplier to purchase your paint.

Other sources of paint-color ideas are car shows and cruise nights. This exposes you to automotive paint colors that you might not see in a new car lot. When you see a color that you like on a vehicle, you can usually find the owner to inquire about the origins of the color. However, you may find that it is a custom mix. In that case, it probably cannot be duplicated exactly—unless someone retained the mixing information.

In some situations, it may be desirable to paint a vehicle a color that was available when that vehicle was new, even if this specific vehicle was never that color. A modern source for vintage paint colors can be found on the internet at autocolorlibrary. com. The content is a collection of

paint-selection charts, dealer information, and assorted information that provides automobile paint-color information dating back to 1924.

It is searchable by year and manufacturer to allow you to find what was available back in the day. While the actual color of anything viewed on a computer has varying degrees of variances, your paint supplier should be able to easily mix a pint of your desired color as a sample with the information captured from this site.

QR Code

Scan this code to go to autocolorlibrary.com.

As a side note, this site also provides similar information for use in the restoration of military vehicles and household appliances.

Be wary of selecting a color that is potentially part of a current fad or trend. While it might look great right now, you may grow tired of it quickly when it is not a color you were not really sold on in the first place. With the time and expense of a paint job, you most likely do not want to change it right away.

Many colors will remain timeless over the life of a vehicle. While these colors might look timeless on one vehicle, it might not seem appropriate on others. While you may desire to stand out in a crowd, you must be willing to accept the criticism when you do.

When doing a complete restoration of a collectable vehicle where resale is always a consideration, color choice can be extremely critical. Factory original colors are usually the only acceptable colors, and regardless of the color name, it must often be the precise shade of that color with no variance. Depending on the vehicle, it may be necessary to determine which secondary colors (stripes, trim, and interior) were used from the factory. If you choose to participate in this world, find a trusted source of accurate information.

What You Like

Of course, paint is meant to be a long-lasting characteristic of an automobile, so you should paint it the color that you want. If you want a blue car, paint it blue. The slickest finish on a red car or any color that is full of custom finishes is not going to be a blue car. Paint is too expensive to paint something a color you do not like.

The Best Coverage

All things being equal, dark colors cover better than light colors, especially when sprayed over dark primer or sealer. When the financial budget is tight, it may be necessary to limit how much paint you can purchase. When the color does not matter, black or dark blue goes further toward a complete paint job than white or light yellow.

What Best Suits Your Skill Level

If there is a reason you see so many hot rod vehicles that are finished in matte or flat black, it may be that the black yields a bit of sinister look, but the non-glossy surface does not reflect any imperfections in the surface preparations. However, glossy black is purely the opposite in terms of reflection. Glossy black paint will most always look great, unless surface preparation is less than perfect

As satin black finishes have gained in popularity over the last several years, most of the paint manufacturers offer their version of hot rod black. It is designed to give the look of black primer that was on vintage hot rods while the owner saved up enough money for a paint job. However, since this is paint, it will provide a more durable finish than primer ever would.

or the vehicle is not kept clean and shiny.

For a daily driver that potentially will see rain and UV rays, black is not a desirable choice. When you want to show off your bodywork skills and have the luxury of a garage and the necessary time to keep the vehicle superbly detailed, black is the only choice.

White typically does not show dust, dirt, and the effects of the weather as much as black. However, professional painters will tell you it is difficult to touch up should the need arise. Primary colors of red, yellow, and blue, along with their secondary colors of orange, green, and purple generally cover bodywork and hold their color well. They will be relatively easy to keep clean, and they photograph well if the color does not get too dark.

Single Stage

For a first-time or budget paint job, using a single-stage paint is a wise choice. For all intents and purposes, it is available in all solid colors. Some manufacturers will have multiple lines of single-stage paints that cater to budget and other characteristics that are appealing to auto body repair shops.

Two common types of single-stage paint are polyurethane acrylic enamel and acrylic urethane. Acrylic enamel is commonly used for fleet vehicles, as it is easy to spray initially, easy to touch up, and is available in a wide variety of solid colors. With proper preparation, it provides good gloss without the need for color sanding after application. Acrylic urethane has all the same features as acrylic enamel but is typically available in a wider variety of colors, including factory metallic colors.

A downside of single-stage paint is that there are only the coats of paint that provide protection to the sheet metal below. Minor scratches can go down through the paint and to the primer or bare metal quite easily. However, with the proper preparation and cure time between coats, multiple coats of single-stage paint can be applied to protect the sheet metal. When color sanding is planned, additional coats of color should be applied.

Fewer Components

In addition to the paint itself, a single-stage paint job requires only hardener specific to the paint and reducer to make it sprayable. Fewer components make the overall project at least somewhat less expensive, as well as less likely to have any mistakes regarding mixing said components.

Can Be Color Sanded (Depending on the Product)

Some single-stage paints can be color sanded after application, while it is not recommended for others. Discuss this with the paint supplier prior to beginning the project. Most single-stage paint products provide a sufficient gloss after application, so color sanding is not required. However, color sanding can be used to perfect the finish, provided that sufficient coats of color have been applied prior to sanding. This can be of great benefit when painting in a home garage or any other location that might be hampered by less-than-optimal spray booth conditions.

Any color sanding should be done only after a full 24-hour cure time. Waiting 90 days is better, when the project allows. Sanding should be done with 1,200- to 2,000-grit sand-

paper and then buffed with a fine buffing compound on a fine polishing pad. Metallic single-stage paint should not be sanded but can be buffed.

Keep Waxed for UV Protection

Since there is no clear coat to fight off UV rays, it cannot be stressed how important a good application of a high-quality wax is for protecting the finish. However, it is equally important that the paint is allowed to fully cure prior to the wax being applied. If the wax is applied too soon, the paint will never fully cure.

Easy to Touch Up

Single-stage paint systems are easy to maintain, as more paint can be applied directly over a properly prepared older finish. The area to be touched up must first be cleaned with wax and grease remover so the new paint will adhere. The area can then be scuffed with 400- to 600-grit sandpaper, cleaned again, and new paint applied.

Base Coat/Clear Coat

If you prefer to have the UV protection of a clear coat, you are applying a multicolor paint scheme, or you are repairing an OEM finish, base coat/clear coat is a perfect choice. It is typically available in all domestic and import factory colors as well as custom-mixed colors. Using a clear coat also opens up the possibilities of an overwhelming array of custom finishes, including pearls, metallics, and others too numerous to mention.

Applying base coat usually requires only two or three coats to achieve coverage. Of course, this depends largely on the color of the

Each component added to the paint job increases the cost due to the materials. Shown is the paint required for a two-tone paint job on an S-15 that I did several years ago. In this case, it was a gallon of silver, a quart of black, and enough hardener/catalyst for both. What is not shown is the reducer than makes it sprayable.

base coat as well as the sealer to which it is being applied. With the relatively quick drying time of the base coat, any drips or runs can be allowed to dry, sanded out, and reapplied, prior to application of the clear coat.

Added Component/Cost

Even with a standard base coat/clear coat repaint, there are more components involved than with a single-stage paint job. This includes the color base coat along with its reducer for the color portion of the paint job. The clear coat requires the clear component as well as reducer and hardener. In most cases, the same reducer can be used for the base and the clear, so you are still looking at four separate components at a minimum. When you add custom finishes, such as pearl, the costs are going to rise. Still, nothing defines a vehicle like a quality paint job regardless of the budget.

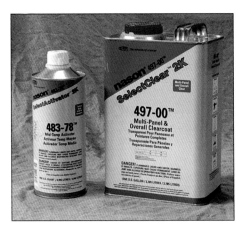

While adding clear, whether it is part of a base-coat/clear-coat system or used as a top coat over color, it adds to the cost and labor time. There is the clear itself, along with activator and reducer.

Additional Time Frame Concerns

When applying a single-stage paint, the time between coats and drying time are the only real time constraints. That changes when base coat and clear coat is involved. The flash time between color coats is still going to be relatively short at between 5 and 10 minutes, but the clear must be applied within a certain time frame, usually within 24 hours. On a single-color paint scheme, that should be no problem.

However, with each additional color and/or effect within the paint scheme, there is some drying time, masking to be removed and/or added, and drying time before applying the clear. When this is not all completed within 24 hours, the color must be sanded and reapplied. You must take this all into consideration and plan your time accordingly.

Wet Sanding Not Required but Is a Possibility

While it is not absolutely required, wet sanding the clear after waiting the proper curing time allows for perfection of the surface. Whenever sanding is planned, additional coats of clear should be applied to prevent sanding through the clear. Sanding should be done with 2,000- to 4,000-grit sandpaper and buffed with a fine buffing compound on a fine polishing pad.

Difficult to Touch Up

A negative of base coat/clear coat is that when a repair is required, the clear must be removed from the area to be repaired. The repair can then be made, paint applied, and clear applied. In some instances, blending the clear may require refinishing an entire panel.

Provides UV Protection

The clear coat does provide considerable UV protection, so with proper washing and waxing, the colors should not fade over time. Certain clears are designed to protect colors more than others and contain higher amounts of UV blockers. Generally, the higher the cost of the clear coat, the higher the protection against UV damage and fading. Of course, keeping the vehicle parked indoors when possible and out of the weather and elements goes a long way toward protecting the finish as well.

Useful for Multicolor Paint Schemes

Clear also enhances a multicolor paint job by covering the various edges of each color with a seamless layer or protection. While the thickness of paint is miniscule, not having coats of clear covering these edges will make the paint job look not as slick.

Any paint job that is going to include multiple colors should include several coats of clear in the overall scheme. Even when that paint scheme is going to be one solid color over another solid color, clear protects the first color from any miscues that might happen when applying the second color. With the clear in place, the second color can be sanded off if necessary without harming the paint below.

Many multistage components (pearl, candy, or metallic flakes) are combined with clear for application. This allows these special finishes to be applied as a layer almost anywhere in the painting sequence.

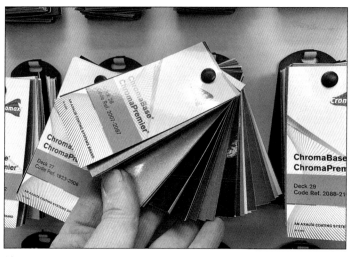

Your local paint dealer has all sorts of color chips to browse through when selecting a color. These are larger, which provides a better sample. When possible, look at the sample color chips in the sunlight to get the best view of the color.

Multistage

Today's factory automobiles and their amazing colors are a result of multistage paint systems. This technology dates to the 1950s when candy colors were common on the custom automobiles of the day. Back in the day, a vehicle received a base coat of silver or gold, and then a translucent color (a mixture of toner for color and clear) was applied. Each additional coat of the translucent color influenced the overall color. When the desired overall color was achieved, multiple coats of clear was applied to protect the surface below. The clear was then sanded and buffed to provide a lustrous, shiny surface.

On contemporary vehicles, the base coats are more varied than simply gold or silver. They may include any of several shades of gray and other colors and may include metallic or pearl in the base. With the wider variety of base applications and the multitude of translucent colors, the overall color effects possible are virtually endless. The OEMs are using more candy colors with several tri-coats available straight off the showroom floor. Ford's code RR, a candy apple red, is one example of many.

Just as with base coat/clear coat, the additional materials add to the cost of the overall paint job. Likewise, more materials add to the complexity of the painting process. It can be done by a nonprofessional but should not be attempted as your first automotive paint job.

Metallic

Metallic automotive paint is certainly nothing new, but now, it is more common than ever. With the refinement of the size of the metallic flakes and advances in robotic paint application in factories, a metallic finish can offer shine and gloss to most paint schemes. When repainting a vehicle, you can use a factory metallic paint code when ordering your paint or create your own custom metallic paint.

Metallic flakes are available in bulk in diverse sizes and can be added to most any paint. When doing this, the flakes are spooned out of the package and added to the paint blend based on weight. Opt for too little rather than too much, as more can always be added. The paint is then mixed, and a test panel is sprayed. When the flakes are spaced too far apart in the test panel, more metallic can be added to the mix, and another test panel can be sprayed. The process is repeated until the results are as desired.

When working with metallics, there are some things of which to be aware. Depending on the size of the metallic flakes, a spray tip with a larger orifice may be required to prevent the spray gun from becoming clogged. Shake the paint containers vigorously prior to filling your spray gun to ensure the metallic is equally suspended within the paint. Most professional painters shake their paint gun after each pass to ensure that all particles remain thoroughly

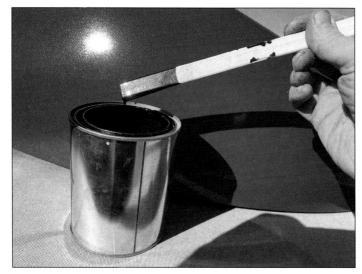

When using metallic paint, it is important to stir the paint thoroughly before pouring it into your spray gun. Gently shake your spray gun on a regular basis while spraying to keep the metallic suspended within the paint.

Pearl additives are available in multiple color combinations. Each of these color combinations yield a different effect when used with the same color of paint. The amount of pearl additive also influences the outcome. When spraying pearl, be sure to mix enough for the entire project or ensure you are consistent when mixing each batch.

suspended and dispersed. This ensures uniform metallic coverage over all parts of the vehicle that is being painted.

Pearl

Another common additive to contemporary OEM paint jobs is pearl paint. When viewed from different angles, light reflection off pearl finishes causes painted surfaces to reflect unusual colors. As with metallics, pearl can be part of a factory color or added to a custom paint mix. The pearl effect is created by tiny chips of synthetic inorganic crystalline substances that are painted on one side and are clear on the other.

This additive is available in assorted colors and is premixed into a paste that can be added to the paint when mixed. The color presented is determined by the color of the pearl additive. Check paint chips at the paint and supply store to select the combination of color paint base and pearl additive to use for whatever color you desire.

Working with Clear

Whether applying clear atop a single-stage paint as part of a base coat/clear coat system, or as part of a multistage system, it does add a bit of complexity along with its durability. Film build is important because too little will cause a poor appearance, and too much will cause adhesion failure or cause previous applications of paint to not cure properly.

Unlike color, clear is difficult to see, so you must spray each panel in a logical manner to ensure proper coverage. When applying a high-solids clear coat, two coats may be adequate, but a value-priced product may require three coats to achieve the same coverage. When the clear is going to be buffed, more must be applied to maintain the necessary thickness required to provide UV protection. On multi-color or custom paint schemes, clear coats should be applied so that polishing and waxing do not directly touch or adversely affect exotic color blends, metallic flakes, pearl additives, or custom graphics.

Choose the Best Clear for the Task

A multitude of clear products are available for the various needs of the auto-collision repair industry, where getting repairs made and the vehicle back to the customer in a timely manner is key. For this reason, many clears are rated based on the speed of their application. A faster clear will ultimately be better for a collision repair facility, but for a full repaint, a slower clear that requires up to 24 hours to dry is perfectly acceptable.

As with every choice, weigh the pros and cons to make a good decision. When it comes to paint products, common considerations are how much time is available to complete the task and if a spray booth with a heater option is available.

When you do not have the luxury of a spray booth, you may be forced to use a clear with a faster flash and drying time. When this is the decision that you must make due to the drying times, you may need to spray the clear on one or two panels at a time to be able to buff them in the required timeframe.

For a superior gloss or a larger paint job, a slower clear will yield a better finish. However, that requires more time between coats and a significantly longer drying time. If you have access to a spray booth with an oven, you can speed up that process. The best results ultimately require finding the best characteristics for your circumstances.

Something else worth mentioning is that the longer the clear is allowed to cure, the harder it gets. When your cutting and buffing is done within the recommended guidelines, this is not a real problem. However, as you exceed that time frame, cutting and buffing requires more effort.

While intermixing automotive paint products from different manufacturers is never really recommended, there is nothing wrong with asking professionals what they are using. When those you trust are having good results with various products, ask what they used and how they used it. When the results are good, it is sometimes okay to break the rules.

Clear Characteristics

Air Dry	Speed	General Purpose	Show/Glamour
Quick flash time	3-to-5-minute flash time	5-to-10-minute flash time	10-to-15-minute flash time
30-minute air dry time	90-minute air dry time	4-hour aid dry time	Overnight dry time
Quick to buff time	Short/low baked option	Bake most common	Best suited for bake
Spot repairs, one panel	One to three panels	Multipanel jobs	Large jobs/complete paint jobs
Same day turnaround	Fastest overall/most popular	All-purpose	Superior gloss/high temperature and humidity climate

When painting a show car and/or doing a complete repaint, a slower glamour clear provides the best finish. This will require longer times between coats and an even longer dry time. However, it will ultimately provide a superior shine and finish.

Common Defects and Their Causes

Defect	Cause
Solvent Pop	These are tiny pinholes where solvent gets trapped in the clear coat. These can be caused by incorrect flash time, too much film build, or incorrect spray pressure. An additional cause is using a solvent (reducer) that is too fast for the spraying conditions.
Dieback	This lack of gloss is usually attributed to a lack of proper flash time, improper film build, or using a reducer that is too fast for the conditions.
Sags	Also known as runs, these usually occur on vertical surfaces where too much is applied. However, other culprits may be an incorrect mix ratio, causing the solvent to not evaporate fast enough or not get enough flash time between coats.
Orange Peel	This is when the clear or painted surface has a textured finish that resembles an orange. This can be caused by spraying at too great of a distance between the spray gun to the surface, incorrect air pressure that doesn't atomize the fluid correctly, and using a reducer that is too fast and causes the clear coat to not flow properly.

Waterborne

Waterborne automotive paint has improved significantly since its first use in the United States. While you may have not known the reasoning, you have most likely seen automobiles originally manufactured during the 1990s that had paint peeling off in sheets. These examples certainly gave waterborne paint a bad name. Those issues have been figured out and are no longer a problem, which makes waterborne paint common in today's automotive manufacturing plants.

While it is critical to use compatible products with all automotive paint systems, most solvent-based products are designed to work with other solvent-based products. Prior to using waterborne paint, verify that all components are compatible with the waterborne paint system.

Environmentally Friendly

Whether it's used in an automotive collision repair center or a hobbyist garage, waterborne paint is environmentally friendly because there is less odor and air quality is improved. While this is a great benefit to high-volume collision centers, it may make the difference between troublesome neighbors and admirers of your automotive hobby. Keep in mind when deciding between water or solvent paints, the water-based paint is much slower to dry and requires quite a bit more airflow to properly dry.

Accurate Mixing

Traditional solvents are heavy and require virtually constant stirring. If a paint formula is mixed in the morning, some of the components may not be stirred as thoroughly as others, resulting in a slight variance of the color.

A significant advantage of waterborne paint is the ability to mix the paint accurately and consistently, which provides excellent color matching and blending. Instead of the large rack of solvent-based toners that are stirred mechanically, waterborne automotive paint products can be shaken by hand and mixed. There is no settling in the acrylic waterborne latex resin.

Easier Blending

Since no solvent is required, waterborne paint products can be used in a wider range of ambient temperatures. Temperature-specific reducer is not required as it is with solvent-based products. This allows for more consistent color mixing. Additionally, when waterborne paint is stored in a sealed plastic container, its pot life is typically around 90 days. This is convenient for the touch up of minor flaws.

Before You Spray Paint

Regardless of the type of paint or the color to be sprayed, always verify that the surface preparation has been done to a quality that will suit you. Anything that is less than adequate will be easier and cheaper to redo now than it will be after color has been applied. Whether the paint job is a minor collision repair to one or two panels, a simple repaint of a few parts, or a complete frame-off restoration, the attention to detail (or lack thereof) makes or breaks a paint job, so it is worth verifying everything.

Prep Work

Verify that the surface to be painted is as smooth as possible. For the best results, this means the entire

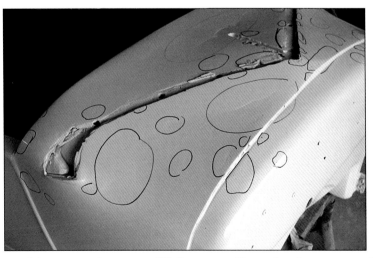

This was a sad day for me. I had done bodywork to a fiberglass roadster body, including plenty of block sanding, and was convinced it was ready for paint. Wrong! After applying a couple coats of Volkswagen Moonglow base coat, all sorts of errors appeared. There was nothing to do but sand it down and redo it.

surface has been sanded with 600- to 800-grit sandpaper. For a vehicle that is purely for transportation, the entire surface should be sanded with 400-grit sandpaper. Any areas of bodywork should be feathered out entirely with no perceptible edges of layers of substrates. Verify that there are no imperfections, especially pinholes, which must be corrected prior to paint application.

Clean the surface with wax and grease remover to remove dust, dirt, oil, or any other contaminants. Wear gloves when spraying to ensure that no fingerprints are inadvertently added to the surface when spraying. Wear an anti-static paint suit when painting to minimize lint or other contaminants landing on the painted surface.

Choose the Color

Verify that the color of the paint is the color that you want it to be, especially when this is a repair to only a portion of the vehicle. Use spray-out cards to ensure that the paint matches and to determine the number of coats to achieve coverage.

Sealer

Verify that all parts to be painted have been prepped with the same color of sealer to help ensure correct and consistent color match. This is especially important when using multistage top coats, translucent colors, and waterborne paint.

Mix the Top Coat

Use an appropriately sized container to mix enough top coat (paint, reducer, and hardener) at one time to maintain color consistency throughout the paint application process. Even if the largest mixing cup available is a quart, pour each quart of mixed top coat into a larger container and stir together. Always stir the top coat thoroughly and use a strainer to filter the paint when pouring it into the spray gun.

When mixing waterborne paint, mix and store in a plastic container. Invert the container twice prior to pouring the mix into the spray gun. Do not shake waterborne paints.

Set the Spray Gun

When using solvent-based top coats, spray a test pattern onto a piece of masking paper taped to the wall. For a full spray, turn the fluid-control knob almost all the way out, squeeze the trigger, and turn the fluid-control knob inward until you feel pressure on the knob. Turn the fan-control knob all the way open to create an elliptical pattern.

When using waterborne paint, periodically check the viscosity of the paint with a viscosity cup and a timer. The product information sheet provides information regarding the correct-viscosity cup to use and the correct amount of time for the cup to empty. If the paint is too thick, it will require more time than indicated to pass through the viscosity cup, and therefore will require thinner.

Verify that the air compressor has been drained of any accumulated moisture and that the drain has now been closed. Verify that the air hose, gauges, and regulators are working properly. Adjust the spray gun to deliver a full, wet, even pattern at 6 to 8 inches from the surface.

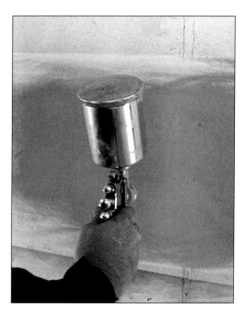

Prior to spraying any paint, spray a test pattern on a piece of masking paper taped on the wall. This gives you a chance to ensure your spray gun is spraying the correct pattern. It is better to adjust on a piece of masking paper than on your car.

With all the various colors and shades of body filler and primer substrates, applying one color of sealer is necessary to provide an even color.

Compressing air causes condensation (moisture) to build up in your air compressor. Get in the habit of draining your air compressor after every use. Moisture in the air compressor will not improve your paint job.

Apply Color

Spray color at the appropriate speed to avoid runs and overlap each pass approximately 75 percent to ensure flow and coverage. Remember that too great of a spray distance and/or too fast of spray gun movement creates a dry spray with a rough texture. Conversely, holding the spray gun too close to the surface and/or moving too slow causes runs.

Refer to the product information sheet for suggestions regarding paint film thickness. As a rule of thumb, light to medium coats work best. Heavy coats will lead to runs and potentially other problems, such as solvents being trapped within the paint as it dries.

For waterborne paint, allow each coat to thoroughly dehydrate (dry) between coats. Waterborne paint dries as air moves across the painted surface. This results from fans built into the spray booth or handheld blowers (specialized nozzles connected to the air hose) aimed at the surface.

Simple Repaint

While a simple repaint might not be simple to some, it is still less complicated than doing a complete color change paint job. The substantial difference in the two is that in a simple repaint, you are using the same color, while the latter is a different color when the job is done. There are reasons for doing each of these, so both are acceptable for various situations. For a simple repaint, the bulk of the labor is prepping the surface and masking prior to painting the vehicle the same color as before.

To clarify, the paint being used might not be the exact same paint code as what is currently on the vehicle. However, the color is sufficiently close enough to the same shade of blue, for instance, that the interior and under-hood area do not require new paint to be acceptable.

Exterior Only

You may be wondering why someone would paint a vehicle without changing the color. A quick answer is that the vehicle has suffered collision damage with multiple panels requiring paint. Depending on the age of the vehicle, it may be easier to prep the undamaged panels to prepare for repaint than to attempt to match the color from one panel to another.

Another reason might be that the owner does not like the existing color of the vehicle. This might be the case when a teenager has received his or her driver's license and is making a plea for a new car. A new coat of paint might be an incentive for them

Before you spray paint, check the product data sheets to determine how long to wait between coats and prior to taping for additional colors. When using clear, verify how soon it must be sprayed. There is a specific window, so the color must be dry, yet still applied within a specified time. When all your spraying is done, give it plenty of time to dry.

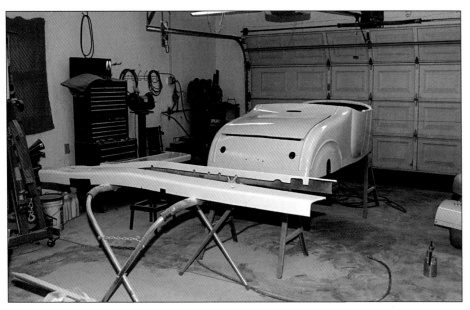

to be more accepting of an older vehicle for their first set of wheels and prompt them to take better care of it.

On a basic paint job, only the exterior is painted. With some vehicles, the complete interior is covered with upholstery and/or plastic panels, so it is not necessary to paint the interior even if you do change colors.

In addition to any necessary bodywork, the complete exterior requires proper preparation. This includes washing the vehicle and cleaning the surface of any contaminants with wax and grease remover. Scuff the surface with 400- to 600-grit sandpaper. Clean the exterior surface again with wax and grease remover.

Mask off or remove any external components such as door handles, headlights, taillights, and trim, along with wheels and tires. There is no need to remove any glass. Simply mask it using masking paper and masking tape. To paint the edges of the hood and trunk lid, open them and cover the engine compartment and trunk area with masking paper secured with masking tape. Almost close the hood and trunk lid to leave the edges of the opening panels exposed.

Apply two coats of sealer to provide a uniform surface and ensure proper adhesion to the existing finish. Allow the proper cure time for the sealer and then apply your choice of single stage or base coat/clear coat. Allow the proper cure time and then remove the masking material. Reinstall any components that were removed.

Color Change/Total Repaint

While spraying a different color is no different, there is significantly more work required both before and after spraying that makes the difference. This additional labor requires more time, but it ultimately leads to a more-professional-appearing paint job. Reassembly is discussed more in Chapter 7.

Exterior

All body trim must be removed, as it may cover up rust that requires repair. Door handles, bumpers (as opposed to front and rear fascia panels), the grille, mirrors, headlights, taillights, and radio antennae must all be removed to enable a smooth flow of paint on the area where they mount.

Even when you are not planning to replace the glass, it should be removed prior to repainting the vehicle, especially when doing a color change or complete paint job.

All glass should be removed because weatherstripping and trim around the windshield and back glass often traps moisture and dirt that causes rust around the window opening. Even though removal of these items requires extra labor, it is less work than attempting to mask these parts to prevent overspray from reaching them. Additionally, these parts often get in the way of painting what really needs to be painted, all the while leaving obvious signs of an amateurish repaint.

To remove all these extraneous pieces requires the use of multiple hand tools to remove nuts, bolts, and various types of clips. When possible,

This area above the windshield is commonly full of rust. When left untreated, any rust will eventually lead to missing metal that will cause the windshield area to leak.

This lower corner of the windshield post is still in decent condition. However, as this area supports the windshield and the back glass, it should be thoroughly inspected and repaired when necessary. It is much easier and less expensive to repair this area prior to applying paint.

For a complete or full color change paint job, getting the vehicle down to its bare bones (or as close as possible) provides an opportunity for the best assessment of the vehicle's true condition. Addressing any collision or rust damage prior to refinishing with new paint is always the ultimate method for beginning a paint job.

temporarily reinstall the nuts onto the bolts from which they were removed to prevent losing them. Some trim pieces or emblems may be secured in place with adhesives and require the use of an adhesive remover to safely remove them without damage. This adhesive remover can typically be purchased at your local auto-parts store.

Develop a plan for efficient storage of these removed parts so that they can be found and reinstalled later. Losing parts or allowing them to be damaged while in storage adds to the cost of the paint job in terms of repair or the replacement of parts. Resealable plastic bags with labels of the contents work great for storing small parts.

Interior

Depending on the age and make of the vehicle, several areas in the interior may require paint. This also means there are several items that must be removed do the necessary paint work. The seats and carpeting or floor mats must be removed. There is hopefully some insulation material below the carpeting, and this must be removed as well. Removing carpeting and insulation may reveal rust issues that requires repair prior to painting.

Various components must be removed, such as seat belts, dash instrumentation, sun visors, interior door and kick panels, the headliner, and dash covers. If desired, the steering wheel can be removed, but the steering column may need to be left in place and masked. This depends on your mechanical expertise, the make and model of the vehicle, and if it is a frame-off rebuild or merely a paint job. On older vehicles, removing the steering wheel provides better access to that portion of the dash and is simple. However, with air bags on newer vehicles, it may be necessary to consult a service manual to avoid inadvertently deploying the air bag, which is expensive to replace.

Any wiring running through the passenger area should be covered to avoid obscuring any color coding with fresh paint. An effective way to do this is to wrap the wire bundle (wires running from under the dash toward the rear of the vehicle, for example) with masking paper and secure with masking tape.

Firewall and Engine Compartment

There are multiple ways to paint the vehicle's firewall and inner fenders, and they all depend largely on whether the project at hand is purely a repaint or part of a frame-off rebuild.

Whether the vehicle is a vintage classic sitting on a full frame or a newer unibody vehicle that has bolt-on cradles for the front and rear suspension, those components should still receive some attention. The amount of effort put into this depends greatly on the vehicle's intended use.

With the suspension and drivetrain components removed and the vehicle securely supported on a lift or jack stands, the underside of the body can be prepped with a wire brush. An orbital sander/grinder affixed with a wire-cup brush works well for this.

The make and model of the vehicle also plays a part in determining the best method. Painting the firewall of a 1946 Crosley with the engine in it is not much of a problem, especially when you have a detail spray gun. On the other hand, painting the firewall of a new Corvette is a major challenge.

When the project is part of a major rebuild, the firewall and bottom side (exterior) of the body should be painted with the body off the frame when possible. This is quite common on frame-off rebuilds of vintage vehicles, whether they are original or reproductions. If possible, pressure wash the undercarriage of the body to remove as much dirt, grease, mud, road tar, and undercoating as possible. When you do

Any high spots or ridges in the sheet metal quickly reveal themselves when prepping with a wire brush. Ultimately, the entire surface should clean up like this high spot. If there are any areas where sheet metal overlaps, check for rust formation or spaces between the layers of sheet metal.

When the underneath surface of the body is cleaned, it can be prepped for the protective covering of your choice. Rust preventative coatings are available in spray or brush applications and provide a simple and effective finish.

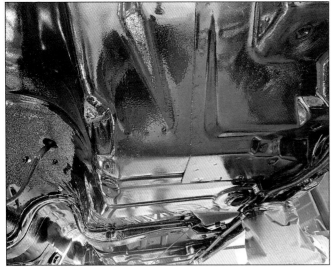

Since there is seldom a definitive break line between the underneath side of the body and the firewall, the same coating should be used for the underhood area. The smooth, glossy finish of this rust inhibitor makes a great backdrop for a nicely detailed engine.

The steering column, various wires, and heater hoses provide plenty of obstacles to paint around. When these cannot be removed or pulled back into the interior of the vehicle, pull as many of the wires as feasible together and cover them with a paper or plastic bag. Seal the opening with masking tape and mask the rest of the wires individually.

not have access to a pressure washer, consider renting one or trailering the body to the local car wash to spray the engine compartment and as much of the underside as possible with the engine degreaser setting. Be sure to rinse thoroughly to remove any residual contaminants.

Any areas where the sheet metal overlaps another piece of sheet metal deserve careful inspection as they are prone to rust. During the life of a vehicle, these panels can begin to separate and allow dirt, debris, and moisture to congregate within. Look for the obvious formation of rust or any areas where there is space between the two layers of sheet metal. Surface rust can be sanded off, while significant rust should be removed and patch panels installed. When the metal is sound but simply spreading apart, hammer the two panels back together when possible. While it may not have been used originally, consider applying a bead of caulk or a layer of brush-on seam sealer. Allow it to dry properly prior to applying the final finish of your choice.

When desired, the undercarriage of the body can be primed and painted, utilizing the exact same methods as those on the top of the vehicle. As you can imagine, this requires a significant amount of work. Depending on the intended use of the vehicle, it may be justified.

Other available finishes are various types of rust-preventative coatings. Some of these yield a smooth finish, while others yield a textured surface. Most of them can be applied with a brush, while others can be sprayed. Due to the thicker nature of these products, they usually require a spray-gun tip with a larger orifice or sometimes even a special applicator designed for the specific product.

Regardless of the product, wear protective gear to protect your eyes and skin. Since the surface being coated is typically above you during application, this is especially important.

When the vehicle is not going to be removed from the frame/chassis, paint the firewall whenever the engine is out of the vehicle. Depending on the schedule for the project, this may mean painting just the firewall at a completely different time than the rest of the vehicle. Still, this is more convenient than painting around the engine in most cases.

When there are no other alternatives, the firewall and inner fenders can be painted while the engine is in

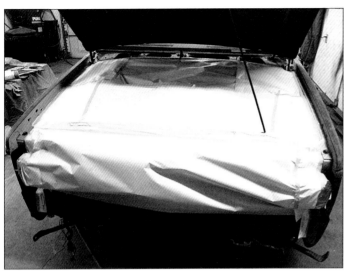

While repainting this S-15 pickup, it was not practical to pull the engine and transmission to do a complete frame-off rebuild. However, to paint the inside edges of the front fenders, the engine needs to be exposed. Getting overspray on the engine was avoided by covering the entire engine compartment with masking paper from fender to fender and firewall to radiator core support.

Painting a Car

When doing a complete repaint, there are two basic schools of thought regarding painting. Both require complete disassembly to allow for adequate access to the entire panel. One thought is to paint each piece individually and reassemble the pieces after painting them. Another is to paint the inside of each panel (hood, trunk lid, doors, and interior), assemble those pieces back onto the body, and paint the entire exterior at one time.

Painting the Removable Inside Panels

Some people cringe at the thought of completely reassembling a bunch of freshly painted pieces and parts. It does require being extremely careful, wrapping parts (specifically edges) with masking tape and foam padding, and knowing exactly how the pieces fit together. This comes from having previously assembled the pieces. Regardless of how careful you may be, some minor touch-up may be required.

Painting all the exterior at one time helps ensure color match, and when the painting is done, you are much closer to being finished with the project. Still, there are valid reasons for either method. A second set of hands help greatly with reassembly, whether the parts are painted or not.

place. Use masking paper or masking film to mask off the engine. Then, use a detail spray gun (doorjamb gun) to spray the firewall and inner fenders. If possible, remove any clips or fasteners that secure wiring to the area being painted and hold this wiring away from the surface while painting.

Regardless of whether the engine is in place or not, take the time to mask any wiring or other accessories in the immediate area that cannot be removed. Overspray on these items looks very unprofessional.

Trunk

The trunk area of the vehicle will be significantly easier to paint, as everything that might be in the way should be removable, since it is a storage area. Remove the spare tire, jack, and anything else that is not part of the vehicle. Depending on the vehicle's vintage, there may be upholstered panels or a plastic/ rubber trunk floor covering to remove.

As always, mask any wiring to avoid overspray. For extra detail points, use splatter trunk paint on vehicles where this was the factory finish. This was common on domestic vehicles from the 1950s through 1970s and is available in spray cans.

The trunk area can be painted to match the exterior, or it can be coated to match the underneath side of the car. Regardless of the coating, it must be thoroughly cleaned for the coating to properly adhere. Use a putty knife to remove anything (previous carpeting or rubber mat) that may be sticking to the trunk floor. Then, prep it with a wire brush.

Prepping and Painting the Inside Removable Panels

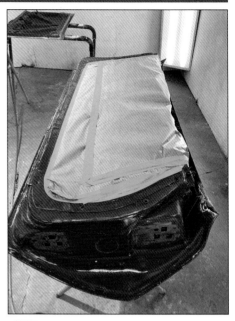

1 With the windshield out, prep-ping the cowl and dash area is much easier. A wire wheel on a die grinder cleans up the area quite nicely. For the most part, this area will be covered, but it should look nice and be the same color as the rest of the car.

2 Remove the interior door panels, door glass, and door-glass riser mechanisms. As it will most likely be replaced, remove the existing weatherstripping. Prep the painted surface with a wire wheel and sandpaper as required.

3 Much of the inside of the door will be covered by the interior panel, so it is usually not painted. However, when the inside of the door is made of metal, it deserves some form of protection from the elements. If the glass is still in the doors, mask the opening with masking paper and tape.

4 Prior to priming and painting the doorjamb and cowl, mask the inside of the door opening. Begin by placing a strip of masking tape around the perimeter. Masking paper can then be secured to this with masking tape to avoid paint overspray from reaching the interior.

5 When masking to paint the doorjamb, the masking tape on the exterior of the car is applied so that approximately half of the width of the tape adheres to the quarter panel and the other half is folded back. This is done to prevent a hard edge on the quarter panel. When the quarter panel is painted, masking will be done in reverse.

Prepping and Painting the Inside Removable Panels *continued*

6 With the exception of the residue left over from an OEM sticker on the inside, the trunk lid is in decent condition.

7 The perimeter of the trunk lid shows some surface rust that was probably caused by moisture being trapped by the weatherstripping used to prevent moisture from getting into the storage area.

8 A wire wheel or Roloc disc on a die grinder makes for easy work of removing the surface rust from the trunk lid.

9 With the surface rust removed, the inside of the trunk lid requires sanding with some 400-grit sandpaper to prep the surface for paint application.

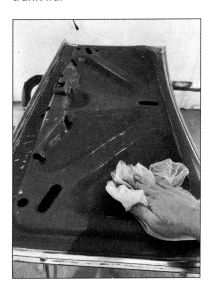

10 After scuffing the surface with 400-grit sandpaper to enhance adhesion, clean the surface with wax and grease remover. After wiping the surface clean, use a clean, dry cloth to wipe away any residual contaminants.

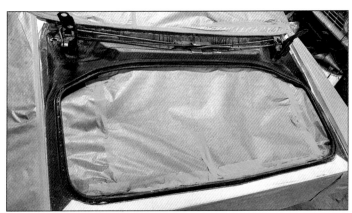

11 Using the same masking techniques as used to mask the door opening areas, mask the external trunk area. This area will be blocked by the trunk lid when the entire exterior is painted.

12 With all areas to be primed, cleaned, and ready for primer, the direct-to-metal primer is mixed in accordance with the mixing instructions. Mix enough sprayable material to apply two coats to the insides of the doors, cowl and door-jambs, and the trunk-lid opening.

13 This specific direct-to-metal high-build primer is designed to be mixed with primer-hardener in a ratio of 4:1.

14 Warm to hot shop conditions call for a slow reducer to prevent the primer from drying too quickly. The reducer is the third component in a mix ratio of 4:1:1/2.

15 Position the doors and trunk lid on stands in the spray area so there is adequate space to move around between them when priming and painting. Having a space large enough to prime or paint several components at one time saves time.

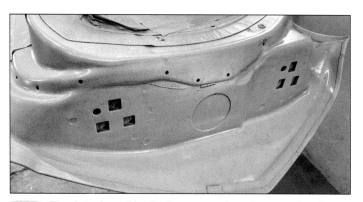

16 The interior of both doors receives two coats of direct-to-metal primer. Ensure that you have adequate coverage all over, especially where the hinges bolt on. It is conceivable that the hinges could trap some moisture, so ample protection from the formation of rust is a good practice.

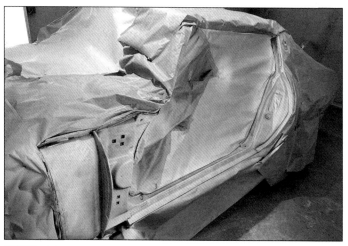

17 After extensive masking of the firewall, upper cowl, roof, quarter panels, and underneath of the car, the side cowl and doorjamb areas can now be primed. Two coats of direct-to-metal primer should be sufficient.

Prepping and Painting the Inside Removable Panels *continued*

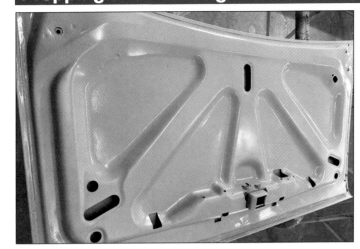

18 *The inside of the trunk lid has now received two coats of direct-to-metal primer and is looking great.*

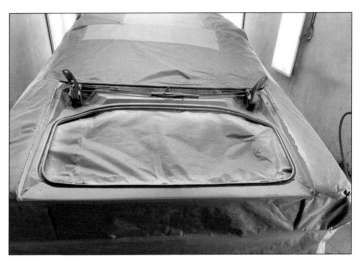

19 *The next area to receive primer is the trunk jamb area of the car that is hidden by the trunk lid when closed but is in plain view when the trunk is open.*

20 *Just as with the doorjambs, the masking tape is adhered to the car's body but then folded over slightly so that the paint does not form a hard line. When the body is painted, there will not be a distinguishable line in the paint when it is masked this way.*

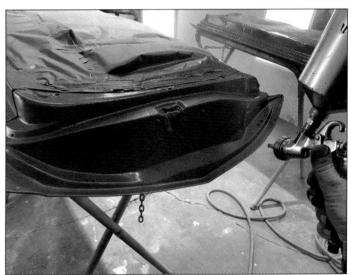

21 *We're making progress. Clean the primer gun, mix some base coat with reducer (1:1 in this case), and then break out the base-coat spray gun. Be sure to use a strainer when pouring paint into the spray gun.*

22 *When spraying base coat, the intent is to spray enough coats to achieve coverage. When the base coat flashes, it will be dull. The shine will be provided by the clear.*

23 When painting large areas, spray the perimeter of the entire panel and then spray the middle. An error common to new painters is easing off the trigger too soon at the edges. Spraying around the perimeter first helps avoid that.

24 Continue painting with an approximate 75-percent overlap on a wet edge to achieve good coverage. Notice that the ring on the air cap of the spray gun is a copper color, indicating that this spray gun has a relatively larger spray tip for spraying color. The one on the clear spray gun is a different color, indicating that it has a relatively smaller tip. The colors of the tips have no significant value aside from differentiating the two spray guns.

25 Adequate lighting is important to ensure full coverage when applying paint. When lighting is inadequate, it is easy to apply more paint than necessary and develop runs or have bare or thin spots. Either one can be fixed, but it requires additional labor.

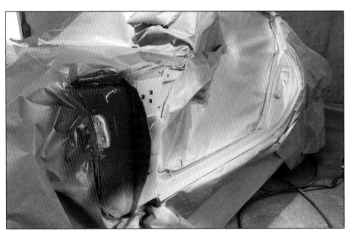

26 A great benefit of having light-colored sealer with dark paint or dark sealer with light-colored paint is that it is easier to see your progress. However, you must ensure the light-colored paint is opaque enough to cover the dark sealer.

27 After awaiting the correct flash time between coats, a second coat of color can be added to the doors and other parts.

Prepping and Painting the Inside Removable Panels *continued*

28 The trunk jamb area has received two coats of base-coat color, and the painting of the inner panels is now complete.

29 With a base-coat/clear-coat paint system, the clear will provide the gloss. However, make sure you have adequate color coverage. Since clear is difficult to see, ensure that it is applied in a systematic method to avoid lack of coverage.

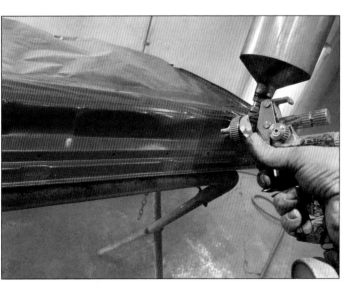

30 Notice the ring around the air cap is different on this spray gun, so it must be the clear spray gun. Whenever you switch spray guns or even refill one, spray a test panel to ensure everything is as it should be.

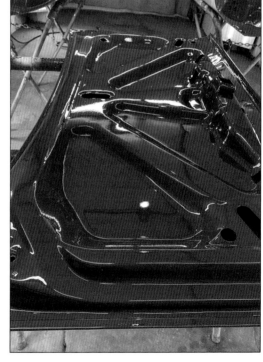

31 With color and clear on the inside of the trunk lid, it is looking great. The lack of thin spots and runs come from experience.

32 One coat of clear is starting to provide some gloss to the finish. Always allow the proper amount of time between coats, whether it is primer, color, or clear.

33 After applying two coats of base coat and a minimum of two coats of clear coat, the doorjamb area is looking very good. When you don't intend to cut and buff the clear, two coats are probably sufficient. However, more coats will be required when additional finishing work is planned.

34 The mica-finish base coat/clear coat sparkles in the sun. Allow for proper drying time before handling.

Cowl, Inside of the Hood, and Fenders

Even though the cowl and inside of the hood are visible only when the hood is open, and the inside of the fenders are visible only when the car is on a lift rack, these panels still need to be protected from corrosion. These sheet-metal panels can be painted the primary body color, a neutral color, or coated with some type of undercoating. Regardless of what material is applied, it should be applied with as much care and preparation as the shiny material that everyone sees.

For this project, the cowl, inside of the hood, and insides of the front fenders will be primed with a direct-to-metal primer and painted with SEM's Hot Rod Black. This is a single-stage, semi-flat black that works very well for areas that are not going to be detailed on a regular basis.

Painting the Cowl, Inside of the Hood, the Front Valance, and Fenders

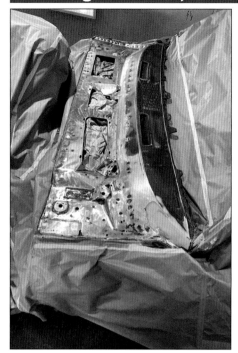

1 The area to be primed and painted should first be cleaned with wax and grease remover. It can then be prepped with a wire wheel or wire cup brush. It then needs to be cleaned again with wax and grease remover.

2 Two or three coats of epoxy primer or direct-to-metal high-build primer should be applied per the manufacturer's directions. If imperfections were covered or any bodywork has been done, the DTM high-build primer might be a better option.

3 After masking the areas to not be painted, apply the primer of your choice per the manufacturer's directions. Be sure to allow the proper flash time (as with any other paint product).

4 Hot Rod Black is offered by SEM and is packaged as a kit, including the paint, reducer, and catalyst.

5 Whenever priming or painting areas that have large openings, such as on this cowl panel, spend the extra time to mask these openings with masking paper. This is one detail that separates the professionals from everyone else.

6 After the appropriate flash time, apply a second coat of Hot Rod Black. It goes on shiny but flattens out as it dries.

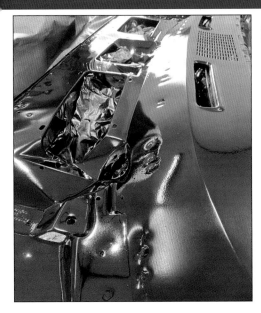

7 This type of finish provides an OEM appearance and is excellent for underhood areas.

8 The underside of the hood deserves the same care as the rest of the vehicle. You do not want someone admiring the well-detailed engine, only to be disappointed in the appearance of the inside of the hood. Attend to any damage that requires attention.

9 Prior to applying primer or paint, the surface must be cleaned and prepped. A wire wheel or wire-cup brush works well to scuff up the irregular contours of the inside of the hood.

10 The swirl marks indicate the effectiveness of being cleaned with a wire-cup brush that is attached to a grinder or drill motor. Sanding this area by hand is quite tedious.

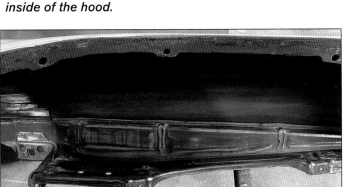

11 The inside of the front fenders requires either primer and paint or undercoating. Regardless of the finish, the surface must be clean and free of contaminants.

12 After a few coats of Tamco primer sealer, the underneath side of the hood was painted the same H8R Orange metallic that the rest of the exterior will receive.

Painting the Cowl, Inside of the Hood, the Front Valance, and Fenders *continu*

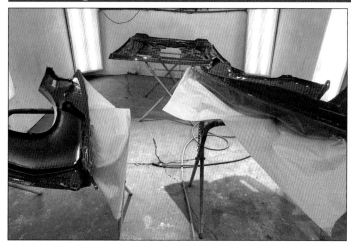

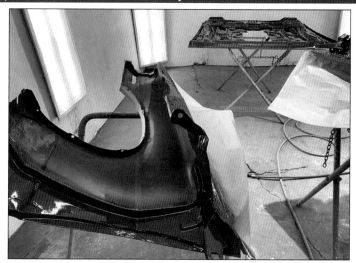

13 *After masking off the exterior of the front fenders, the insides and edges that will be seen when the doors are open is painted the body color. When painting multiple panels at one time, leave enough room to maneuver between them.*

14 *The inner portion of the front fenders will be primed with Tamco black primer and painted with Hot Rod Black.*

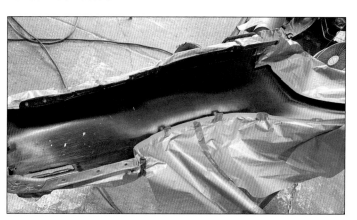

15 *After the new paint on the edges and other visible portions of the fender dries, masking paper and tape are used to cover all areas of the fenders except for the portion that will receive the Hot Rod Black paint.*

16 *The area is prepped just as any other panel. It will receive two coats of black primer that are allowed to flash and dry in accordance with the product directions.*

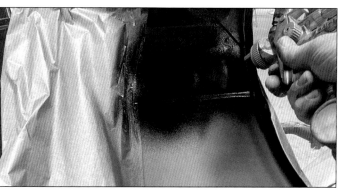

17 *The black primer is followed up with two coats of Hot Rod Black paint.*

18 *After waiting the appropriate amount of time, the masking paper can be removed. The front fenders look very good at this point.*

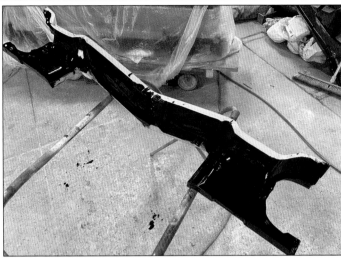

19 Notice that the lip of the fender is still in light-gray primer. The H8R Orange and black areas of the fender will eventually be masked off. The lip, along with the rest of the fender, will be painted the body color.

20 The lower valance panel that fits between the front fenders and below the grille is finished the same as the front fenders. That is black primer and Hot Rod Black on the inside and gray primer with body color on the outside.

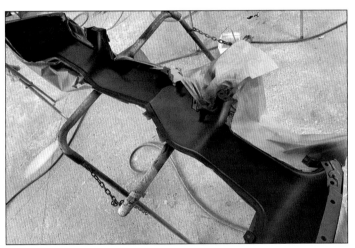

21 The inside of the upper valance also received black primer.

22 The upper valance was then finished with Hot Rod Black paint.

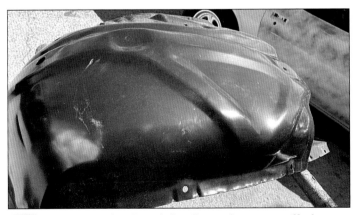

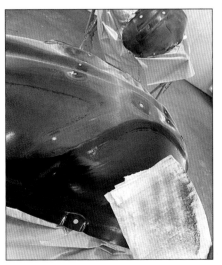

23 The inner fenders (wheelhouse) were scuffed up with 200- and 400-grit sandpaper.

24 They were then cleaned with wax and grease remover.

Painting the Cowl, Inside of the Hood, the Front Valance, and Fenders *continu*

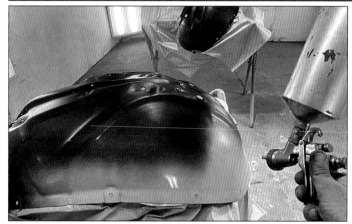

25 Since these pieces will receive the body-color paint, they will be primed with the same direct-to-metal primer.

26 After the primer had time to dry adequately, the H8R Orange body color paint was applied.

27 As anxious as you are going to be to reassemble the vehicle, it is imperative to allow sufficient drying time prior to reassembly. When reinstalling body panels, it may be necessary to install shims on the back side of the panel. Be sure to use fender washers with the body bolts, rather than simple flat washers.

28 With both front fenders loosely bolted onto the cowl so that they will not fall off the body, install the radiator core support.

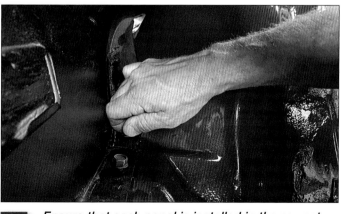

29 Ensure that each panel is installed in the correct order so the parts fit like they should. This can be a finger-pinching opportunity, so be careful.

30 With the core support in place on both sides, loosely install the appropriate body bolts.

31 *The front fenders can now be installed. On vehicles that mount the hood hinges on the fenders, it may be a good idea to mount the hinges prior to installing the fenders.*

32 *With help from an assistant, carefully set the front fenders in place one at a time.*

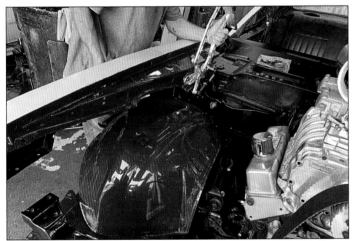

33 *Be careful to not scrape or scratch any paint.*

34 *Loosely secure the front fenders in place with the appropriate body bolts.*

35 *Check that all connecting pieces and parts fit properly.*

Painting the Cowl, Inside of the Hood, the Front Valance, and Fenders *continu*

36 *As you are tightening bolts, check the panel gaps and alignment. Add shims when necessary.*

37 *While the panels may not align perfectly, it is up to you to decide if they fit well enough. Take your time and try not to get frustrated. Sometimes, you must walk away and come back later, and it will fit better. You must get the fit you can settle for before you paint.*

38 *It appears as though the gap is slightly wider above the beltline than below it. This may be a camera-angle issue, but perhaps it is not. The main detail to check is that the belt line is straight from front to back. When it is, that is about as good as it is going to get.*

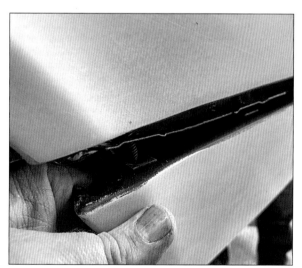

39 *Install the lower valance to tie the front fenders together. In most cases, this involves threading body bolts through holes in the lower valance and into threaded bungs on the back side of the fender.*

40 *Leave all the front-clip body bolts slightly loose until all panels are in place.*

Coat the Trunk with Rust Preventor

There are about as many ways to make the trunk of a vehicle look nice as there are vehicles with trunks. Many show vehicles have trunk panels that are upholstered. Others are painted with splatter paint, as this was a common OEM treatment during the 1950s and into the 1970s. Some are simply painted the same color as the exterior. All of these are perfectly acceptable.

However, there is another practical solution that looks good and is relatively easy. Other than a paint scraper and/or wire wheel that you probably already have, the only piece of necessary equipment is a disposable paintbrush. The wire wheel is to prep the surface, and the brush is used to apply a coat of rust preventative. POR-15 is a similar product.

Rust Prevention on the Inside of the Trunk

1 A quart of this product should be more than enough to coat the trunk of most any passenger car. This product can also be used for coating the vehicle's frame and some suspension components.

2 As with any paint product, a clean surface is essential for proper adhesion. Remove everything from the trunk, prep the metal with a wire wheel, and then clean with wax and grease remover.

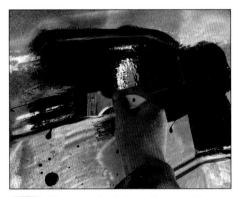

3 Be sure to follow the application directions and safety instructions that are provided with the product. After shaking or stirring as directed, apply with a brush. Wear rubber gloves during application, as it may be difficult to remove from your hands.

4 Apply plenty of rust preventor into all the crevices, as that is where rust is most likely to begin.

5 Having plenty of ventilation is always a good idea when possible. A charcoal mask at minimum should always be used when applying any type of automotive paint product.

Chassis

About the only time the chassis is going to be painted is when it is a new vehicle construction or frame-off rebuild. In either case, remove everything from the bare frame before painting it. Brake lines, the fuel tank, fuel lines, wiring, and all suspension components should be removed.

When this is a vintage frame, take the time and spend the money to have it media blasted to ensure that it has no rust issues. When you suspect the frame is not square, have it accurately measured at a collision repair shop. When it is out of square, they can pull it back to within tolerance. Thoroughly clean the frame, apply a few coats of epoxy primer, and paint with the color of your choice.

There are multiple types of coatings for vehicle chassis. One is the same automotive paint used on the rest of the vehicle. This can be applied using the same practices anywhere else automotive paint is used. There are also ceramic coatings designed to provide extra protection that is often required on the underside of a vehicle. These coatings are available to be sprayed or brushed on. Some of these require special primers, while others do not. Be sure to research and use compatible products prior to coating the chassis. Powder coating is also a good choice for chassis parts. The frame, suspension parts, radiator support, and other parts were media blasted and powder coated for this project.

Even a slightly bent frame can cause fitment issues. However, a bent frame can usually be accurately measured and pulled back into square by a collision repair shop with a frame rack. This vintage truck frame required a bit of heat persuasion during the pulling process. This is evident from the discoloration.

After the straightening work was done, the entire frame was cleaned and sprayed with two coats of epoxy primer.

After the epoxy primer was allowed to dry, two coats of black single-stage polyurethane were applied. The polished suspension components highlight the frame quite nicely.

REASSEMBLY

Although there is still plenty of work left to do, you have now reached a major milestone of an automotive painting project. Rust issues and collision damage have been addressed, the sheet metal is straight and smooth, and there are many freshly painted parts to be reassembled and/or have parts assembled to them. You, your family, and your friends are all looking forward to seeing this completed project in all of its radiant splendor.

Do not give up, but now is not the time to get into a big hurry, either. Hurrying may result in a piece or two being scratched, and that is not a good thing. You have come too far on this project to be required to go back and touch-up paint.

Tape the Edges

To help avoid scratching or scraping any paint during reassembly, apply masking tape to any surfaces that you suspect may contact each other during reassembly. Since the paint is still fresh, wearing soft gloves when handling panels during reassembly helps avoid damage as well. When the panels are aligned and secured in place, remove the masking tape.

Enlist Some Help

Two great sources of assistance at this point are a factory service manual for the vehicle on which you are working and a second set of hands. The service manual provides information such as how many and what type of fasteners to use. If that second set of hands belongs to someone who is knowledgeable regarding the reassembly of vehicles, all the better.

It is probably a stretch, but perhaps you thought ahead enough to take photos during the disassembly process and wrote some detailed notes during that process. If you did, refer to them because this is why you went to the trouble to do that.

Reassembling the Heavy Parts

Several pieces and parts are too large to fit into place by yourself. Any of the hinged mechanisms, such as the hood, trunk lid, and doors, fit into this category. Bumpers fit into this category also. While one person can usually pick these up easily enough, doing so does require two hands, so another person is required to secure the panel in place with the appropriate attaching hardware.

Hood and Trunk Lid

There are typically two hinges for the hood and two hinges for the trunk lid. Each of these are typically secured to the body by two or three bolts that thread into threaded holes. The hinges may have slotted holes in the portion that bolts to the body or where the hood or trunk lid bolts to. The slotted holes are what allow for adjustment of the respective panel.

First, secure the hinges to the body with the appropriate hardware. If there are slotted holes, begin with the hinge located in the middle of the available adjustment. Have one person hold the hood or trunk lid in place while another person secures the panel to the hinge. Tighten all the fasteners snug, but do not fully tighten them.

Slowly and carefully close the hood or trunk lid and watch for any interference during the entire closing movement. If the panel does not scratch or rub any paint and has even gaps around it, the positioning is good. Open the panel to double check the fit. When all is good, fully tighten all the related hardware. When the fit is not as it should be, loosen the mounting hardware enough to adjust as necessary, then snug the hardware again. Check for proper fit and alignment again. Repeat as necessary until the fit is as it should be, and fully tighten the hardware when the fit is correct.

With the hardware fully tightened, verify the fit again.

As long as you leave the decklid hinges on the car when the decklid is removed, it is fairly easy to reinstall, as only four or six bolts are required in most applications. Depending on the size of the vehicle, having a sec-

ond person to assist is a good thing. On some of the land barges from the 1950s through 1970s, a third person may be a requirement as some of those hoods and trunks were huge. Since we are working with fresh paint, prevention of damage is better than repair.

Installing the Decklid

1 *Placing some padding around the area to protect the paint if anything slips is a good idea.*

2 *On a relatively small car like this Camaro, one person can reinstall the decklid. From one side of the car or the other, move the decklid into position.*

3 *Get at least one bolt started through the hinge and into the decklid. It will probably be easier to get a bolt started on the side closest to you while supporting the decklid with the other hand. Hand-tighten the bolt at first.*

4 *Install the bolts on the opposite side and then tighten all bolts with a wrench or socket.*

Installing the Decklid *continued*

5 *With the decklid bolts tightened enough to prevent any movement while opening and closing the decklid, close it to check for fitment.*

6 *Adjust and recheck if necessary or tighten the bolts to their final torque value. The rust inhibitor coating applied to the interior of the trunk makes for a simple yet good-looking area.*

Doors

Mounting the doors follows the same basic process as the hood and trunk lid. The significant difference is that the doors are mounted to a vertical axis, so they are naturally going to pull themselves down on the side opposite the hinge due to gravity. This makes it especially important to have an assistant help with the doors. If necessary, a door can be installed by one person, but doing so may require the use of a floor jack or another adjustable lifting device.

Most passenger cars are going to have two hinges per door, but older cars and/or some trucks may have three hinges. When proper alignment of the hinges was addressed in the bodywork stage, the doors should not be difficult to install. Proper alignment is undoubtedly the toughest part of the procedure, as the doors tend to have more adjustability than the hood or decklid.

While it should be obvious, the doors should have the door glass, glass riser mechanisms, and anything else removed from the doors prior to installing them. It will make good sense to align the doors as accurately as possible at this point, but it is worth mentioning that they may require adjustment after the weatherstripping is installed.

If a door does not close all the way, it could be that a hinge pin is corroded or bent, or that a portion of the hinge has been bent. When this is the case, remove the door and the hinge pins. Verify that the hinge is not bent. If it is, repair or replace it. Verify that the hinge pins are straight and replace them if necessary. If they are corroded, clean with emery cloth, apply a fine coat of lubricant, and reinstall.

Hanging the Doors

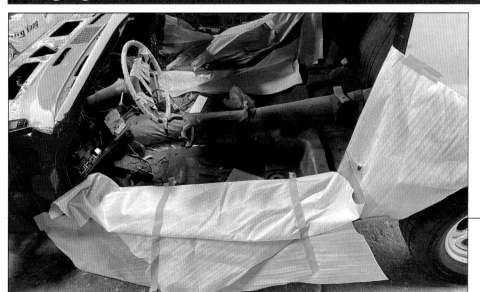

1 *Since the doors are mounted on a vertical axis, they are going to be more prone to sagging on the opposite end, which makes padding and masking more important to protect the sheet metal. Thin foam used in packaging works wonders for this.*

Hanging the Doors *continued*

2 *Multiple configurations of hinges are used for car doors. These aftermarket hinges are designed to better deal with the weight of the Camaro doors. They bolt to the door in a set location but allow for adjustment where the hinge mounts to the cowl.*

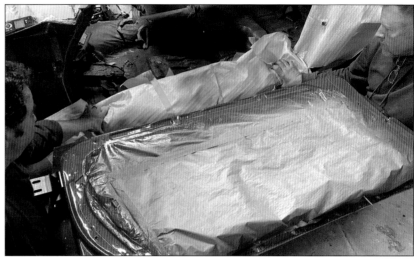

3 *Tape the padding in place to minimize any undesired movement when positioning the door. Most doors require two people to hold it in position and secure to the car.*

4 *Carefully set the door in place to check for fitment and ensure nothing is in the way.*

5 *Unfold the hinge and secure it to the cowl with the appropriate hardware. Before installing the door, verify that the intended bolts fit into the cowl as they should. Since there may be an excessive amount of paint on the cowl, it may be necessary to chase the threads with a tap prior to installation.*

6 *These aftermarket hinges are heftier than the OEM units to better address the weight of the relatively long doors. Three bolts secure each hinge to the cowl.*

7 *Some hinges use hex bolts, while others use recessed bolt heads of various types. Ensure that you use the correct type to avoid any obstructions that may prevent the door for opening or closing.*

8 *When the door is secured to the cowl and is fully supported by the hinges, any protective material must be removed to check the actual fitment.*

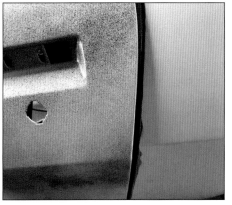

9 *Supported by the hinge, the back edge of the door is hanging a bit low, as evidenced by the bodyline that runs from front to back.*

10 *When adjusting doors, remember that while it appears that the back of the door must move up, it may require the front of the door to move down slightly. The door is not going to change shape, so all mounting bolts must be loosened slightly. Then, fit the door into the opening.*

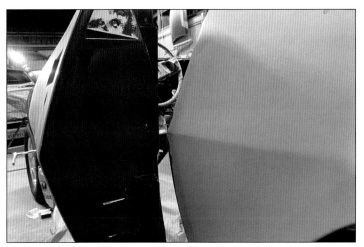

11 *In addition to aligning bodylines, it is essential that opening or closing the door does not scrape off any paint from the door or doorjamb.*

12 *It may take a while to get the fitment correct, but it can be done. Realize that it may require patience. Remember that when it is not working, there is nothing wrong with walking away and coming back later with a fresh perspective.*

Block Sand and Prime the Exterior Panels

Although all the body panels may have received some bodywork, for a truly custom paint job, bodywork is not complete until just before the paint goes on. None of this remaining bodywork should be significant, but it is these minor things that make the difference.

Since you are getting very close to being ready for paint, now is the time to get all bodywork exactly the way you want it. Test-fit the headlight bezels and any trim to ensure that these pieces will all fit as they should without any gaps. This may mean sanding off a bit of body filler that may have been applied a little too thick in some places.

Block Sanding and Priming the Bodywork

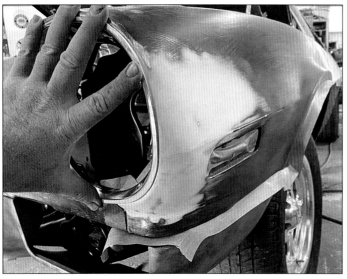

1 Test-fit the headlight rings to ensure that they fit the opening correctly. A slight bit of body filler was required at the front of this fender.

2 Verify that the mounting tabs are not full of body filler. Ensure that the headlight bezel fits exactly as it should.

3 A slight bit of body filler was required to get the right front fender as smooth as it should be. The dark spots indicate areas that were higher than the surrounding area. With the added body filler, it is all the same level.

4 Feather out any areas of body filler so that it is impossible to distinguish any layers of filler.

Block Sanding and Priming the Bodywork *continued*

5 *Verify that any opening panels (hood, doors, and decklid) clear any protrusions, such as an air scoop. You must also verify these panels close completely without hitting anything that does not protrude through them.* With the hood hinged, it was determined that more clearance was required for the hood.

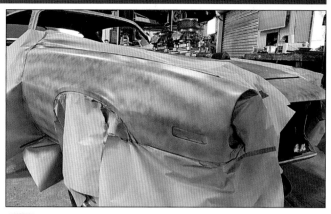

6 Apply a guide coat of contrasting-color paint to any areas that received bodywork.

7 There are specific guide-coat products available, but most any rattle-can enamel will work just as well. The goal is not to cover the panel as you would with final paint but merely make a uniform dusting over the entire panel.

8 Successful block sanding requires a sanding block, the proper grit of sandpaper, and patience. Just any old sanding block will not suffice. Since the purpose of the block is to make full, even contact with the surface, the block's surface must match the contour of the area to be sanded. This DuraBlock has a teardrop profile to give it both a curved and flat surface.

9 The correct grit of sandpaper is also important. At this point, 600-grit wet-or-dry paper is appropriate.

10 On a flat surface, use a flat block. On a surface that has been primed with a catalyzed primer, use plenty of water to obtain the smoothest surface.

Block Sanding and Priming the Bodywork *continued*

11 *In this concave area, use the rounded portion of a block so that you do not flatten out the curve.*

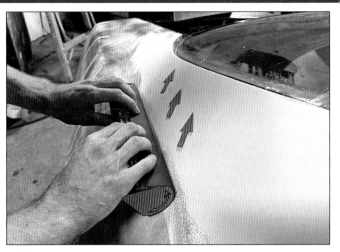

12 *Roll the sanding block on the curved surface and move it diagonally across the panel. Avoid sanding a rut in the panel. Keep the panel moving.*

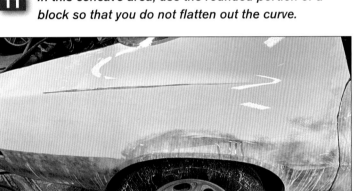

13 *Sand the guide coat until it is all gone. Places where the guide coat remains indicates a low spot. A high spot is indicated by a spot where the guide coat is quickly removed but the guide coat remains around it. The dark line on the rear quarter panel is the unsanded guide coat. Leaving that area for last shows that the line is straight and that it doesn't need to be re-primed.*

14 *After block sanding, ample light helps reveal any imperfections. The better the reflection, the better the surface finish.*

15 *Since there is no glass in the car at this time, a paper towel or sponge can be soaked in water and squeezed out onto the area being sanded. In this situation, having a bucket of water handy is a good idea.*

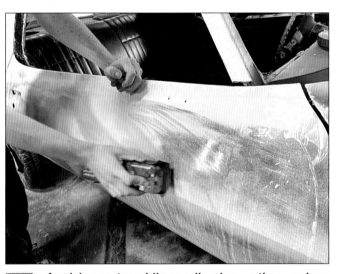

16 *Applying water while sanding keeps the sandpaper lubricated, makes it easier to push, and helps prevent the sandpaper from loading up.*

17 When the block-sanding process indicates a low area, now is the time to fill it. Mix the required amount of filler and then apply it. Be careful to get it as smooth as possible to avoid unnecessary sanding that can cause gouges.

18 A slight low spot on a body line can be magnified greatly if it was not filled prior to paint. Now is the time to fix or address all imperfections.

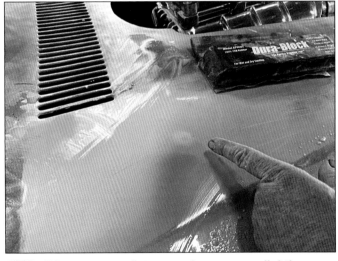

19 Use the largest sanding block available for the area you are sanding to get the best overall finish.

20 When you can tint your primer, use a slightly different color of tint on each layer of primer to see when you have removed the most recent application of primer and exposed the lower substrate. When it blocks flat and looks like this, you are fine to paint it. When you hit metal or filler, it is time to touch up the bodywork and re-prime.

21 Do not be afraid to rub your hands over the finished surface to feel any imperfections. Just remember to thoroughly clean the surface with wax and grease remover prior to spraying any paint.

Layout and Mask for Custom Paint: Part 1

With the insides of the sheet metal painted and all the pieces assembled and bolted together, the final push of painting the entire exterior can finally begin. This method of assembly and then painting the exterior can prevent scratches and other damage that can occur when parts are painted and assembled. However, when painting an assembled car, it requires lots of masking. This masking can take a fair amount of time but is a requirement unless you are okay with getting overspray on places where you do not want it. You should not be okay with that.

When the overall paint scheme is anything but one color (simple two-tone paint, multicolor paint, and/or graphics, such as flames or scallops), the masking task gets even more complicated and time-consuming. It becomes imperative for the person doing the masking work to have a clear image of the process in their mind, as some additional masking must be done for each color that is applied. While all masking tape is temporary, some applications of tape must be removed prior to others during the painting process. So, be careful when any masking tape crosses another piece of masking tape. You do not want to spend hours laying out a design and then ruin it by removing a piece of tape that may have been applied as a guideline.

Masking and Painting a Custom Paint Job: Part 1

2 Wider masking tape (3/4- or 1-inch wide) is used to outline any areas to be masked off to prevent overspray. This tape is applied to the sheet metal and serves as a foundation for additional masking tape and paper.

1 At this point, the tape is just part of the design process, determining what the graphics will look like. Notice that the front header panel hasn't been final sanded yet.

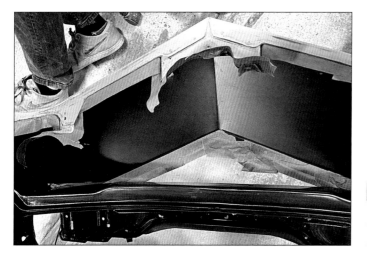

3 Since other masking materials will be attached to this outline tape, take your time and pay attention to details. Ensure the tape is firmly pressed into place and that it will form a nice, clean edge.

Masking and Painting a Custom Paint Job: Part 1 *continued*

4 *The rough design has been finalized. The tape is removed so that final prep can be done.*

5 *Starting with masking tape to outline the opening in the hood, the carburetors and hood scoop are masked with masking film. This thin polyester film is more flexible than masking paper, and therefore is more suitable for this application.*

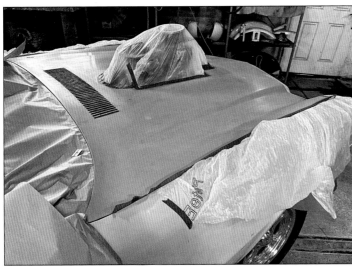

7 *To serve as a guideline and rather than masking, a strip of 1/8-inch masking tape is applied to indicate the centerline of the hood. This serves as a baseline for measuring to ensure that the pattern is identical from side to side.*

6 *All tape has been removed, and final masking is being done.*

8 *Narrow masking tape is available in widths down to 1/8-inch wide at your favorite auto-body paint-and-supply store. Have plenty on hand before you start any extensive layout.*

9 *The final layout can now take place.*

Masking and Painting a Custom Paint Job: Part 1 *continued*

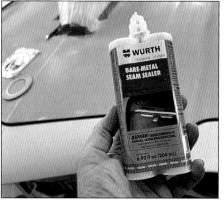

10 The design and construction of the valance panels creates some seams. While it is not desired to weld these together, the seam should receive some seam sealer to prevent moisture from getting in between the two parts and causing rust.

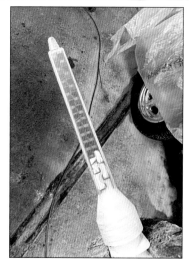

11 This brand of seam sealer is a two-part epoxy applied with a special application gun. The product is packaged in two separate bottles that are wrapped together to flow through one opening. The application nozzle threads onto this opening and blends the two components together during application.

12 Prior to applying the seam sealer to the vehicle, squeeze enough onto a piece of disposable material to ensure the product is mixing properly.

13 The application device for this type of product is essentially a double-barreled caulking gun. As you squeeze the trigger, the two seam-sealer components flow through the mixing nozzle and into the seam.

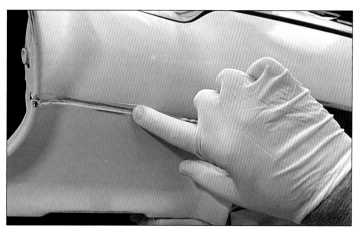

14 I forgot to seam seal prior to taping the graphics. Notice the tape roll. I had to stop taping and apply the sealer. If you forget a step, try to correct it before moving on.

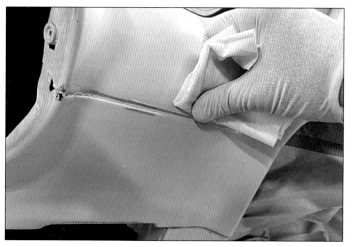

15 To wipe away any excess seam sealer, use a cloth slightly dampened with urethane reducer. With a light touch, wipe away the excess.

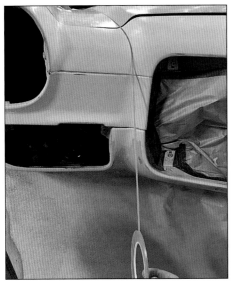

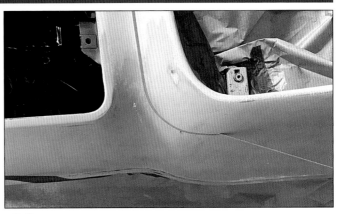

16 *After the seam sealer has been applied, the outlining can continue.*

17 *In this case, the outline continues downward from the hood, down the valance, and horizontally beneath the valance to the opposite side.*

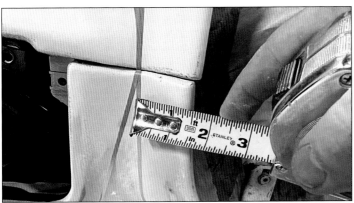

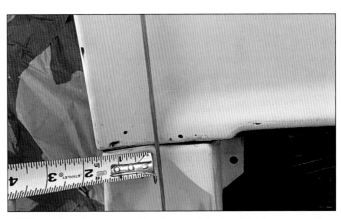

18 *To ensure the pattern is the same on both sides, the location of the tape is measured at repeatable locations and matched on the opposite side.*

19 *A key to measuring from side to side is measuring at locations that are repeatable, such as at a seam, body line, or reference line indicated by another piece of masking tape.*

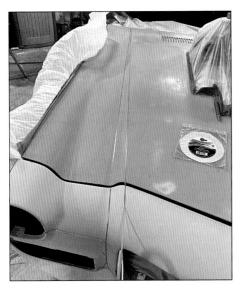

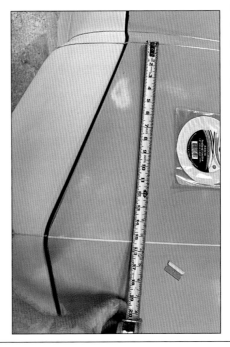

20 *The pattern is continued by running another line along the inside edge of the sloped area of the hood from back to front.*

21 *To ensure the opposite side matches, a measurement near the front of the hood is taken from the centerline tape.*

Masking and Painting a Custom Paint Job: Part 1 *continued*

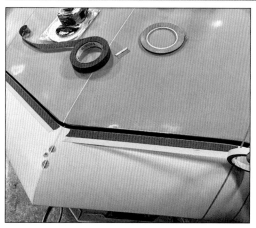

22 While it requires additional masking tape, offset widths can be established by laying down strips of wider masking tape adjacent to the line to be offset from. In this case, to offset the outline 1¾ inch from the hood opening, a strip of 1-inch-wide tape and a strip of 3/4-inch-wide tape provides uniformity.

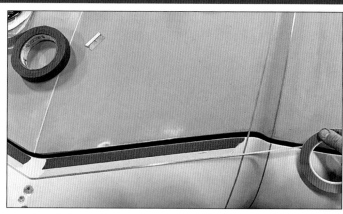

23 Note that these pieces of offset tape are kept short so that they do not interfere with the narrower outline tape. The purple and green tape are relatively temporary and will be removed before painting begins.

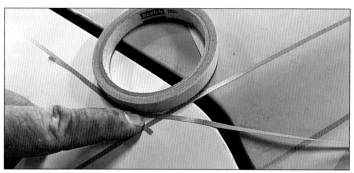

24 To serve as a template for masking a round corner, use a round object of the desired radius, such as a roll of masking tape. Be sure that you tape all the curves before you use any more of the tape from the roll so that the radius stays the same. Paint mixing cups and various sizes of paint cans can also be used for this task.

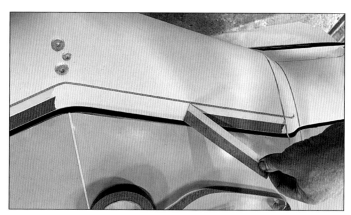

25 With the outline tape in place on the upper valance panel, the offset tape can be removed.

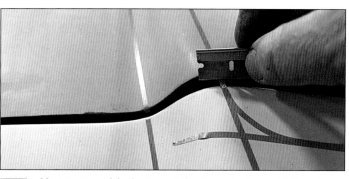

26 Use a razor blade to cut the tape in the middle of any openings, such as between the hood and valance panel. Then, wrap the ends of the outline tape around the edge of the panel (in this case, the hood and valance panel).

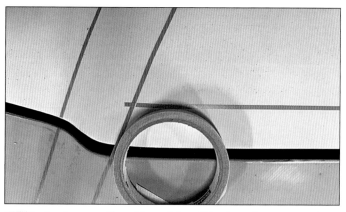

27 Just as on the other side of the hood, a convenient radius template, such as a roll of masking tape, is used to lay out the short piece of outline tape that will go around the corner.

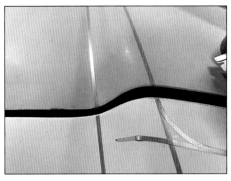

28 Be sure that the curved tape perfectly overlays the longer tangents and is pressed down sufficiently to remain in place.

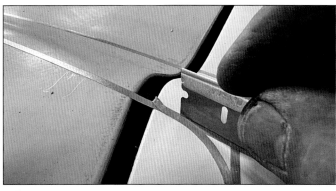

29 Use a razor blade to cut through the tangent pieces of outline tape that form the original corner. Then, remove and dispose of the extra pieces of outline tape.

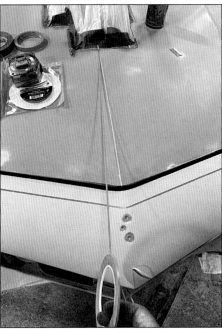

30 To mimic the outline created onto the center of the hood, begin with a piece of outline tape at the front of the hole in the hood and pull it forward toward the valance. Since the hood is flat leading to the center, this first side should be placed by eyeball to where it is visually appealing.

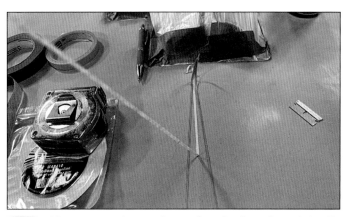

31 After measuring to determine the location of the first piece of tape, the outline tape can be applied on the opposite side to match. With that completed, the tape that represented the hood centerline can now be removed.

32 Using the same process as before, the outline tape is applied to form a smooth curve between the front-to-back and side-to-side tangents. The excess tape is cut off and removed.

33 The outline for the hood paint is now complete. Now is a good time to run your thumb or fingertip over every bit of outline tape to ensure that it is firmly pressed into place.

Masking and Painting a Custom Paint Job: Part 1 *continued*

34 This outline just completed will be the outer edge of an area that will be painted white pearl. The rest of the hood, front fenders, and valance must be masked before applying that paint. Begin by applying wider masking tape to the outside of the area that will receive paint.

35 The area to be masked has now been outlined with 1-inch-wide masking tape. Masking paper will be secured to this masking tape.

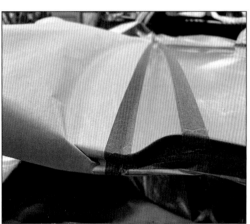

36 Align an edge of the masking paper with the middle of the 1-inch-wide masking tape to which it will be secured. Then, secure the paper in place with another strip of masking tape. Ensure this second strip of masking tape is pressed down firmly and does not leave any gaps where overspray could get through.

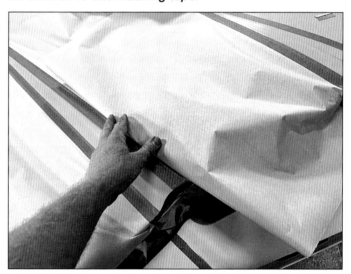

37 Fold and/or cut the masking paper as required for it to fit into the desired area.

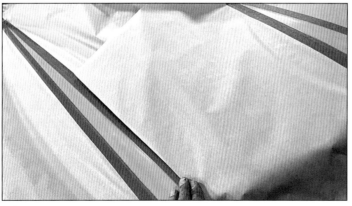

38 Where the masking paper has been folded to fit into the area, ensure that it is pressed flat so there are no bubbles for paint to get into.

39 Secure all the edges of masking paper with masking tape.

40 For the white pearl paint that will be applied to the hood, the masking is now complete.

41 Use a lint-free paper towel wetted with wax and grease remover to clean the area to be painted.

42 It may have looked clean, but the dirt on the towel shows that it was not pristine. Be sure that no wax and grease remover is allowed to dry on the surface.

43 The white paint to be applied is a custom mix of DBC1684 base coat with some orange and a bit of black mixed in. With the paint mixed, stained, and in the spray gun, spray a test pattern and adjust the spray pattern if required.

44 With the spray gun adjusted properly, begin spraying the area to be painted. Begin with the area in the middle of the hood first, as it will be the most difficult to reach.

45 Apply the paint evenly to the rest of the area. Refer to the instruction sheets for the paint you are using for the recommended number of coats, time between coats, and other pertinent information.

Masking and Painting a Custom Paint Job: Part 1 *continued*

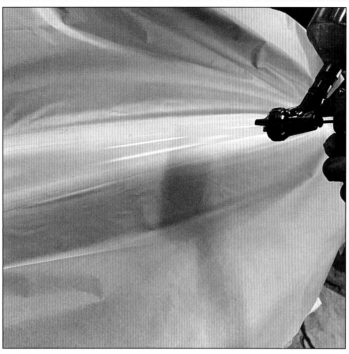

46 *Apply the second and successive coats as required. Be sure to allow the required amount of time between coats.*

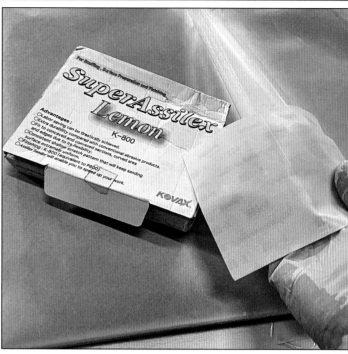

47 *K-800 is a super flexible sandpaper designed for nibbing the base coat between coats. It is flexible, so you won't have any sharp edges digging into your color.*

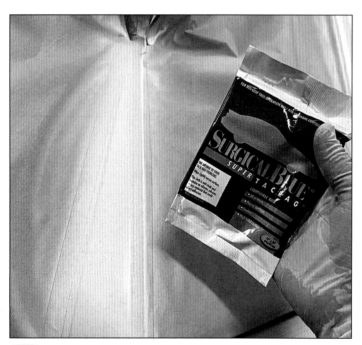

48 *White tack rags are more aggressive and stickier, and they are designed for use with primers and sealers. The blue tack rags are not as sticky and have a finer mesh for use with base coats.*

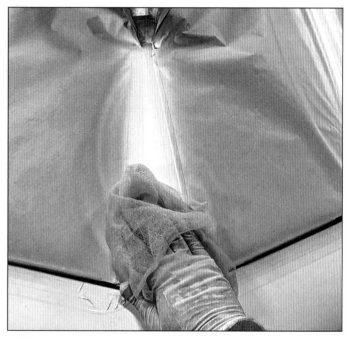

49 *Use the blue tack rags between each coat and nib with the K-800 between every two to three coats of base coat. Once you have coverage, only use a tack rag. Do not use sandpaper.*

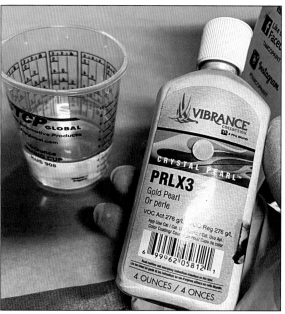

50 *Allow the base coat to dry sufficiently prior to applying the clear coat. Be sure to thoroughly review and understand the instructions for base coat and clear coat so you know what your window of opportunity is between applications.*

51 *Pearl is added into an "inter-coat" clear (not a top-coat clear). The inter-coat clear dries fast and doesn't need to be re-sanded prior to subsequent layers of material.*

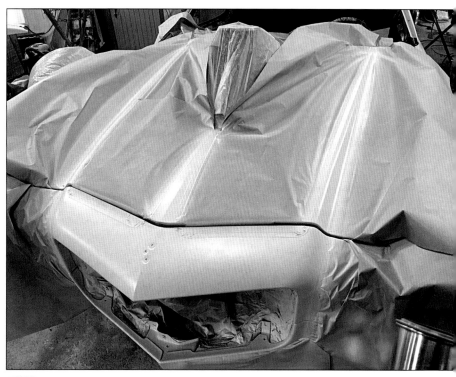

52 *Traditional top-coat clear would leave too much MIL build, making it very difficult to get a smooth finish with final clear.*

53 *Leave the masking material in place and allow the base coat and clear coat to dry for the recommended time. Depending on how extravagant your paint scheme is, be aware of the time to tape, sand, and apply the top coat.*

Layout and Mask for Custom Paint: Part 2

The complexity of the custom paint scheme increases the cost of the paint job in both materials and labor time. When you are doing the work yourself, the financial impact is less. However, it may take considerable time when you consider the time spent masking, spraying paint, and waiting for paint to dry before moving forward. You may or may not have that time to spend, but that is for you to decide. Material costs for masking tape and masking paper increases with each application, not to mention the actual cost of the paint and the necessary additives.

Masking and Painting Your Custom Paint Job: Part 2

1 *For marking layouts or measuring marks on the surface to be painted, use a Stabilo pencil. These can be purchased from most art supply stores. Do not use permanent markers or any dye-based pens. They will bleed through.*

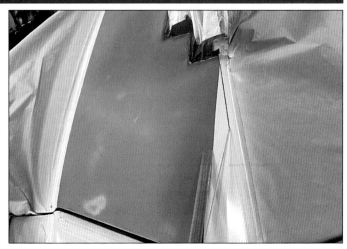

2 *As the complexity of the paint scheme increases, you will find yourself removing some masking paper before applying paint. You must have a clear vision of the overall paint scheme in your mind the entire time that you are masking and painting.*

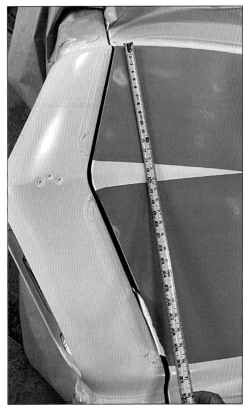

3 *The area that is in gray primer at this point will receive a black base coat, followed by a final body color with pearl added and some other special effects. Note that some masking material must still be removed from the top of the upper valance.*

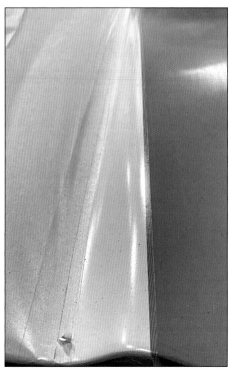

4 *Since it has been removed previously, another strip of 1/8-inch fine-line tape is applied between the gray primered area and the pearl white paint to delineate the area for the black base coat and body color.*

Masking and Painting Your Custom Paint Job: Part 2 *continued*

5 The pearl white area must be masked off prior to the next application of paint. The narrow, pointed area in the center of the hood can be masked with tape, but the excess width must be trimmed away near the point. Cut the tape along the outside of the fine-line tape with a razor blade using light pressure. You do not want to cut into the paint.

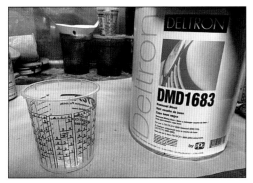

7 Deltron DMD1683 base-coat black toner is used beneath the color that will be applied to the hood.

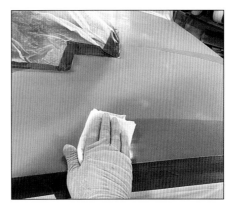

6 After masking the outer sides of the hood with masking paper and tape, clean the surface with wax and grease remover. Wipe off any residue with a clean towel.

8 Prior to spraying any paint, always spray a test pattern to ensure that your spray gun is adjusted properly. It is much better to test on some masking paper than on your painting surface.

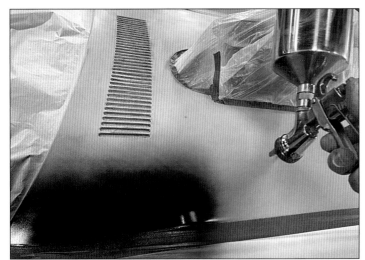

9 Apply the base coat and keep the spray gun perpendicular to the surface and approximately 6 to 8 inches away from the surface. Conventional wisdom says to apply paint to the edges of the surface first and then to the rest of the area.

10 The black base coat has been applied to the entire hood and the small areas on the upper valance panel.

Masking and Painting Your Custom Paint Job: Part 2 *continued*

11 After awaiting the proper amount of drying time, sand off (nib) any imperfections such as drips, runs, or dust that appear in the base coat with 800-grit sandpaper.

12 For this project, a second base coat (custom-mixed dark brown) is going to be applied as well. This is essentially the color coat. The previous black was applied to slightly alter the appearance of this dark brown color. Allow the paint to dry completely.

13 To provide a custom effect to the dark brown, a spray container filled with water was used to spray it onto the dark brown base coat. To achieve the droplets, open the tip quite a bit and pull the trigger gently. Practice this on some other surface to verify the correct method for obtaining the water droplets on the surface.

14 This is what the water droplets look like on the painted surface. You can work with a uniform effect, heavy around the edges, or purely random. Whatever you desire. This is something that should be practiced on a scrap piece of metal prior to performing it on your dream car.

15 A slightly different custom shade of dark brown is applied to the water drops. It is first over-reduced 2:1 when mixed and then applied with reduced air pressure so that the water droplets do not get blown around. Narrow the spray pattern and keep the spray approximately 10 to 15 degrees from the surface (not perpendicular). Spray an even pattern until you see the color buildup on the droplets.

16 Wait for the water to evaporate. The color used for the water droplets can be a contrasting or complimentary color to the color beneath it.

17 *After the water evaporates, you will end up with a pattern like this. If you mix and spray a light color from the opposite direction, it will intensify the water-drop effect. After allowing the proper drying time, apply two coats of your favorite clear to lock it all down prior to laying out the next graphics. The drops are very fragile and can be damaged easily by taping over them or using a tack rag.*

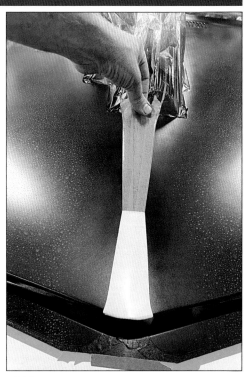

18 *After the proper drying time, masking paper and tape can be removed as dictated by the paint scheme. As the masking material is removed, the paint scheme comes to life.*

19 *Unmask the white and apply top-coat clear to all of the graphics. This seals it all and helps level the surface between the white and the brown.*

20 *First, look at the finish in the sun after the clear coat has been applied. Now, it can be sanded with 600 grit and then 1,000 grit.*

Layout and Mask for Custom Paint: Part 3

When planning a paint scheme, take your skill level and available money into consideration. The more complicated the scheme, the more skill is required. When you are painting for a customer, you must feel confident in performing the work the customer requests. Of course, you learn by experience, but you must be able to provide the customer with some estimate as to what the cost will be. When the cost becomes more than what they are willing to pay, you have done a lot of work for which you may not get paid. However, if the work brings in

more paying work for you, it may be worth the extra time required. When you are working on your own vehicle, it becomes a rolling portfolio. With additional paint materials (paint, primer, reducer, and masking tape), a more complicated paint scheme costs more, whether it is for a paying customer or for yourself.

In the next section, we will show you how to paint flames. While flames are not required to be a perfect match from one side to another, they should be similar and balanced. You can read that last part as being very similar from one side to the other. We will show you how to do that too.

Masking and Painting Your Custom Paint Job: Part 3

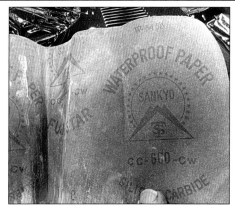

1 *Before laying out the flames, nib the surface to remove any blemishes (runs, drips, or dust particles). Since there is plenty of paint on the vehicle at this point, water is not going to hurt anything.*

2 *When nibbing the surface, use 600-grit sandpaper (or finer) with plenty of water. Confirm that the sandpaper is suitable for use with water. When it is, it will say so on the back.*

3 *After nibbing, the brown panels are free from any defects. Remember, applying additional layers of paint is not going to remove any imperfections beneath it.*

4 *Laying out flames takes skill and patience. Whenever you see a vehicle with flames you like, take a photo of it for future reference. There are many different styles of flame layouts. Some look great, while others are something less.*

Masking and Painting Your Custom Paint Job: Part 3 *continued*

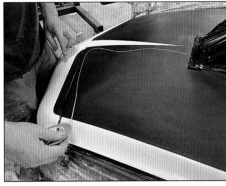

6 Begin with the tip of the first flame and pull the tape toward the belly of the flame. In this flame layout, the tip of the first flame is near the center of the hood in front of the blower and will continue all the way to the exterior edge of the hood.

5 Lay out the flames with 1/8-inch fine-line tape. In this case, the area to be flamed will be the brown panels on the hood. Start at one side of the panel and work your way across that panel. We will show you how to transfer the layout to the other side after the first panel is completed.

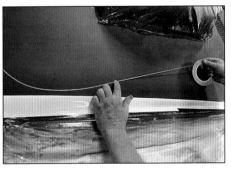

7 The balance of the flames lies between these two edges. Hold the tape roll in one hand while pressing the tape down with your other hand. Both hands must work in coordinated effort to ensure you have smooth, flowing curves. Press the tape down firmly as you go.

8 With the extent of the layout defined, each individual flame lick can be created. Start at the tip of the first flame and pull the tap down the belly and form some curves along the way.

9 Note that the flames are gradual in their width, narrow at the tip and wider at the belly. There is no formula or anything to measure. It must be done by eye. From the tip of one flame to the tip of the next, only one piece of tape is used.

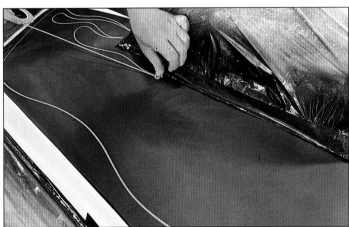

10 Begin the next flame lick at the previous tip and overlap the tape somewhat beyond the flame tip. You will trim the tape at the tips later. Ensure that you press the tape down firmly at the tip so it does not pull loose.

Masking and Painting Your Custom Paint Job: Part 3 *continued*

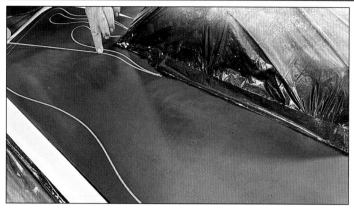

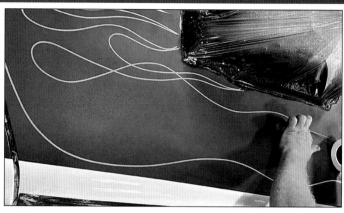

11 Pull the tape toward the belly and increase the width of the flame along the way. Press the tape firmly into place when you like the layout. When you lay down a piece of tape and do not like the layout, pull that piece of tape up and discard it.

12 Just as with real flames, paint flames can overlap at some point. While you lay out the flames, keep an overall image in the back of your mind or in a sketch or photo for reference.

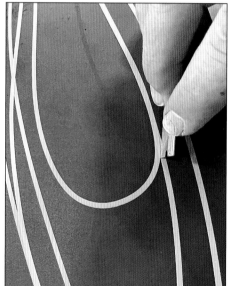

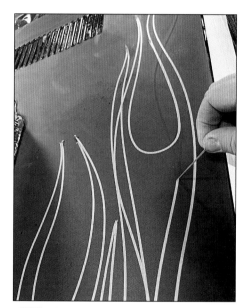

13 The design isn't done until paint is applied. Small tweaks in the layout can make a big difference in the flow of the design.

14 Use a safety edge razor blade to cut the fine-line layout tape where required.

15 Remove any unnecessary tape by pulling it back on itself and off the surface to be painted. If you look closely, you can see a faint image of where tape has been removed.

16 Extreme care must be taken when removing excess tape in overlap areas to ensure you remove the correct pieces of tape. One cannot stress enough the importance of having the overall layout firmly etched in your mind at this point.

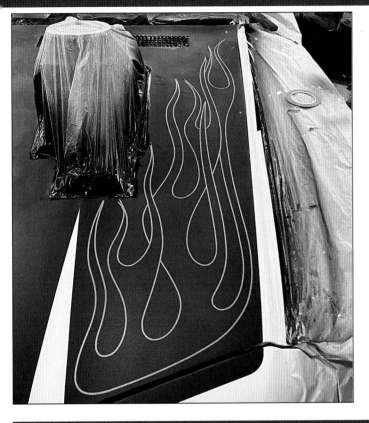

17 With the cutting and trimming completed, we now have an overall look of the completed layout on one side of the hood. The next step is to transfer this layout to the other side.

Transfer a Pattern for Custom Paint

Transferring a flame or scallop layout or any other graphic layout from one side to the other of a vehicle is not as complicated as it may sound. It merely requires some masking paper, masking tape, a pounce wheel, pounce powder and, most importantly, some common reference points. Without these common reference points, there is no way to align the pattern on the other side.

Transferring a Layout Pattern

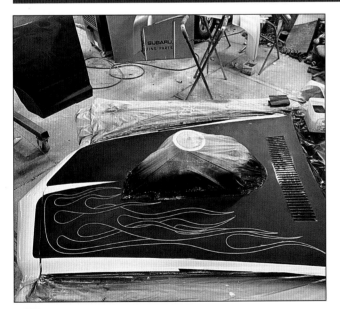

1 Ensure that the first layout is as you want it and is complete. In this case, the flame layout has been created on the driver's side of the hood with 1/8-inch fine-line tape. Cover the area with masking paper and tape it in place.

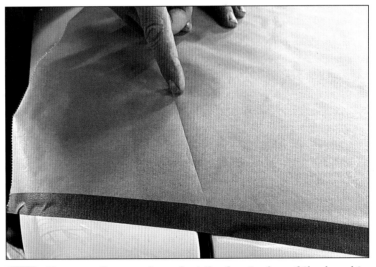

2 Use your fingernail against the front edge of the hood to press a reference line where the hood and front valance come together. At this point, it is easy to see that this line is the front edge of the hood opposed to the back edge of the front valance. Make notes if you need to, and you may need to use a permanent marker to indicate the centerline of the hood or other panels used as reference points.

Transferring a Layout Pattern *continued*

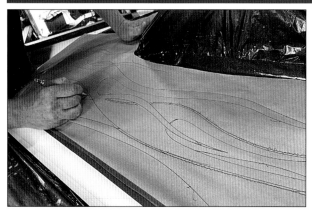

3 Although you may not be able to see the fine-line tape through the masking paper, you can feel it. Use a pen or pencil to trace the entire layout onto the masking paper.

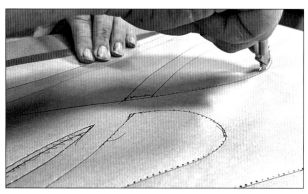

5 After laying a piece of cardboard on a flat work surface, move the masking paper from the vehicle to this work surface. Using a slight downward force, trace over the pen or pencil lines drawn onto the masking paper. Since the cardboard below the masking paper is permeable, the pounce wheel creates a series of small holes in the masking paper where the pounce wheel is rolled.

7 Shake the pounce container to ensure that the pounce is not clumped. Then, pour some pounce into a pounce block.

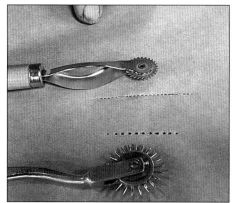

4 A pounce wheel is a metal wheel with spokes or spikes protruding from it and a handle to push or pull it along a pattern. The protrusions from the wheel provide different spacing, depending on size of the wheel and the number of protrusions.

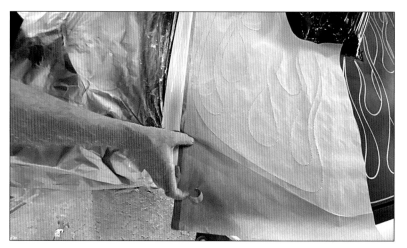

6 Move the masking paper with the holes in it to the location where the pattern is to be duplicated (in this case, the other side of the hood). However, remember that the masking-paper template must be flipped over and aligned on the pattern using the common reference points. When it is placed properly, tape it down enough so that it does not move.

8 Rub the pounce block over the masking paper where the pattern is to be transferred. The pounce (a fine powdery material) falls through the holes made in the masking paper onto the area where the pattern will be.

9 After ensuring that you have covered the entire design with the pounce block, remove the masking paper. The pounce will provide a chalk-like pattern.

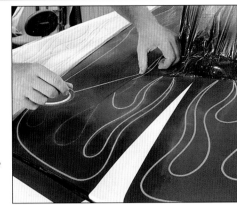

10 Just as when creating the original layout, lay down 1/8-inch-wide fine-line tape over the top of the pounce line.

11 The pattern is now copied as closely as possible from one side to the other.

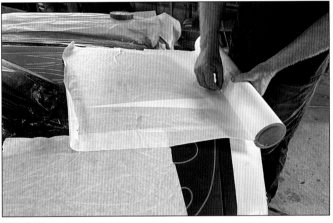

12 Now that the layout has been copied, the surrounding area must be masked prior to painting. Rather than attempt to mask the irregular and intricately shaped area with strips of masking tape, use self-adhesive frisket paper. This comes in rolls and can be spread quickly over a large area.

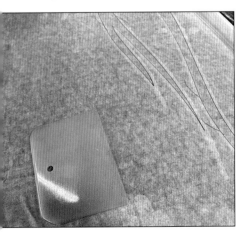

13 After covering the entire area to be masked with frisket paper, use a body-filler spreader or a squeegee to press out any bubbles.

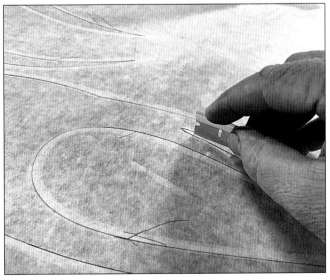

14 You will be able to see the fine-line tape through the frisket paper. Use a single-edge razor blade to cut along the outline. Remain conscious of the area that will be painted when you have removed the frisket paper and consistently cut on the correct side of the tape.

Transferring a Layout Pattern *continued*

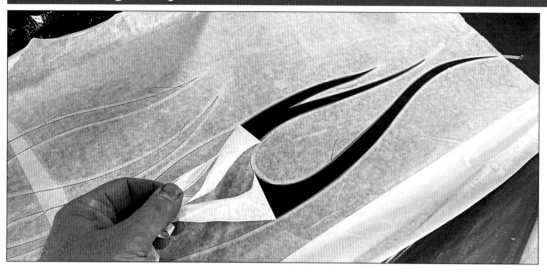

15 *Carefully remove the frisket paper in the area that is to be painted by pulling the frisket paper back on itself.*

16 *As desired, we have a somewhat-complicated and intricate design laid out and masked on both sides of the hood.*

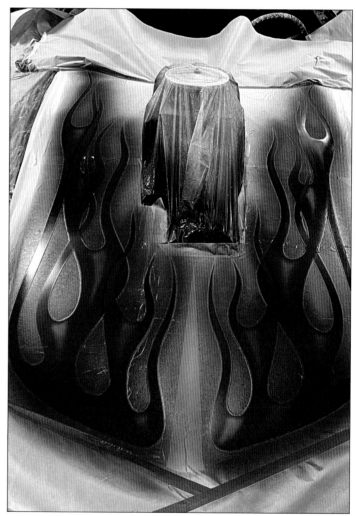

17 *After verifying that all edges are fully pressed down and the surface is clean, the next coats of paint can be applied to the flames.*

Apply the Final Paint

Depending on the paint scheme, you may already be to this point or still have details to address. For this project car, the hood and decklid have received their multiple layers of various-colored paint. It is now time to apply the overall color coats and clear coats to the car. If you have not yet done this, now is the last chance to look the vehicle over and confirm that everything is as you want it. Once you start applying paint, turning back will require lots of rework. Strap in because here we go.

Final Masking and Painting

1 Prior to applying the final coats of paint, ensure that all the necessary masking is done correctly. You do not want any overspray getting in between panels and messing up the finish to the panels below.

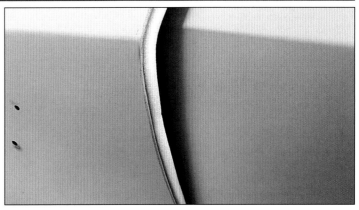

2 Apply the masking tape to the back side of the exterior panels where the paint is going to be applied. Common applications of this back taping are at the back of the front fender/door front, front fenders/hood, and decklid/rear quarter panel.

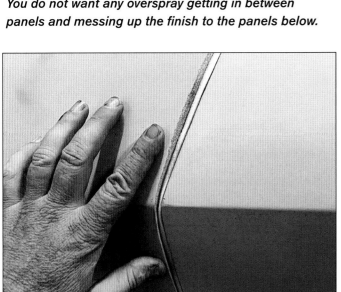

3 With the masking tape applied correctly, the opening between the door and front fender will look something like this. None of the overall body color will be allowed to fall on the area between these two panels.

4 Using the widest masking paper available, start in one corner of your paint spraying area and cover the floor. Tape the seams with masking tape. Be sure you do not create a trip hazard. While this step is not necessary, masking the floor ultimately creates a cleaner working environment.

Final Masking and Painting *continued*

5 Move the vehicle into the spray booth. Finish masking anything that still requires masking. Turn on all the lighting that is available. Turn on the exhaust fan and the air compressor. Mix the paint. Ensure that you are wearing all of your health and safety equipment (spray mask, paint suit, and gloves).

6 After filling the paint cup, spray a test pattern to verify that the spray gun is adjusted as desired. Begin applying paint. Some painters choose to start at the top and work their way down the vehicle. Others start at the bottom and work their way up. That decision is up to you.

7 Keep the spray gun perpendicular to and at a consistent distance from the surface. Keep the spray gun moving at the correct speed to obtain good paint coverage but still avoid runs. Ensure that you cover all the area to be painted, especially edges of wheel wells and panel edges. Apply a complete coat and then wait the required time between coats. Repeat this process until full coverage is achieved.

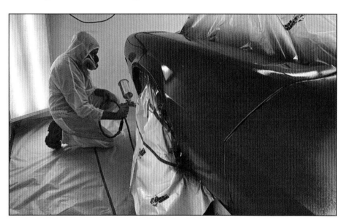

8 After all paint has been applied and you have waited the appropriate drying time, carefully remove any masking paper that is covering any areas that need applications of clear.

9 After waiting the required time but still within the base coat/clear coat time frame, apply the necessary coats of clear. Ensure that you wait the recommended flash time between each coat. If you plan to do lots of wet sanding and buffing afterward, ensure that you apply enough coats of clear to avoid burning through.

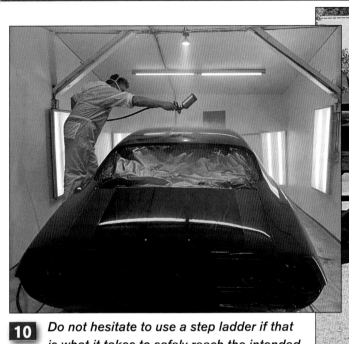

10 *Do not hesitate to use a step ladder if that is what it takes to safely reach the intended surface when applying paint or clear. Ensure that the hose remains clear of the vehicle.*

11 *After spraying everything, clean out your spray gun. After waiting the appropriate dry time, carefully remove all of the masking material. Let the vehicle sit for the appropriate time prior to doing any wet sanding and/or buffing.*

Bumpers

On vintage automobiles that feature real bumpers, they are relatively easy to install with the help of an assistant. There is often a bumper bracket that attaches to the vehicle frame with two bolts. The bumper bracket typically attaches to the bumper with two bolts near the frame-mount location and with one or two bolts at a more outboard location. The bolts that secure the bumpers in place are typically in clear view, so it is merely a matter of installing all the bolts through the bumper and bumper bracket and then securing them with a lock washer and nut on the back side. Align the bumper as desired and then fully tighten the nuts and bolts.

On some reproduction bumpers and/or bumper brackets, the holes may not align properly. When the bumper is chrome, any modifications will need to be made to the bumper bracket unless you plan to have the bumper rechromed.

On vehicles from the 1940s and 1950s, front and rear bumpers may be quite large and heavy. Because of the size and weight, an assistant (and possibly a floor jack) will be required. These bumpers typically have more fasteners than smaller bumpers. Install all of the mounting hardware. Then, move from one fastener to another as you gradually tighten them. Avoid tightening any one fastener down all the way until they have all been snugged up to avoid have one side sticking out more than the other. An assistant can lift, push, or pull the bumper into the correct position while you tighten the fasteners.

Glass

Working with glass can be a challenge for several reasons. Besides the fact that it can easily be broken during storage and installation or made more likely by improper installation, it can cause damage to your fresh paint when it breaks. Prior to installing glass, protect the window frame edges by applying strips of masking tape on the surrounding area.

Another challenge is the means of securing the glass in place. There are many methods to secure glass in place. While some are held in place with urethane sealers, others require rubber moldings or are held in place with metal clips. When the fixed glass is secured by urethane sealer, it is designed to add structural strength to the passenger compartment of the vehicle. In some vehicles, butyl sealant is used instead of urethane. In vehicles where rubber molding is used, the glass sits in a groove in the rubber molding. A second groove in the rubber molding fits around a pinch weld formed by the sheet metal around the window opening.

Another challenge is ensuring that each piece of glass maintains a watertight seal around the perime-

Unless you are experienced at installing glass, this should probably be left to professionals who are trained on how to install it. If a professional breaks your glass, they pay for it. If you break it, you pay for it. Plus, you do not want to cut off your thumb.

ter. Any leaks allow moisture to get into areas where rust can form. This is often compounded by being hidden by trim and is therefore allowed to go unchecked until it is past the point of being repairable.

When installing fixed glass, clean the window opening with wax and grease remover to eliminate any contaminants that might cause the sealer to fail. If using butyl sealant only, lay a full bead of sealant on the mounting surface. When urethane sealant will be used also, slope the butyl sealant away from the glass and fill the triangular void with urethane sealant. With the help of an assistant, set the glass in place. The butyl sealant secures the glass in place while the

urethane fully cures.

Movable glass is usually held in place by multiple pieces of metal that clamps to the bottom of the glass. These clamping pieces are then connected by the mechanism that opens and closes the window, whether the windows are closed manually or by power. Be sure to install new window rubber and felt as required by the vehicle.

Even though the necessary tools and materials are available at the local paint-supply store, installing glass is not for everyone. Glass can be expensive, and it creates a mess when it gets broken. When installing glass is beyond your comfort level, do not hesitate to hire a professional glass installer.

Install Fixed Glass

1 To secure fixed glass (the windshield and rear window) in place, a quick curing urethane, such as 3M's Windo-Weld, is an excellent choice. This type of product is usually available where you purchase paint products.

2 Use a safety blade to cut the tip off the nozzle. The nozzle is tapered, which means if you cut closer to the tip, you will get a narrower bead. If you cut farther back from the tip, you will get a broader bead. If you are new to this, start narrow and work up to where you feel comfortable.

Install Fixed Glass *continued*

3 Some glass installers notch the nozzle so that it yields a triangular-shaped bead when dispensed.

4 Doing this lays down a sizable bead to make direct contact with the sheet metal. When the glass is pressed into place, the tip of the sealer spreads out and provides a good contact patch (but not so much that it oozes out of control).

5 Unless you are installing a small rear quarter window, always enlist some help to install a windshield or back glass.

6 To help avoid damage caused by scratches or excess sealer reaching the paint, outline the window opening with wide masking tape. Be sure the glass is seated in place and then gently press it into place.

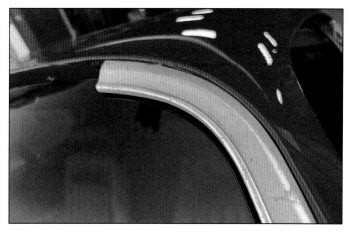

7 Reinstall the exterior window trim and be sure to install the pieces in the correct order when there are any pieces that have any sort of overlap.

Factory Trim

Prior to reinstalling metal trim, inspect the trim carefully to determine if it requires any straightening or other repair. It may need to be rechromed or polished to look its best. Now that the vehicle has been repainted, trim that is dirty or grungy is going to look bad. It may simply need a good cleaning and scrubbing with an old toothbrush.

If the trim includes any painted sections, touch those up too. Clean vinyl or rubber trim by scrubbing it with an all-purpose cleaner and a soft brush, and then apply a coat or two of vinyl dressing.

Verify that all mounting clips are installed on the back side of the trim before you begin the reinstallation process. Determine how the mounting clips attach prior to installing the trim.

To prevent damaging the trim or the paint, have someone help you when reinstalling pieces that are longer than your arm span.

Take extra care when reinstalling door handles and key locks, as they fit directly into a hole in the painted surface. There is no way to protect the edges. The hardware to secure door handles, key lock cylinders, and door-mounted mirrors must be

---

After detailing and cleaning any old trim or unpackaging new trim, ensure that you know how it is to be secured in place. Ensure that you have the correct hardware and carefully install the trim.

Reinstall any necessary hardware that must be used to reinstall trim.

While the chrome on the hood emblem is in good condition, the color in the bowtie is worn quite a bit. This can be made to look like new by taking it off, scuffing up the area to be painted, applying some primer, and then applying paint.

accessed through openings on the inside of the door. Determine the correct-size wrench for the fastener beforehand to make your reassembly tasks easier. It is a great idea to have a flexible magnetic retrieval tool handy.

Remove old wax and dirt from emblems and badges by using an old toothbrush and a mild cleaner. When paint or lettering requires a touch up, touch-up paint in the correct color can be used.

Grille

The grille of a vehicle typically attaches with screws that thread into metal clips. These clips typically slide over the edge of a piece of sheet metal with a hole in it. Sometimes the clip is threaded, but sometimes it is simply a larger hole on one side of the clip and a smaller hole on the other side. If the clip is threaded, it accepts a machine screw. If it is the smaller hole kind of clip, it is designed for use with a sheet-metal screw.

Although the grille, headlight buckets, and trim rings may appear to be one assembly, they are usually separate pieces. This allows for replacing a headlight when necessary without removing the entire front of the vehicle. However, in some vehicles, the smaller LED headlight bulbs are installed through the back of the headlight assembly.

Miscellaneous Parts

Additional parts to reinstall may include windshield wipers, weatherstripping, side reflectors, headlights, taillights, radio antennas, and license

In most situations, it is not necessary to remove the entire grille to replace a headlight. There is usually a headlight bezel (four holes for mounting screws are clearly visible here) that when removed will provide access to the screws that secure the headlight bulb. Ensure that you remove the screws that secure the headlight and not the ones that adjust it.

plates. These are all relatively simple to install. Take your time to avoid doing any damage.

The coolest paint job will not look its best until all the necessary trim is reinstalled. But when it is all complete, you will have completed a job of which you can be proud.

PERFECTING AND MAINTAINING THE FINISH

Presuming that you have verified that the paint you used is compatible with being wet sanded, it will go a long way toward improving the finish. It will eliminate any dust and dirt that may have landed in the paint and flatten most orange peel in the finish. Merely as a reminder, paint that is not designed to be wet sanded can probably still be polished to increase its shine.

Wet Sanding

When wet sanding a painted surface, remember to use exceptionally fine sandpaper. Nothing coarser than 1,200 grit is generally used for sanding dust nibs flat. Most of the wet sanding will be done with 1,500-, 2,000- and 3,000-grit wet or dry sandpaper with plenty of water.

Begin by filling a bucket with water. Let it sit for about 15 minutes to let any hard-water deposits settle

to the bottom of the bucket. When hard water is an issue, use bottled water with a small hole poked in the lid so that you know there are no contaminants in the color-sanding water. A large case of bottled water is only a few dollars, so it is money well spent. If desired, add a small amount of car-wash soap or liquid dish soap to help lubricate the sandpaper. Even though the sandpaper is much finer, it is still essential to use a sanding block when sanding. Wrap the sandpaper around a wooden paint stir stick, dip it in the water bucket, and begin sanding in a circular motion and with a light touch. Dip the sandpaper in the water often to reduce material buildup.

Begin wet sanding with 1,500-grit wet-or-dry sandpaper. See if that removes the dust or dirt specks and if it flattens out the orange peel in the paint. If it doesn't flatten out the surface, move backward to 1,200

until the surface is flat before moving to 1,500. If the 1,500-grit sandpaper flattens it all out, sand the entire vehicle with the 1,500 grit and then finish with 2,000-, 2500-, and 3000-grit sandpaper as desired. When the 2,000-grit sandpaper does not adequately remove the imperfections in the paint, go back with 1,500-grit sandpaper, and finish with the finer grits. There's nothing wrong with bouncing between grits in certain areas to ensure a flat surface. Just remember which grit has been used in which area.

It is not a desire to be redundant, but it is important to remember now that paint is on the vehicle, wet sanding must be done with very fine grits of sandpaper with a very light touch and lots of water. The goal is to remove any imperfection in the coats of paint and clear, which are very thin. You are no longer doing bodywork.

Wet Sanding the Paint

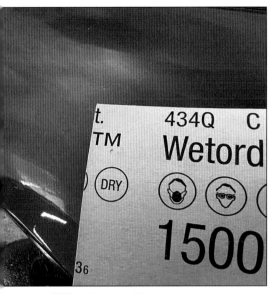

1 After waiting the appropriate time for the paint system to dry and cure, wet sanding can begin. In most cases, you must wait 30 days from the day the last top coat was applied, but 90 days is better. Begin with 1,500-grit (or finer) sandpaper.

2 Wrap the sandpaper around a paint stick. Dip the sandpaper in a bucket of water (or use a spray bottle to keep the surface wet) and begin sanding in a circular motion with light pressure. The location where you start on the vehicle does not matter, but it will make sense to start and finish one panel before moving to the next. As you sand, the paint will start to get dull. That is okay and is to be expected.

3 These are the products required to achieve that custom show-car finish. As an overview of the wet sanding process, start at the lower left with 1,500-grit sandpaper, move on to 2,000 grit, and then on to 3,000 grit. For the buffing process, start at the upper left with rubbing compound, then follow with machine polish. If desired, follow with ultrafine machine polish. These products (or something similar) are available where you purchase automotive paint.

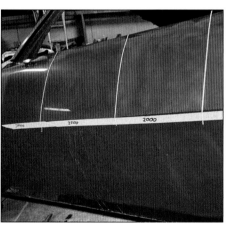

4 You certainly do not need to tape your vehicle in sections. However, this photo provides a look at what to expect the surface to look like after sanding with the designated sanding grits. After using with the 1,500-grit sandpaper, the surface looks dull. After the 3,000 grit, the surface looks significantly smoother as indicated by the reflection.

5 You can wet sand by hand with sandpaper wrapped around a paint stick, or you can use a pneumatic palm sander. Either one will get the job completed. Use the same sanding grit regardless of which method you use. Be extremely cautious when using a pneumatic sander, as it will be extremely easy to burn through the paint.

Rubbing Compounds and Buffing

Rubbing compounds basically do the same thing that wet sanding does, but it is simply a different method used for different paint products. Applying a gritty compound to a single-stage urethane paint will dull the surface but greatly improve the finish of a catalyzed urethane (most multistage paints). Always verify with the paint supplier what can or cannot be done with the paint system being used to finish it to perfection. Some rubbing compounds are designed to be applied by hand, while others require the use of a buffing machine.

Most auto-parts stores and all automotive-paint stores have a selection of rubbing compounds, polishes, and glazes for perfecting the finish on your new paint job. The best one depends on the type of paint on the vehicle and whether the compound will be applied by hand or machine.

Polishing Compound

Whether the newly painted surface has been wet sanded with wet sandpaper or rubbed out with rubbing compound, it will most likely benefit from polishing compound applied by hand or with a buffer. When polishing by hand, use a soft, clean cloth and follow the directions on the polishing product. Polishing in a straight line with a back-and-forth motion reduces the chances of creating swirls. While this can technically be done by hand, it will translate to a long day or month and very sore arms. Consider purchasing an inexpensive polisher that is capable of low speeds in the 600- to 1,200-rpm range. Faster speeds run the risk of burning the fresh paint.

When polishing with a buffer, apply a few strips of polishing compound a few inches apart. Work an area no bigger than about 2 square feet at a time. Do not allow the buffer pad to get dry. Ensure there is always wet polishing compound between the buffing pad and the painted surface. Keep the buffer spinning at a moderate speed and in motion relative to the surface to avoid burning through the paint. To help avoid burning through the paint on ridges or edges, apply masking tape to the high point. Buff to the tape edge and then remove the tape and polish the ridge or edge by hand. Continue buffing each section until the polishing compound is gone and the paint is shiny.

A power buffer will fling polishing compound everywhere, so you may need to cover everything in the surrounding area with a drop cloth. More importantly, any of this excess polishing compound must be removed from the paint before it is allowed to dry because it can cause damage.

To prevent the cloth buffing pads from loading up with dried compound, clean the pad with a pad spur on a regular basis. While holding the pad spur securely, push the pad spur into the buffing pad while it is slowly spinning. This will break up the loose polishing compound.

Rub and Buff

Other than a periodic wash and wax, buffing your new paint is basically the last chore of a paint job. There will most likely be some minor reassembly, but the heavy lifting is behind you now. To bring out the most in the paint job, you must take your time and do this job correctly. Do not get in a hurry because it is easy to burn through the paint, which causes rework. Be patient, do it right, and you will see the difference.

Rubbing and Buffing the Paint

1 *After wet sanding the entire exterior of the vehicle, begin the buffing process. This is somewhat easier, as buffing is usually always done with a pneumatic or electric buffer. Do it by hand if necessary. When going this route, purchase a rubbing compound designed for hand buffing.*

Rubbing and Buffing the Paint *continued*

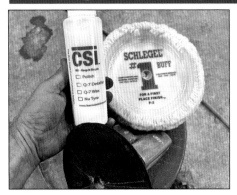

2 Rubbing compound should be applied with a general-purpose wool bonnet. Buffing and polish com-pounds are typically sold in bulk-sized bottles, so a smaller squeeze bottle may be more convenient when buffing. Label any bottles that you put any compound in. While these products are very fine, they are an abrasive, so do not mix them up.

3 Some prefer to apply the rubbing compound directly to the sheet metal and begin buffing, while others apply the compound directly to the wool polishing bonnet. Regardless of how you choose to do it, always keep wet compound between the surface and the buffer and do not allow the compound to dry in the polishing bonnet.

4 Various buffing pads are recommended for differ-ent buffing compounds, so consult with the people where you purchase your paint products for their recom-mendations for your specific application. When using the correct combination of products and some labor, you will see some progress.

5 When sanding or buffing along ridges in body lines, mask over these high spots and wet sand or buff them by hand.

6 With the reflections of the overhead shop lights glistening in the new paint, the painting process is complete.

Overspray

Meticulous and proper masking will eliminate most overspray issues, yet they do happen. Overspray on sheet-metal surfaces can usually be removed by polishing and buffing. Overspray on wheel wells can also be removed by polishing, but on a daily driver, covering the overspray with spray on undercoating will usually suffice. Chrome polish, such as Simichrome, works well to remove overspray from chrome or stainless pieces, such as wheels, bumpers, and exhaust tips. It may be necessary to apply the chrome polish with 0000 steel wool in stubborn areas. Use a single-edge razor blade to scrape overspray from glass.

Extra Details

Extra details, such as flames, scallops, pinstriping, or lettering can be applied almost anytime, but wax needs to be removed so that the new paint can properly adhere. Therefore, if you know you are going to add any paint products, it is better to do so prior to applying any wax. Custom graphics, lettering, scallops, and flames can all fill a book of their own, so we will not go into those items here.

Pinstriping

Pinstriping is a common method to enhance a paint job, whether it is a one-color paint scheme or to cover the color-change seam on scallops or flames. Painted pinstripes are applied using a pinstriping brush (pinstriping dagger) and slow-drying enamel paint. Other brands of pinstriping paint are available, but 1-Shot Sign Painter's Enamel is probably the most common. While the professional stripers make it look easy, pinstriping

takes considerable practice to become accomplished.

To lay down some pinstriping, clean the entire area that will be striped with wax and grease remover because striping paint will not adhere to wax or any other contaminants.

Multiple brands of paint are suitable for pinstriping, but 1 Shot Sign Painter's lettering enamel is probably the most common. This can is a pint size, so you can see that a striping brush is tiny.

Flames and scallops are two forms of graphics used to enhance a painted surface. These flames with their intertwined layout suggest being three dimensional but may not be fully comprehended as they are. Outlining them with a pinstripe greatly enhances the appeal.

Pinstriping brushes are typically made of camel hair and are small. They are available in a variety of sizes, with the smaller brushes enabling the user to lay down finer lines that are more intricate than those done with a larger brush.

At the risk of oversimplifying the process, the pinstriping brush is first dipped into pinstriping enamel to load the brush. The brush hairs are then pulled along a pallet to shape the brush. Some stripers squeeze the brush hairs to the desired shape. After the brush hairs are shaped as desired, the pinstriping paint is applied to the surface.

With the pinstriping applied to the edges of the flames, the overall design is greatly enhanced, and the flames take on a more realistic three-dimensional appearance.

Since pinstriping covers such a small area relative to the entire vehicle, stripers usually have a few primary colors of striping enamel and custom mix the desired color for each striping job.

Fine-line tape can be used to layout a desired line to be painted. That tape is outlined by tape on each side, and the middle piece of tape is removed. The area between the two pieces of tape is then painted. Before the striping paint is dry, the remaining tape can be removed. Pulling the tape before the paint is dry allows the edges to relax and lay down. Pinstripers commonly use tape for guidelines, but much of their striping work is done freehand.

Add Painted Stripes

After painting a vehicle, there may be a desire to add more graphics for personalization. Flames, both traditional and realistic, and scallops have been around for a long time. Stripes of various types are a form of graphics that can truly wake up a paint job and separate it from the rest. Stripes are typically a simpler design than flames or scallops and therefore are easier to layout.

Regardless of the style of graphics, a key to the success of the layout is working with the body lines of the vehicle. It is typically never a good idea to have a paint line crossing a body line in a perpendicular fashion. Rather, crossing at somewhere between 15 and 30 degrees typically looks better. This does not suggest that you layout flames with a protractor. Graphics must be visually appealing and therefore laid out by eye, but if you follow this guideline, you can lay them out easier.

A second key is visual balance. This does not imply that flames must be perfectly symmetrical from one side of the hood to the other, as flames are fleeting and not perfect. Still, they need to be similar in layout from one side to the other. With scallops being more geometric in design, they must be more perfectly matched.

To enhance this Kia sedan, some stripes to match the owner's motorcycle will be applied. As with any paint project, begin by cleaning the surface. Wash the surface with car-wash soap and water, dry, and then clean again with wax and grease remover to remove all contaminants. After that, it is pretty much designing the layout, masking, and applying paint. Follow along as this Kia receives a relatively easy but striking set of stripes that will set it apart from all others.

Adding Painted Stripes

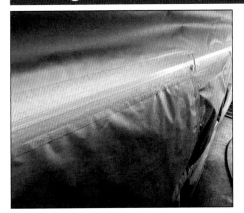

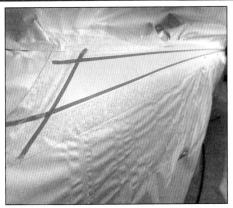

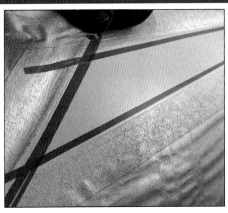

1 Use 3/4-inch masking tape to outline the area to be painted. If this were a more intricate layout, 1/8-inch fine-line tape would be used, as it holds tight to curved lines more accurately. Press the masking tape down firmly to the surface. Attach all other masking paper that is used to cover areas that are not part of the stripe to this.

2 Following the body lines and headlight shape, the stripe on the sides has an angular shape instead of the round corners on the hood. As on the hood, this 1/8-inch tape line establishes the space between the edge of the white and a gold metallic stripe.

3 To establish the width of the gold metallic paint line, 1/16-inch-wide fine-line tape (orange) is applied adjacent to the 1/8-inch-wide fine-line tape (blue).

4 When pulling masking tape along a straight line, begin by securing it at one end. Then, pull it taut along the desired line with one hand and press it in place with your other hand. This results in a straighter line than pushing the tape down along the desired line.

5 To avoid confusion, the orange tape in this photo will eventually be removed and the area painted gold metallic. Prior to laying out a design, think it through and determine which tape will mask and which will serve as a spacer.

6 To establish the inside line of the gold metallic stripe, a strip of 1/8-inch-wide fine-line tape (blue) is applied adjacent to the orange tape that will eventually be removed.

7 The 1/8-inch-wide fine-line tape (blue) is applied at the ends and along the length of the stripe as well.

8 Where the layout is narrow, 1/8-inch-wide fine-line tape (blue) can be used to mask the very narrow portion of the layout. Where room allows, 1/2- or 3/4-inch-wide masking tape can be used.

Adding Painted Stripes *continued*

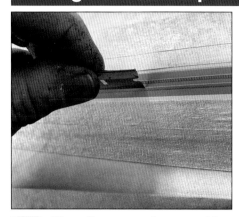

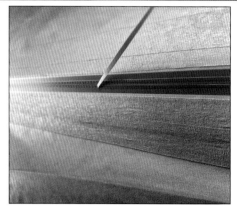

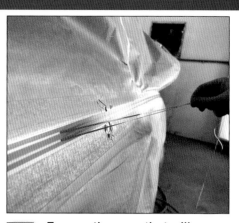

9 *Since the orange tape must be removed, any masking tape that covers it must be removed. Use a safety razor blade and a light touch to slice the upper layer of tape.*

10 *Pull the upper layer of masking tape back on itself and away from the surface to remove it.*

11 *Expose the area that will receive the gold metallic paint by removing the orange masking tape.*

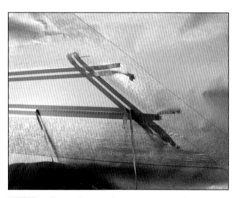

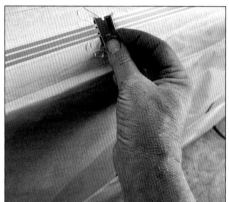

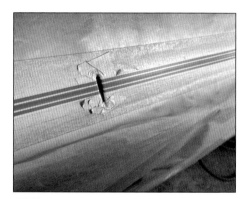

12 *Anywhere the tape overlaps, a razor blade is required to trim it as necessary.*

13 *Where tape crosses a gap (near the doors, trunk, or hood), use a safety razor blade to slice the tape in the middle of the gap.*

14 *Push the ends of the masking tape into the gap and push down the ends of the tape firmly. The narrow white areas will be painted gold metallic.*

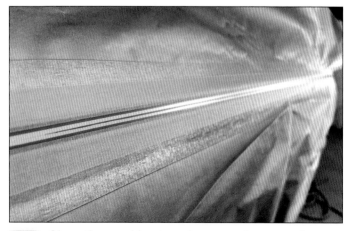

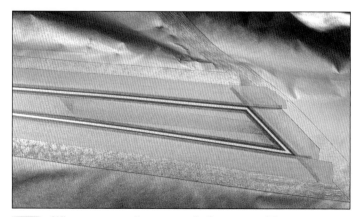

15 *Since the masking tape is narrow in some places, make sure that it is firmly pressed into place before spraying any paint.*

16 *Where room allows, mask the area with 3/4-inch-wide masking tape. Ensure that there are no slivers of unprotected areas that should be masked.*

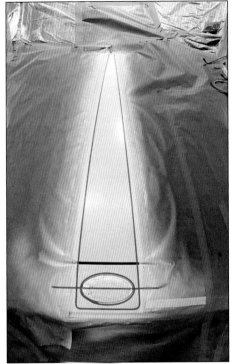

17 *After masking off the hood emblem and attaching the masking paper to cover the rest of the vehicle, the white color for the stripe was applied to the hood and each side. After waiting the proper amount of time to tape, the 1/8-inch-wide (blue) fine-line tape was applied. This line establishes the space between the edge of the white and a gold metallic stripe.*

18 *Prior to painting the gold metallic, the wide white area on the hood must be masked off. This can be done with a narrow piece of masking paper and masking tape or multiple strips of masking paper. Since this stripe tapers, it is just as easy to use multiple pieces of 2-inch-wide masking tape.*

19 *Begin by applying a strip of 1/8-inch-wide (blue) fine-line tape adjacent to the inside of the 1/16-inch-wide (orange) fine line. Follow that up with a strip of 3/4-inch-wide masking tape. Make sure the 3/4-inch-wide overlaps the blue fine-line tape slightly to avoid any slivers of unprotected sheet metal.*

20 *Use a touch-up (doorjamb or detail) spray gun to apply the gold metallic paint to the small areas.*

21 *This is a lot of masking paper and tape to paint these stripes, but it is better than removing any unwanted overspray.*

Adding Painted Stripes *continued*

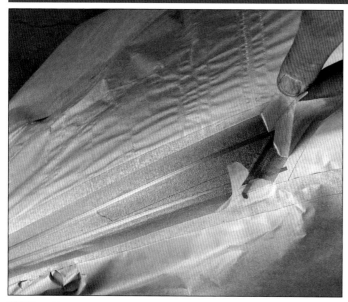

22 *After awaiting the proper dry time, carefully remove the masking materials.*

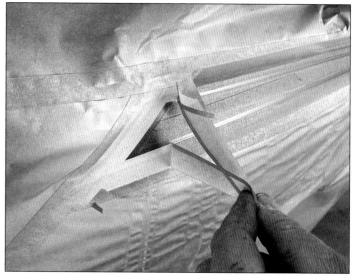

23 *Overall, there are several layers of masking material used in this process. Remove them in the opposite order in which they were applied.*

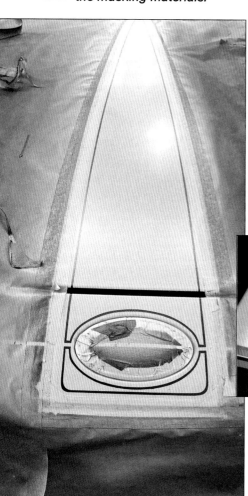

24 *The stripes will receive another pinstripe, so the masking material on the outsides of the hood and the hood emblem is left in place.*

25 *A narrow stripe of light blue lettering enamel will be applied 1/8-inch outside of the gold metallic stripe.*

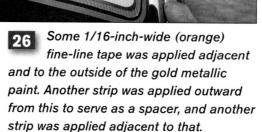

26 *Some 1/16-inch-wide (orange) fine-line tape was applied adjacent and to the outside of the gold metallic paint. Another strip was applied outward from this to serve as a spacer, and another strip was applied adjacent to that.*

27 *The middle strip of 1/16-inch-wide (orange) fine-line tape was removed. Using a pinstriping brush, the light blue lettering enamel was applied between the strips of fine-line tape. Notice that the striper uses his pinky finger against the vehicle to aid in steadying the striping brush.*

28 *After the paint has had adequate time to dry, carefully remove the masking tape.*

29 *The hand-painted light blue pinstripe serves to cover the seam of paint between the overall blue and the new white. If the newly applied stripes were going to be covered with clear, the hand-painted pinstripe would not be necessary because the clear would provide a smooth surface. When clear is not used, a hand-painted pinstripe is perfectly acceptable.*

30 *Striping adds a nice bit of detail to personalize an otherwise common four-door sedan.*

Repairing Small Nicks

Whenever you take your vehicle out of the garage, it is quite possible the paint will receive a nick or chip eventually. When the damage does not go through the paint, it can probably be buffed out, and everything will be fine. However, if the scratch or nick goes to the primer or to the bare metal, it should be repaired as soon as possible. Any time bare metal is exposed to the elements, it will begin to corrode.

If you have any of the paint left over from when you sprayed the vehicle, you can use it. Touch-up paint is available for most newer vehicles, so if you are using one of those colors, you are in luck. The parts department at your local auto dealer for the brand of vehicle your paint is using should be able to acquire a bottle of touch-up paint for you if you can provide the paint code. The touch-up bottles have a small brush attached to the cap for applying the paint. You can also use the clean end of a paper matchstick to apply the paint.

Begin by cleaning the damaged area with wax and grease remover. Use a clean dry towel to wipe away any residue. Mask off the surrounding area

Touch-up paint can be purchased in small bottles that include a brush attached to the cap. Some auto-parts stores carry touch-up paint, but you can always purchase it through a car dealer. Having the paint code from the VIN/Options tag of the vehicle is necessary to obtain the right color.

so that you do not inadvertently get paint drops where you do not want them. Use a piece of 800-grit-or-finer sandpaper to scuff the area where the paint will be applied. Avoid scuffing any undamaged paint. Apply a light coat of touch-up paint to the damaged area and let it thoroughly dry. Use the same sandpaper to get the touch-up paint smooth. Apply another coat of touch-up paint if necessary, let it dry, and sand it smooth. Continue these steps until the damage has been repaired.

Keep it Clean

With the time and effort you put into a high-quality paint job, the last thing you want is for dirt and clutter to detract from it. Not only do you need to wash and wax the vehicle on a regular basis but there are also other cleaning and detailing chores that help keep your vehicle looking new.

Wash and Dry

Frequently washing a vehicle that is coated with a good application of wax is one of the best things you can do for your new paint. However, prior to washing the newly painted vehicle, you must wait a while. Multistage paints can be washed after a few days, but uncatalyzed enamels must be allowed to cure for a few days to a week before being washed. This is to ensure that the paint's solvents have completely evaporated. Always use a mild automotive soap when washing a vehicle. Most automotive car-wash products are liquid so that there is no worry of dry granules scratching the finish.

Begin the wash process by pouring a small amount of car-wash soap into a bucket and fill it with warm

Liquid car wash and a soft sponge are about all you need to wash your car, along with a bucket and some water. Keeping your car's painted finish clean goes a long way toward making it look good for a long time.

water. Using a wash mitt, wash the horizontal areas (hood, roof, and trunk lid) first and rinse each section after washing. Wash the vertical sides next. Then, finish with the lower portions all around the vehicle. Rinse the wash mitt often and when finished washing.

Thoroughly rinse the entire vehicle starting at the top and work your way down. Dry the vehicle with soft, fluffy towels.

Clay-Bar Detailing

A relatively new method of detailing a vehicle is cleaning the painted surface by using a clay bar. This should not be done on a freshly painted vehicle. When it is done, it should be between the wash and wax steps. Clay bar detailing should not be done until after the vehicle has received a complete coat of wax. When the vehicle remains outside most of the time, clay-bar detailing needs to be done three or four times a year unless there is lots of contami-

nation in the air. Once or twice a year is plenty for a vehicle that is in the garage most of the time.

Clay-bar detailing is a cleaning process to remove minute contaminants but should be done only after a thorough washing of the vehicle. Clay bars come in two grades: fine and medium. If you are new to this, use the fine grade of clay to prevent any damage. Medium clay is typically used by professional detailers on vehicles that have gone a while since their last detailing.

Begin by purchasing a bar of automotive detailing clay and the lubricating spray that goes with it. Warm the clay by rolling it back and forth in your hands and form it into a ball to make it more pliable. When the clay is pliable enough to work with, form it into a flat, round shape about 3/4-inch thick. This round disc should be a size that fits comfortably beneath your fingers.

Work in sections that are about 2 feet square and start in the cleaner portions of the vehicle (roof, hood, trunk lid). Apply the lubricating spray over the area so that it is saturated and spray the clay as well. With the clay flattened beneath your fingers, slide the clay up and down or side to side. Add more lubricant if the clay gets difficult to slide across the surface.

Two important things to remember are to not slide the clay in a circular motion, as this is more likely to cause scratches. Do not use clay on a dry vehicle as this will break the clay apart and scratch the surface.

Continually check the clay surface to see if it has picked up contaminants. If it is full of contaminants, fold the clay over, apply more spray lubricant, and continue working the area until it is free of contaminants.

When an area is thoroughly clean, move to another area. Be sure to use plenty of spray lubricant. As you move to a new section, overlap the first by a few inches. Ensure that you are always using a clean area of the clay, keep the surface lubricated, and use a light touch. When finished, remove any lubricant with a clean microfiber towel.

Wax

Protecting your vehicle's painted finish with a high-quality Carnauba wax is important. While the wax helps protect the paint from harmful UV rays to an extent, it also makes washing the vehicle easier. The non-stick surface of wax repels bugs, bird droppings, tree sap, and other contaminants that could have a negative effect on the paint.

Prior to applying the first coat of wax to a new paint job, wait approximately three to four months. Since the wax forms a protective layer over

Automotive wax is available as a liquid or paste wax. The manner of application is purely a personal preference. Products such as Meguiars Quik Detailer are great for vehicles that already have a good coat of wax but you want to bring out the shine for a show, parade, or other special occasion.

the paint, it slows or prevents evaporation of the solvents in the paint. Whenever those paint solvent vapors are trapped in the paint, a buildup of pressure causes the paint to blister. When the weather is hotter, the solvents take less time to fully evaporate; therefore, less time is required to wait to apply wax. In cooler weather, more time is required for the solvent to evaporate.

You must also remember the difference between polish and wax. Oxidation and other contaminants are cleaned from the surface with polish. Wax protects the surface. Using the wrong products on a new or old paint job will do more harm than good.

Detailing

After washing the exterior of your vehicle, open the doors and clean the doorjamb area. You cannot really use a wash bucket and hose to clean this area, but you can use a soft, damp sponge to clean the painted portion. Scrub the tires with soapy water and a brush, and then apply a protectant designed for tires to give them a nice shine. Clean the wheels. Polish any chrome or stainless trim with an appropriate cleaner. Going to the trouble to clean all these other surfaces will make your paint job look even better.

Clean the glass, inside and out, with a glass cleaner and newspaper. Many paper towels are coated with something that smears when used to clean glass, and newspaper works well. This is another reason to pay close attention to what towels you use to wipe down your panels prior to paint. Do not use a paper towel that leaves more contaminants than it picks up.

Interior

Clean windows look better and are also safer than windows that are dirty or smeared. A good glass cleaner and newspaper or streak-free towels make cleaning the glass in your car very easy.

Begin with a strong vacuum cleaner to pick up any sanding dust that may be in the interior. Use a soft brush attachment on the vacuum to clean the dash. Then, use a crevice attachment to get into the tight spots. Vacuum the trunk. Use a small amount of an all-purpose cleaner to clean the steering wheel and any plastic interior panels, sun visors, and vinyl seats.

Engine

Degreasing and detailing the engine goes a long way toward making your car look better. Admittedly, the engine compartment does not really have any effect on how your paint looks, unless you are a car enthusiast. Then, you understand. If you keep the water spray away from your fresh paint and the distributor, some time with the engine degreaser setting at your local car wash will typically improve the appearance of your engine compartment.

Many cleaner/ degreaser liquids are available at auto-parts stores, grocery stores, or department stores. Depending on what you are trying to clean, it may take some effort on your part, but a clean car will always look better than one that is dirty.

Final Words

Whether the next vehicle you paint after reading this book is your first automotive paint job or the most recent of an extensive list, be proud of your accomplishment. There are probably some things you will consider doing differently the next time. That is okay, as that shows growth in experience. Regardless of how well the project turned out or did not, you can still take pride in having done it yourself. That should provide significantly more personal satisfaction than paying someone else to do the work.

Source Guide

Automotive Technology, Inc.
544 Mae Ct.
Fenton, MO 63026
800-875-8101
636-343-8101
automotivetechnology.com
Details: paint booths, equipment, and supplies

Eastwood Company
263 Shoemaker Rd.
Pottstown, PA 19464
800-343-9353
eastwoodcompany.com
Details: automotive restoration tools, equipment, and supplies

Hemmings Motor News
P.O. Box 100
Bennington, VT 05201
800-227-4373
hemmings.com
Classified ads for vehicles, products, and services

High Ridge NAPA
2707 High Ridge Blvd.
High Ridge, MO 63049
636-677-6400
Details: automotive parts, DuPont paint products

Jerry's Auto Body, Inc.
1399 Church St.
Union, MO 63084
636-583-4757
Details: auto-body repair

Licari Auto Body Supply, Inc.
2800 High Ridge Blvd.
High Ridge, MO 63049
636-677-1566
Details: PPG paint products and supplies

Meguiars
17991 Mitchell S.
Irvine, CA 92614-6015
800-347-5700
meguiars.com
Details: car-care products

Miller Electric Manufacturing Company
1635 W. Spencer St.
Appleton, WI 54912-1079
920-734-9821
millerwelds.com
Details: welders, plasma cutters, tools, and accessories

PPG Refinish Group
19699 Progress Dr.
Strongsville, OH 44149
800-647-6050
ppgrefinish.com
Details: paint products

Trim Parts
2175 Deer Field Rd.
Lebanon, OH 45036
513-934-0815
trimparts.com
Details: GM restoration parts

Year One
P.O. Box 129
Tucker, GA 30085-0129
800-932-7663
800-950-7663
yearone.com
Details: automotive restoration parts